The Industrial Revolution

Recent Titles in
Greenwood Guides to Historic Events, 1500–1900

The Second Great Awakening and the Transcendentalists
Barry Hankins

The Age of Napoleon
Susan P. Conner

The American Civil War
Cole C. Kingseed

The Scientific Revolution and the Foundations of Modern Science
Wilbur Applebaum

The Mexican War
David S. Heidler and Jeanne T. Heidler

The Abolitionist Movement
Claudine L. Ferrell

Maritime Exploration in the Age of Discovery, 1415–1800
Ronald S. Love

The Trail of Tears and Indian Removal
Amy H. Sturgis

Darwin's *The Origin of Species*
Keith Francis

The Age of Romanticism
Joanne Schneider

The Reformation Era
Robert D. Linder

Slave Revolts
Johannes Postma

338.903 Wya
Wyatt, Lee T.
The industrial revolution

$45.00
ocn193174548
12/10/2008

The Industrial Revolution

LEE T. WYATT III

Greenwood Guides to Historic Events, 1500–1900
Linda S. Frey and Marsha L. Frey, Series Editors

GREENWOOD PRESS
Westport, Connecticut • London

Library of Congress Cataloging-in-Publication Data
Wyatt, Lee T.
　The industrial revolution / Lee T. Wyatt III.
　　p. cm.—(Greenwood guides to historic events, 1500–1900, ISSN 1538-442X)
　Includes bibliographical references and index.
　ISBN 978-0-313-33769-7 (alk. paper)
　　1. Industrial revolution—Great Britain—History—18th century. 2. Industrial revolution—Great Britain—History—19th century. 3. Industrial revolution—United States—History—19th century. 4. Agriculture—Economic aspects—Great Britain—History. I. Title.
　HC254.5.W93　2009
　　338.9'034—dc22　　　2008029501

British Library Cataloguing in Publication Data is available.

Copyright © 2009 by Lee Wyatt III

All rights reserved. No portion of this book may be reproduced, by any process or technique, without the express written consent of the publisher.

Library of Congress Catalog Card Number: 2008029501
ISBN: 978-0-313-33769-7
ISSN: 1538-442X

First published in 2009

Greenwood Press, 88 Post Road West, Westport, CT 06881
An imprint of Greenwood Publishing Group, Inc.
www.greenwood.com

Printed in the United States of America

The paper used in this book complies with the Permanent Paper Standard issued by the National Information Standards Organization (Z39.48–1984).

10　9　8　7　6　5　4　3　2　1

Contents

Series Foreword by Linda S. Frey and Marsha L. Frey		vii
Preface		xi
Chronology		xv
Chapter 1	Historical Overview	1
Chapter 2	The Way We Were: On the Eve of the Industrial Revolution	11
Chapter 3	The Agricultural Revolution in Great Britain	25
Chapter 4	The Industrial Revolution in Great Britain	39
Chapter 5	The Industrial Revolution in America	79
Chapter 6	The Industrial Revolution on the Continent in the Late 19th Century	119
Chapter 7	The Industrial Revolution beyond the West	143
Biographies		157
Primary Documents		205
Annotated Bibliography		243
Index		255

Photographs follow page 156.

SERIES FOREWORD

American statesman Adlai Stevenson stated, "We can chart our future clearly and wisely only when we know the path which has led to the present." This series, Greenwood Guides to Historic Events, 1500–1900, is designed to illuminate that path by focusing on events from 1500 to 1900 that have shaped the world. The years 1500 to 1900 include what historians call the early modern period (1500 to 1789, the onset of the French Revolution) and part of the modern period (1789 to 1900).

In 1500, an acceleration of key trends marked the beginnings of an interdependent world and the posing of seminal questions that changed the nature and terms of intellectual debate. The series closes with 1900, the inauguration of the twentieth century. This period witnessed profound economic, social, political, cultural, religious, and military changes. An industrial and technological revolution transformed the modes of production, marked the transition from a rural to an urban economy, and ultimately raised the standard of living. Social classes and distinctions shifted. The emergence of the territorial and later the national state altered man's relations with and view of political authority. The shattering of the religious unity of the Roman Catholic world in Europe marked the rise of a new pluralism. Military revolutions changed the nature of warfare. The books in this series emphasize the complexity and diversity of the human tapestry and include political, economic, social, intellectual, military, and cultural topics. Some of the authors focus on events in U.S. history such as the Salem witchcraft trials, the American Revolution, the abolitionist movement, and the Civil War. Others analyze European topics, such as the Reformation and Counter-Reformation and the French Revolution. Still others bridge cultures and continents by examining the voyages of discovery, the Atlantic slave trade, and the Age of Imperialism. Some focus on intellectual questions that have shaped the modern world, such as Charles Darwin's *Origin of Species*, or on turning points such as the Age of Romanticism. Others examine defining economic, religious, or legal events or issues such as the building of the railroads, the Second Great Awakening, and abolitionism. Heroes (e.g., Meriwether Lewis and William Clark), scientists (e.g., Darwin), military leaders (e.g., Napoleon Bonaparte), poets (e.g., Lord Byron) stride across the pages. Many of these events were seminal in that they marked profound changes or turning points. The Scientific Revolution, for example, changed the way individuals viewed themselves and their world.

The authors, acknowledged experts in their fields, synthesize key events, set developments within the larger historical context, and, most important, present well-balanced, well-written accounts that integrate the most recent scholarship in the field.

The topics were chosen by an advisory board composed of historians, high school history teachers, and school librarians to support the curriculum and meet student research needs. The volumes are designed to serve as resources for student research and to provide clearly written interpretations of topics central to the secondary school and lower-level undergraduate history curriculum. Each author outlines a basic chronology to guide the reader through often-confusing events and presents a historical overview to set those events within a narrative framework. Three to five topical chapters underscore critical aspects of the event. In the final chapter the author examines the impact and consequences of the event. Biographical sketches furnish background on the lives and contributions of the players who strut across the stage. Ten to fifteen primary documents, ranging from letters to diary entries, song lyrics, proclamations, and posters, cast light on the event, provide material for student essays, and stimulate critical engagement with the sources. Introductions identify the authors of the documents and the main issues. In some cases a glossary of selected terms is provided as a guide to the reader. Each work contains an annotated bibliography of recommended books, articles, CD-ROMs, Internet sites, videos, and films that set the materials within the historical debate.

Reading these works can lead to a more sophisticated understanding of the events and debates that have shaped the modern world and can stimulate a more active engagement with the issues that still affect us. It has been a particularly enriching experience to work closely with such dedicated professionals. We have come to know and value even more highly the authors in this series and our

Series Foreword

editors at Greenwood, particularly Kevin Ohe and Michael Hermann. In many cases they have become more than colleagues; they have become friends. To them and to future historians we dedicate this series.

Linda S. Frey
University of Montana

Marsha L. Frey
Kansas State University

PREFACE

There is no drudgery about labor unless you make it your master.
—From *Manufacturer and Builder*, Vol. 24 (November 1892), 242

Beginning in the last half of the 18th century and extending into the early 20th century, first Great Britain and then Western Europe, the United States, and several other parts of the globe experienced the vibrant stirrings of a major technical and economic transformation. This development was in great measure the culmination of forces that had gained momentum in Western civilization during the Renaissance of the 14th and 15th centuries and continued with the dramatic discoveries of the Scientific Revolution over the next 200 years. The theoretical and analytical mysteries unlocked by the scientific community laid the foundation for the application of more practical techniques and approaches to harness the new sources of power, the reduction on the sole reliance on traditional sources of labor, and the creation of new organizations and enterprises. The result was the emergence of a new demographic, economic, political, and social map of the Western world and the unparalleled increase in wealth and national prosperity after 1750.

In the 1820s British and French writers coined the phrase *Industrial Revolution* to identify the changes in manufacturing and production that had initially occurred in Great Britain and by the early 19th century had appeared in the new American republic and on the continent of Europe. These writers compared the dramatic impact of industrialization to the political and social upheaval caused by the French Revolution. Two decades later, Friedrich Engels reinforced the use of the term in his influential work, *The Conditions of the Working Class in England*. Indeed, historians have long debated the causes, characteristics, expansion, and results of the economic and industrial developments after 1750, even to the point of identifying two industrial revolutions: the first one dominated by the British prior to 1850 and the second characterized by the rapid advance of industrialization outside of Great Britain after 1850. Yet despite the efforts of some scholars to revise the initial historical interpretation of the Industrial Revolution, the term itself has retained its legitimacy in the literature as no adequate substitute has yet been advanced to better encapsulate the industrial and economic changes of this dynamic era.

This work has as its purpose to survey the scope and impact of the Industrial Revolution, an age that some historians argue is comparable to earlier important epochs that changed mankind. The book is organized into a chronology of selected key events and seven chapters that address important aspects of nearly two centuries of industrialization. It should be emphasized that on occasion there are discrepancies in various sources regarding the rich statistical information related to the Industrial Revolution. Areas such as population growth, number of power looms, and horsepower production, for example, can be illustrated or interpreted in several different ways. As such, I have chosen to present the data using a more conservative approach but one that most assuredly emphasizes the dramatic change of the era. Chapter One provides a historical overview of themes appearing in the work. In addition, it introduces the reader to a brief, and admittedly selective, survey of some of the larger important historical questions and debate surrounding the construct of the Industrial Revolution.

The second chapter sets the stage for an onset of industrialization. The life of Europe as it existed on the eve of the Industrial Revolution is examined. Rising population, the growing impact of science and technology, the appearance of early capitalism and consumerism, and the pre-industrial lifestyle of Europeans are among the themes that set the opening of the Industrial Revolution into perspective.

Chapter Three reviews the influence of the Agricultural Revolution on the emergence of the Industrial Revolution. This topic has drawn serious scrutiny by historians who have debated the scope and depth of its impact. Was it a critical precursor and stimulus to industrialization, or did it evolve simultaneously during the era? The long-standing enclosure movement, advent of modern farming practices such as the Norfolk system and livestock breeding techniques, and the shift of labor from the rural to urban areas play key roles in analyzing the relationship of changes in the agrarian world to the new environment of factories and cities.

Preface

Chapter Four surveys the Industrial Revolution in Great Britain. There is little debate regarding Great Britain's role as the powerful engine that started the world on the road to industrialization. This chapter reviews the all-important conditions that existed in Great Britain and paved the way for that nation's rapid transition to new economic realities. In addition, the growth of infrastructure (roads, canals, and railroads) and the role of cotton textiles, iron production, and mining industries are briefly reviewed to emphasize how quickly Great Britain's industrialization advanced in comparison to its continental counterparts. Other topics include the rise of the middle class, the plight of the workers, and the environment in the new industrial city, with a particular emphasis on Manchester.

Chapter Five addresses the Industrial Revolution in the United States. A brief look at colonial America provides a point of origin to compare how quickly the United States began to embrace industrialization. This transition occurred notwithstanding a heated debate in the early republic between Alexander Hamilton and Thomas Jefferson regarding the merits of manufacturing and the later disruption of the Civil War. Despite these potential impediments, the United States marshaled its many resources and distinct advantages such as a plentiful agriculture, an unlimited labor supply assisted by millions of immigrants who flooded the nation after 1840, and a remarkable array of inventors. By the late 19th century the United States had for the most part matched and surpassed Great Britain in almost all measurable categories related to industrialization.

Chapter Six depicts the spread of the Industrial Revolution to the continent of Europe. The nations of Western Europe faced a number of factors, most particularly the havoc wreaked by the Napoleonic era, a period of upheaval that initially impeded their ability to compete with Great Britain. However, after the middle of the 19th century, economic stability and the transfer of British technology to the continent began to change the situation. In spite of starting well behind the more advanced position of Great Britain, Belgium, France, and the German states particularly found the necessary resources and created their own sophisticated industrial bases and began to challenge British industrial supremacy by 1900.

Chapter Seven addresses the impact of the Industrial Revolution on several areas of the non-Western world. To be sure, the growing number of Western nations that industrialized in the 19th century dominated areas such as India, the Middle East, and Latin America as they made feeble attempts to transform their economies. Russia and Japan were the exception. The Russians made remarkable strides in a brief period of time to overcome centuries of conservatism.

However, by the early 20th century the rapidity of change and the disappointment and devastation brought about by the Russo-Japanese War and World War I pushed that nation to revolution and a new economic direction. Japan, on the other hand, made a national decision to embrace industrialization, one that ensured a successful transition through the adoption of Western techniques and adapt them to the Japanese culture.

The conclusion of the book includes biographies of fifteen persons, some well-known and others more obscure, who made important contributions to the Industrial Revolution. In addition, a variety of primary documents such as government reports, literary pieces, and period journal articles survey a variety of topics related the Industrial Revolution in order for the student to gain better perspective, clarity, and a first-hand impression of its complexity and impact without the filter of the present. The work also contains a number of illustrations that provide a visual reinforcement of themes addressed in the book. Finally, a selected bibliography is presented to encourage further study of the Industrial Revolution as a means to gain additional understanding of this important historical era, one that continues to influence our world today.

I wish to thank several persons for their support during this project. I am forever indebted to the series editors, Linda and Marsha Frey, who asked me to become a participant in the series. These outstanding scholars applied a welcome critical eye to the manuscript. They also provided often-needed encouragement and retained remarkable faith in me over the years. Mariah Gumpert at Greenwood Press exhibited extraordinary patience and kindness, especially as my family faced several challenges and crises during the completion of this work. I also sincerely thank the staff of the Prints and Photograph Section of the Library of Congress who assisted me in obtaining important documents and illustrations to supplement the book. Claude El-Khouri and Amanda Davis of the Brevard Community College library staff worked diligently to obtain a number of sources for the work. Eileen Trobaugh, secretary of the Liberal Arts Department at Brevard Community College, helped me to overcome several technical difficulties during the preparation of the manuscript. Finally, my wife Patsy provided constant understanding and generous support as I labored to bring the book to press.

Chronology

1654	Otto von Guericke experiments with atmospheric pressure machine.
1690	Denis Papin develops primitive steam device.
1694	Bank of England founded.
1698	Thomas Savery invents the "Miner's Friend."
1700	European population reaches 120 million.
1709	Abraham Darby introduces process of coke blasting iron.
1712	Thomas Newcomen invents the atmospheric engine to pump water from mines.
1727–1845	Major era of Enclosure Movement—4,000 Parliamentary Enclosure Acts.
1731	Jethro Tull publishes *Horse Holding Husbandry*.
1733	John Kay invents the "flying shuttle" to increase output of woolen cloth.
1750	European population reaches 140 million.
1752	Benjamin Franklin conducts electricity experiments.
1761	Bridgewater Canal opens.
1769	James Watt patents steam engine.
1764	James Hargreaves invents the "spinning jenny."
1779	Richard Arkwright develops the water frame to increase the number of spindles.
1776	Adam Smith publishes *The Wealth of Nations*.
1775–1783	American Revolution.

1779	David Bushnell's "Turtle"—first prototype submarine.
1779	Samuel Crompton invents spinning "mule" to work numerous spindles at once.
1784	Henry Cort patents his "puddling" process to convert pig iron to wrought iron.
1784	Arthur Young publishes first of his forty-five-volume *Annals of Agriculture*.
1787	Edmund Cartwright invents his wool-combing machine and early power loom.
1787	John Fitch demonstrates steam-powered paddle boat for the Constitutional Convention.
1789	The French Revolution begins.
1790	Samuel Slater operates mill in Pawtucket, Rhode Island using reproductions of Richard Arkwright's machinery.
1790	First U.S. patent is issued to William Pollard—rove and spinning cotton machine.
1790	European population reaches 190 million.
1791	Alexander Hamilton presents *Report on the Subject of Manufactures* to Congress.
1794	Eli Whitney patents cotton gin to separate seed from the fiber.
1794	First important U.S. turnpike opens: Philadelphia to Lancaster, Pennsylvania.
1798	Thomas Malthus publishes *Essay on the Principle of Population*.
1800	U.S. population reaches 5 million.
1800	Eli Whitney demonstrates interchangeable parts for Thomas Jefferson.
1801	Joseph M. Jacquard develops the silk loom.
1802	Richard Trevithick develops high pressure steam engine for transportation.
1806	Benjamin Thompson invents the coffee pot.
1807	Robert Fulton's *Clermont* steamboat travels New York to Albany at 5 mph.

Chronology

1809	First woman issued a U.S. patent: Mary Kres for straw weaving silk device.
1811	Luddite movement in Great Britain.
1811–1839	Construction of Cumberland or National Road in the United States.
1812–1814	War of 1812 between Great Britain and the United States.
1814	George Stephenson develops the first steam-powered locomotive.
1815	Napoleonic Wars end with defeat of Napoleon at Waterloo.
1817–1825	Erie Canal constructed.
1819	Peterloo Massacre.
1819–1836	Thomas Telford supervises construction of the London–Holyhead Road.
1825	The Stockton–Darlington Railway opens with Stephenson steam locomotive.
1826	Lowell, Massachusetts is founded, and six textile mills are established.
1830	The first locomotive in America (*Tom Thumb*) is in service in Baltimore, Maryland.
1831	Severe cholera outbreak in Great Britain's urban areas.
1832	The Great Reform Bill revises Parliamentary representation.
1833	The Factory Act places limitations on child labor in Great Britain.
1834	Cyrus McCormick obtains patent for his mechanical reaper.
1834	British Parliament passes the Poor Law.
1834	*Zollverein* or German Customs Union established.
1835	Railroad mania begins in Great Britain.
1836–1841	Isambard Kingdom Brunel oversees construction of the Great Western Railway, connecting London and Bristol.
1838	People's Charter drafted.
1839	Charles Goodyear patents vulcanization of rubber.

1840	U.S. railroad mileage equals canal mileage.	
1841	First edition of *Punch Magazine* published.	
1841	Queen Victoria takes her first ride on a railroad.	
1842	Sir Edwin Chadwick publishes *The Sanitary Conditions of the Labouring Population*.	
1844	Samuel Morse demonstrates telegraph—also developed independently by Wheatstone and Cook.	
1844	Friedrich Engels publishes *The Conditions of the Working Class in England*.	
1844–1845	U.S. railroad mania begins (5,000 miles of track laid); Irish potato famine.	
1846	Elias Howe invents the sewing machine.	
1846	The Corn Laws are repealed.	
1846	George H. Corliss perfects four-valve steam engine (later displayed at the U.S. Centennial Exposition in Philadelphia).	
1847	The Ten Hours Act passes.	
1848	Karl Marx publishes *The Communist Manifesto*.	
1848	Revolutions occur across Europe.	
1848	Parliament passes the Public Health Act.	
1849	Samuel Colt and Elisha Root collaborate to manufacture interchangeable parts.	
1850	European population reaches 270 million.	
1851	The Great Exhibition (Crystal Palace) attracts 6 million visitors to London.	
1851	Major census in Great Britain.	
1851	Manchester, cotton textile capital of Great Britain, reaches population of 300,000.	
1851	Isaac Singer develops first consumer sewing machine.	
1853–1856	Crimean War.	
1853	Commodore Matthew Perry (United States) enters Tokyo harbor and contacts with Japan.	
1856	Henry Bessemer develops process to convert pig iron into steel.	

Chronology

1860	U.S. population reaches 31 million.
1861	Russia emancipates serfs.
1861–1865	U.S. Civil War.
1866	Cyrus W. Field lays the first transatlantic telegraph cable.
1858	The "Great Stink" in London.
1867	Reform Bill extends suffrage in Great Britain.
1868	Meiji Restoration in Japan.
1869	First Transcontinental Railroad completed in the United States.
1876	First gasoline engine patent issued to August Otto.
1876	U.S. Centennial Exposition in Philadelphia.
1876	Alexander Graham Bell invents the telephone.
1879	Thomas Edison invents incandescent light bulb.
1880–1914	Twenty million immigrants enter the United States.
1882	Thomas Edison constructs station to generate electricity in New York City.
1883	Karl Benz develops first gas powered "automobile."
1884	Last of 19th century reform bills gives suffrage to almost all males in Great Britain.
1884	Arnold Toynbee lectures on the Industrial Revolution.
1884	Construction begins on first U.S. skyscraper in Chicago.
1886	Karl Benz and Gottlieb Daimler separately develop internal combustion engines.
1886	Haymarket Square Riot in Chicago.
1889	Eiffel Tower opens in Paris.
1892	Rudolf Diesel patents heavy oil engine.
1892	Frank and Charles Duryea patent first gasoline powered engine in the United States.
1892	Homestead Strike in Pennsylvania.
1900	Value of U.S. manufacturing output reaches double that of agricultural output.
1901	Queen Victoria dies.

CHAPTER 1

HISTORICAL OVERVIEW

The Industrial Revolution was a major turning point in world history. Historian Eric Hobsbawm believes that it represents the seminal event in the history of man.[1] While not all scholars agree with Hobsbawm, most support the claim that it ranks alongside the Neolithic Revolution in terms of its dramatic effect on all aspects of human life. In the Neolithic example, man made the transition from being a hunter and gatherer and adopted agriculture as the means to sustain life and organize his world. Neolithic man settled down and formed agricultural communities and then early cities and survived on the agrarian surplus provided by the new economic realities. Likewise, within the short span of three generations, the Industrial Revolution marks a major historical discontinuity. It stimulated the first major transformation of lifestyle in thousands of years because of the emerging technological developments, new enterprises and their related business organizations, the restructuring of labor, and massive demographic shifts that created a modern urban society with its foundation not based on agricultural but rather on the industrial production, exchange, and consumption of a seemingly endless variety of consumer goods. It opened a passage to an era of previously untapped energy. Furthermore, the Industrial Revolution resulted in a phenomenal growth of national and personal wealth and, like the Neolithic Revolution, stimulated responses that fundamentally changed existing political, economic, and social institutions. However, the scope, scale, and impact of the Industrial Revolution far surpassed in its breadth, depth, and speed of change the more gradual diffusion of the Neolithic era.

Although the Industrial Revolution had no definitive start date like its French Revolutionary counterpart, it is apparent that beginning in the early 18th century, economic and technological developments supported by political establishments coalesced to alter fundamentally the landscape of Western civilization, and then by a process of diffusion spread to other societies across the globe. These factors included the ability of agriculture to support a rapidly growing population and mobile society, specialization of economic pursuits and class distinctions, the mutual support of scientific inquiry and technical innovation and their application to commercial applications. There is no dispute that this phenomenon occurred first in Great Britain. Perhaps no single image embodies the spirit of the first century of this new age better than the International Exhibition of the Works of Industry of All Nations, opened formally by Queen Victoria at Kensington in London on May 1, 1851. This six-month-long exhibition housed in an impressive glass and iron structure dubbed the "Crystal Palace" was a soaring monument to the power and vision of the Industrial Revolution and Great Britain's dominant role in the era. It demonstrated the paramount industrial and engineering milestone that Great Britain had achieved in the first century of the Industrial Revolution, a position that surpassed that of its neighbors and brought the nation extraordinary wealth and material success. On the eve of the Great Exhibition, Queen Victoria penned a diary entry that summed up the bursting confidence and optimism of the country with the simple notation, "We are capable of doing anything."[2]

After 1815 the Industrial Revolution spread methodically but unevenly from the British Isles to northwestern Europe, northern Italy, the United States, central Europe, Russia, Japan, and ultimately portions of the wider world such as India, the Middle East, and Latin America. It had a dramatic impact on the political, economic, and social life of Western civilization and a lesser one on the peripheral areas. The Industrial Revolution stimulated a major increase in production and mass consumption. The ancient sources of power—human, draught animal, wind, and water—were replaced by coal and steam and eventually gas and electricity to construct and operate more sophisticated machinery and stimulate new inventions and increasingly higher levels of productivity. These changes required modified forms of labor organizations to ensure sustained profits and resulted in the growth of factory enterprises and new business arrangements to replace the former widely dispersed domestic workshops and cottage industries.

As the impact of the Industrial Revolution deepened, Europe, the Western world, and then selected portions of the globe underwent a distinct transition from an agrarian and handicraft society to one fueled by factories, machines, and more specialized labor. Factory owners and industrial financiers at first resorted to any means available to stoke the industrial engine with little regard for human or environmental consequences. As a result, conditions for the workers took an initial step backwards as the factories were dirty, monotonous, unsafe, and difficult places in which to toil. As people moved from the farm areas to the growing industrial cities, bulging populations erased large portions of the rural landscape and the more simple, traditional, and personal characteristics of agrarian life. This rapid and uncharted growth of the urban areas placed new challenges on political authorities who attempted to cope with housing shortages and overcrowding, poor sanitation and recurrent epidemic disease, and nagging social issues such as abandonment of children, crime, alcohol abuse, and prostitution. Relief for these disturbing social ills and blemishes of industrialization did not appear until courageous and dedicated reformers spurred governments to legislate improvements in the later 19th century. Other changes were the rise of a wealthy and politically influential middle class and the massive growth of an urban proletariat whose initially faint voice slowly became loud as the 19th century progressed, a clamor that eventually transformed the nature of Western politics. Finally, this new environment stimulated in Western nations a fresh and insatiable appetite for raw materials and new resources to pursue ever-increasing levels of economic growth. As a result, fundamental changes occurred regarding the relationship of Western states with each other and the rest of the world as industrial power became the major vehicle by which nations attempted to subdue wide portions of the globe and compete for economic, territorial, and strategic advantage. In summary, the Industrial Revolution was the culmination of complex changes churning in Europe beginning in the 18th century. The marriage of invention and entrepreneurship, a shifting labor supply, the growth of international trade, new and enterprising business ventures, and eventual government involvement and direction contributed to the explosion of economic growth known as the Industrial Revolution and, despite fits and starts, a heretofore unknown level of progress and prosperity.

What the Historians Say: Selected Viewpoints

No serious historian doubts that the Industrial Revolution had its origins in Great Britain, and that by the middle of the 19th century significant industrial activity had spread to the areas of northwestern Europe and the new republic of the United States. Over the course of the next half century, the stirrings of some degree of industrialization had appeared in portions of southern, southeastern, and Eastern Europe, Russia, parts of the former British Empire, a few areas of Latin America, and Japan. The impact and momentum of the Industrial Revolution was maintained throughout the 20th century and has continued to influence developments in other parts of the globe. In all cases the Industrial Revolution stimulated significant economic, political, and social changes in countries or regions in which its reach was felt, at times through the adoption or imitation of earlier developments or perhaps in the establishment of unequal partnerships.

But what does the term Industrial Revolution actually entail and how has the transformation that it represents been interpreted by historians? The Industrial Revolution remains the subject of intense debate amongst historians. Scholars agree that observable economic, technical, political, and social change can be observed in the 18th and 19th centuries. However, significant historical questions continue to generate reappraisal of the era. When did the Industrial Revolution begin? Was the Industrial Revolution indeed a "revolution" or merely a longer evolutionary process? What were the significant pre-conditions or causes of the Industrial Revolution? At what point had the Industrial Revolution run its course? Was there one Industrial Revolution or two? What roles did technology or politics play? How does one evaluate nations that industrialized later in comparison to those who experienced the phenomenon initially? These and other questions remain fundamental to understanding the full implications of the Industrial Revolution. Indeed, the term Industrial Revolution itself, although initially appearing in the first quarter of the 19th century, only assumed a firm place in the historical literature in the 1880s. And, even though some later historians have expressed disdain for the term, they generally have been unable to shed its widespread use in the literature and admit that no alternative designation better encapsulates the true essence of the period.

Arnold Toynbee began the serious historical discussion of the role of industrialization in his 1884 *Lectures on the Industrial Revolution in England*.[3] He argued that beginning in the late 18th and early 19th centuries a visible, dynamic change swept first across Great Britain and then moved almost simultaneously to the European continent and the United States. Toynbee opined that several factors had coalesced by the 18th century to produce this distinct phenomenon: a rapid rise in British population, a significant increase in agricultural productivity, the emergence of the factory system, the growth of internal and worldwide trade, and a visible and dramatic redistribution of wealth in the nation. The result was the collapse of the economic regulation that had prevailed since the middle ages and its replacement with a new spirit of competition. He emphasized that 1760 marked a distinctive, sharp break with the past and that the subsequent accelerated pace of industrialization had run its course a century later. Toynbee died before he could further revise or refine his views; however, his thesis established a baseline upon which later historiography has been evaluated.

Historical Overview

Toynbee's study soon influenced other historians to make a closer inspection of the Industrial Revolution, and they offered a number of challenges to the scope and nature of his thesis. Over the course of the last century, there has been an ebb and flow of historical commentary in response to Toynbee. These historians, while often disagreeing with Toynbee, appeared for the most part either to advance new views regarding the chronological framework of the era or to offer fresh interpretations of its impact on various aspects of society by using modern methodologies. The survey that follows is not intended to be a complete account of the vast historical commentary on the Industrial Revolution post-Toynbee but to introduce the student of the era to several areas of debate regarding its complexities and controversies and to encourage further study.

One of the first responses to Toynbee came from S. Webb and B. Webb and from J. Hammond and B. Hammond.[4] These scholars, writing in the late 19th and early 20th centuries, did not challenge the notion of the Industrial Revolution. Instead they advanced the idea that the Industrial Revolution had as it crux the dualism of the creation of increased wealth but also more poverty, as each of these developments brought significant change to British society. The tension created by the issues of continuity and revolutionary action as opposed to an evolutionary pace of progress toward industrialization also gained much attention. In the 1920s Paul Mantoux argued that industrialization had its roots in a long series of modifications occurring in British society without which the nation could not have experienced an economic transformation by the late 18th century.[5] In the 1930s Arthur Redford appeared to concur at least partially with Mantoux. He argued that Toynbee's identification of a specific start point and the implication that it represented a definite rapid upturn in industrial activity was inaccurate. Rather, Redford suggested that important industrial activity had begun earlier in the 18th century and that 1760 merely represented the moment that those key changes had slowly progressed to the visible point that important industrial change could proceed further.[6] At the same time, J. H. Clapham abandoned use of the term "Industrial Revolution." He argued that no general industrialization was visible by the mid-19th century because no real transformation in the nature of British labor had taken place, although a few industries such as cotton textiles and iron had made great strides.[7] John U. Nef also criticized Toynbee and stressed the idea of continuity and argued that his selection of 1760 for the commencement of the Industrial Revolution was too late. Nef stated that Great Britain had an inherent long tradition of progress and economic change with origins in the commercial and maritime activities that had gained momentum by 1550 and had run their course by the middle of the 19th century.[8] T. S. Ashton sought the middle ground. His work argued that modern capitalism had its beginnings before 1760 and had become fully developed by 1830. Ashton also emphasized that several factors impeded the ability of earlier historians to see the course of the industrialization process: the normal ups and downs resulting from unproductive investment and expenditures, initial entrepreneurial mistakes that later industrialists could study and avoid, and the uncertainty and unpredictability in the natural order of the political process.[9] E. Lipson also believed that the Industrial Revolution was merely another phase of the progress of historical development and represented its constant nature of continuity and change in which old ways and techniques did not wither away but rather joined with the newly evolving ones as the nation experienced industrial growth.[10] Herbert Heaton expanded this view, arguing that the Industrial Revolution had a long 300-year history—150 years of preparation, and another 150 years to run its course.[11] Charles Wilson reinforced these views by arguing that Great Britain's accelerated industrial growth was not revolutionary and, like Heaton and Nef, saw its origins in the 17th century.[12]

These strong challenges to Toynbee's thesis did not fray it beyond repair. A resurrection of the idea of a dramatic break appeared in the 1950s and 1960s, particularly with the publication of W. W. Rostow's important work, *The Stages of Economic Growth*.[13] Rostow, in an apparent effort to reconcile the views of Toynbee, Clapham, and Nef, took a different approach in interpreting the historical evidence. He studied the developed and industrialized nations to determine how their economic progress and modernization might aid underdeveloped nations to achieve the same level of success. In so doing, Rostow identified five stages of economic growth: (1) traditional society, (2) preconditions for a take-off, (3) take-off, (4) move to maturity, and (5) era of mass consumption.

Yet, Rostow's work, like the narrative of his predecessors, also generated careful historical scrutiny. A new group of scholars, steeped in emerging techniques of statistical analysis and referred to as the new economic historians, arose to challenge his assumptions and conclusions. These historians stressed a long, steady process of evolutionary change rather than a revolutionary event to characterize the Industrial Revolution. Phyllis Deane, for example, emphasized that a grouping or clustering of inventions and innovations beginning in the 18th century was the stimulus for change as opposed to one or two industries, such as textiles or mining, leading the transformation. Interestingly, the very title of her work, *The First Industrial Revolution*,[14] revitalized the notion that this label for the era had achieved a restored legitimacy.

Other writers moved away from looking at the Industrial Revolution as a whole phenomenon and analyzed its particular parts. These approaches, following similar lines of inquiry in other areas of the discipline, for example, highlighted finite slices of industrialization such as per capita income, wages, and productivity rates. In addition, it emphasized regional studies, surveyed specific industries such a textiles, iron, and mining, analyzed the shifting standards of living for workers, and studied demographic shifts, urbanization, social change, and the political component in the age of industrialization. Scholars who embraced these lines of inquiry often used a variety of evidence such as census reports (particularly beginning in 1831), documents from parliamentary and royal commissions, mining and manufacturing operations reports, literary sources, newspaper and periodical articles exposing factory and city conditions, and eyewitness accounts to support their contentions.[15]

For the last three decades the debate about the Industrial Revolution has taken on new energy. In the 1980s scholars such as N. F. R. Crafts and E. A. Wrigley reemphasized the gradual advance of industrialization. Crafts stressed that Great Britain had reached a significant level of industrialization by the early 18th century, and the rate of growth throughout the remainder of the century was slow. Wrigley argued that economists such as Adam Smith and Thomas Malthus who lived in the early phases of the Industrial Revolution pointed to the obvious economic changes occurring around them as the beginning of a potential economic collapse for Great Britain. Wrigley argued that in the midst of rapid change these economists could not ascertain the true direction that industrialization had charted for Great Britain and that the modifications taking place underneath the surface in Great Britain eventually proved their pessimism to be misplaced.[16] On the other hand, Toynbee's view that the Industrial Revolution can be seen as a break with the past found new life in David Landes' important 1969 work, *The Unbound Prometheus*.[17] Landes took a fresh look at the early views regarding the Industrial Revolution. He argued that new inventions and revolutionary procedures adopted in the production processes in the cotton, iron, and mining industries stimulated phenomenal economic change and rapid industrial growth in the half century after 1750. He emphasized "modernization," although many historians have since rejected this term. The speed and depth of these changes brought about a reorganization of the workforce into factories and ultimately reshaped the political and social landscape of first Great Britain and then the Western world at large. Thus, the Industrial Revolution as Landes defined it was a watershed moment and indeed a revolutionary event. More recently, in the 1990s, Maxine Berg and Pat

Hudson reinforced Landes' revolutionary view in opposition to the gradualists by arguing that the fundamental nature of the change during the Industrial Revolution had already become obvious to millions of people in Great Britain living in its midst by the early 19th century.[18] Nathan Rosenberg and L. E. Birdzell argued that the growth of legal and commercial support for enterprising adventurers ensured the long term success of the Industrial Revolution.[19] Joel Mokyr proposed that industrialization depended heavily on a combination of technical development and change coupled with the ingenuity and inquisitive nature of the inventors who could bring these two trends together to increase productivity. Mokyr believes that the British leadership role is directly attributable to the government's early protection of private interests.[20] Robert S. Dublessis approached the issue from the aspect of demand-driven industrialization. Consumer demand, in his opinion, created the conditions for enterprising entrepreneurs and inventors to fill the void with new schemes and approaches.[21] Finally, Keith Pomeranz opines that the strong European tie to the Americas provided a favorable climate for industrial growth as it led to ready export markets and economic expansion unavailable to the more inward focused areas such as China.[22]

Although scholars have long accepted the use of the term "Industrial Revolution," it is certain that the debate surrounding the Industrial Revolution will continue as new evidence and analysis provide grounds for fresh interpretations. Indeed, no clear cut beginning or ending of the Industrial Revolution has been agreed upon by all scholars. The unique feature of the Industrial Revolution not only frames the debate but also reveals the difficulty in defining the complexity of the era. It was not solely based on a specific or closely related cluster of events but rather involved the development of certain processes over time such as mechanization, political reform, and urbanization, etc. Then, too, some of the difficulty in its interpretation stems from the fact that more recently much of the scholarship on the Industrial Revolution has been the domain of economists as well as historians. Yet the Industrial Revolution not only touched the economic realm but also had a major impact on the political, social, and cultural ones as well. The opportunity for revisionism and widespread disparity in interpretation perhaps has been a natural development, as the long history of the era provides ample opportunity for a variety of research, reflection, and commentary. In addition, it is certainly true that the British experience with industrialization provided a model for other nations to follow but each did so according to their own specific political environment, cultural norms, and expectations. Therefore, the pace, characteristics, and impact of industrialization in France, Germany, the United States, Russia, and Japan, for example, while sharing similar characteristics and components with Great Britain, also proceeded at times along strikingly different lines. But whether the Industrial Revolution represented a sharp break or proceeded in an evolutionary and gradual fashion, the fact remains that its footprint created fundamental alterations in the modern world among the societies which it has touched.

Notes

1. E. Hobsbawm, *The Age of Capital* (London: Weidenfeld and Nicolson: 1st Vintage Books, 1975).

2. As quoted in *The Pulse of Enterprise: Timeframe 1800–1850* (Alexandria, VA: Time-Life Books, 1993).

3. A. Toynbee, *The Industrial Revolution* (London: Green and Co., 1894).

4. S. Webb and B. Webb, *The History of Trade Unionism* (London: Green and Company, 1884); J. L. Hammond and B. Hammond, *The Rise of Modern Industry* (London: Methuen, 1925).

5. P. Mantoux, *The Industrial Revolution in the Eighteenth Century: An Outline of the Beginnings of the Modern Factory System* (London: Cape, 1961).

6. A. Redford, *The Economic History of England, 1760–1860* (London: Longman, 1931).

7. J. H. Clapham, *An Economic History of Modern Britain* (Cambridge: Cambridge University Press, 1930).

8. J. U. Nef, *The Rise of the British Coal Industry*, 2 vols. (London: Routledge, 1912).

9. T. S. Ashton, *The Industrial Revolution, 1760–1830* (Oxford: Oxford University Press, 1948).

10. E. Lipson, *The Economic History of England* (London: Longman, 1934).

11. H. Heaton, "Introduction" in R. M. Hartwell, ed., *The Causes of the Industrial Revolution in England* (London: Methuen, 1967).

12. C. Wilson, *England's Apprenticeship, 1603–1763* (London: Longman, 1965).

13. W. W. Rostow, *The Stages of Economic Growth* (Cambridge: Cambridge University Press, 1960).

14. P. Deane, *The First Industrial Revolution* (Cambridge: Cambridge University Press, 1965); see also M. W. Flinn, *Origins of the Industrial Revolution* (London: Longman, 1966).

15. For these viewpoints see such works as E. P. Thompson, *The Making of the English Working Class* (London: Penguin, 1968) or B. Inglis, *Poverty and the Industrial Revolution* (London: Hoddler, 1971).

16. N. F. R. Crafts, *British Economic Growth during the Industrial Revolution* (Oxford: Oxford University Press, 1985); E. A. Wrigley, *Continuity, Chance and Change: The Character of the Industrial Revolution in England* (Cambridge: University Press, 1985).

17. D. Landes, *The Unbound Prometheus, Technological Change and Industrial Development in Western Europe from 1750 to the Present* (Cambridge: Cambridge University Press, 1965).

18. M. Berg and P. Hudson, "Rehabilitating the Industrial Revolution," *Economic History Review*, 45 (1992).

19. N. Rosenberg and L. E. Birdzell, *How the West Grew Rich* (New York: Basic Books, 1986).

20. J. Mokyr. *The Lever of Riches: Technology Creation and Economic Progress* (New York: Oxford University Press, 1992).

21. R. S. Dublessis, *Transformation to Capitalism in Early Modern Europe* (Cambridge: Cambridge University Press, 1997).

22. K. Pomeranz, *The Great Divergence: China, Europe and the Making of Modern World Economy* (Princeton: Princeton University Press, 2000).

CHAPTER 2

THE WAY WE WERE: ON THE EVE OF THE INDUSTRIAL REVOLUTION

After 1500 a number of factors gradually coalesced to pave the way for the age of industrialization that swept across Europe beginning in the middle of the 18th century. First, the long, uncertain, but ultimately successful road to recovery following the crises of the 14th century led to an eventual period of rapid population growth and a subsequent demographic shift from rural to urban areas. This development transformed and improved living patterns, particularly for the upper and middle classes. Second, the stimulus and inquiry generated by the Scientific Revolution in the 16th and 17th centuries influenced the spirit of invention and creation of technologies to increase the production of power around which industrialized organizations could be constructed. Third, the expansion of long-distance trade and commerce which began with the age of exploration and discovery resulted in favorable trends in commerce and finance which created unparalleled economic expansion and a consumer revolution initially for nations and regions of northern and western Europe.

Population Growth

During the 14th century, plague, foul weather, war, famine, and peasant uprisings devastated European society and resulted in the death of perhaps one quarter of the population. By the early 1500s, England's population stood at 4 million, France at 15 million, Italy at 11 million, and Spain at 6 million. By the beginning of the 17th century, these crises had generally abated and, despite a brief period of renewed stress in the first half of the 1600s, Europe sat poised for unparalleled economic growth. As conditions improved after 1650, population surged and changed the economic dynamics of Europe, setting the stage for the coming period of industrialization. From the late 16th century to the beginning of the 19th century, population in France, Spain, and the Italian and German states grew by 50% to 80% while that of the British Isles soared by 280%. The most dramatic increase occurred in the 18th century. In 1700 Europe's total population stood at 120 million, grew to 140 million in 1750, and soared to 190 million in 1790. In the same nine-decade period the population of Great Britain rose by 33% to 9 million, France by 33% to 27 million, Spain by 60% to 10 million, Prussia by nearly 300% to 5.5 million, and Russia by 100% to 28 million. This phenomenal increase resulted from improved food production and better diets and a decrease in death rates due to reduced famines and the gradual waning of plague (the last major outbreak occurred in 1720 and was confined primarily to southern France).[1]

The 18th century population increase was felt most acutely in the cities and generally in a relatively small number of urban areas. And, although the percentage of urban residents in Europe increased only slightly from 8% in 1650 to 10% in 1800, the actual numbers actually doubled when placed in the context of the overall rapid increase in European population over the same period. Furthermore, between 1650 and 1750 the number of European cities with a population of 10,000 or more increased by 44%. In 1500, half of the people living in cities of this size had resided in the Italian states, Spain, and Portugal. Beginning in 1700 and in an obvious indication of what was to come, population shifted north and west as cities on the continent with populations of 5,000 to 10,000 actually declined in this period, while those in Great Britain doubled in number. Indeed, in 1800 five of the six largest towns in Great Britain (newcomers Manchester, Liverpool, Birmingham, Leeds, and Sheffield) had been small and insignificant urban areas in 1600. By 1700, 11% of all persons in Great Britain resided in London and an untold number of persons constantly passed in and out of the city conducting business, settling legal issues, participating in the political life of the nation, and enjoying social pursuits. More than three percent of Frenchmen lived in Paris, but like London the capital exerted an influence disproportionate to its population over the surrounding countryside and beyond. Even if one counts the populations of Moscow and Istanbul in that of Eastern Europe, the region was noticeably less urban than Western Europe by 1750. Warsaw, for example, had only 23,000 inhabitants by that date. On the other hand, Amsterdam had become the new Venice, and Antwerp served as a major hub of trade and commerce. London's population had reached

675,000, Berlin had 90,000 inhabitants, and Paris doubled in population in the corresponding period. From 1750 to 1800, nearly 70% of all urban growth in Western Europe was occurring in Great Britain. London, always the largest city in Great Britain, was not even among the top ten cities in Europe in 1550, but by 1800 it was larger than any urban area on the continent.[2]

Changing Lifestyles

This rapid growth reshaped the appearance, lifestyle, and culture of the cities by the 18th century. In this new environment, one's social status was not an abstract concept but rather a reality demonstrated on a day-to-day basis. The large landowners usually kept impressive residences in the towns and lived in rich districts boasting wide streets, airy homes, and often possessing gardens. The wealthiest of this group spent their time dining on fine food, sporting the latest fashions in dress, riding in coaches throughout the city in order to flaunt status, reading books, or going to one of the growing number of social events such as the theater or opera. Dress often readily identified one's economic and social position. For example, lawyers wore dark robes, and masons and butchers had special aprons. The upper classes possessed multiple outfits in a variety of fabrics with designs and colors for adornment. Middle class families consisted of merchants and professionals who, depending on their level of wealth, might also possess some land in the countryside. By 1700, London boasted about 20,000 middle class families, which made up approximately one-sixth of its population.

The growing cities had a voracious appetite for consumption, particularly amongst the upper and middle classes, the latter whose rituals settled into a pattern and often emulated the upper classes and maintained a sharp distinction from the lower classes. But the middle class also occasionally influenced the behavior of the upper class. For example, the adoption of calico clothing by the English middle class in the late 1600s began as a bourgeois fashion statement that eventually found its way into the royal court. And, while the middle classes did not dine in as fine a manner as their upper-class counterparts, meals nonetheless became more varied and rich. For example, breakfast was light and consisted of toast or some form of bread. By the early 18th century, the middle classes in Great Britain had adopted tea as the fashionable drink. Dinner was taken in the middle of the day and comprised roasted or boiled meat or poultry, pork, and vegetables. The dinner meal was also light, perhaps bread, cheese, cake, and pie. Beer was the main drink in London, and many families brewed their own. Children partook of beer, as it often was safer to drink than the water. Not surprisingly, the French retained a preference for wine. By the early 1700s middle-class houses had a number of rooms, pictures and mirrors in most rooms, and a variety of items such as coffee and teapots, several clocks, and some form of a china service.

By the late 17th century, literacy made great progress among upper- and middle-class residents of cities, despite the fact that the number of schools and trained teachers remained woefully inadequate until the late 18th century. Great Britain and the Netherlands led the way with well over 50% of men and 25% of women in the upper and middle classes being literate by the beginning of the Industrial Revolution. France lagged behind, but about 50% of men and 27% of women could read by 1780. The growing evidence of an educated population is found in the cultural diffusion that accelerated in the 18th century. London displayed large numbers of printed advertising in public spaces by the late 1690s, and within a few years France and other regions on the continent had adopted the practice. Furthermore, Great Britain established procedures to license and control publications such as newspapers and magazines. The first London daily newspaper appeared in 1702. By 1780, more than three dozen British towns had daily publications, and Britain's first literary magazine appeared in 1709. It is estimated that when Europe's population surpassed 100 million in the 18th century, newspaper circulation had reached 7 million copies. Another example of the improved literacy level was the postal service. In 1660 mail was transported by boat between London and Amsterdam twice a week. Amsterdam in turn delivered postal materials overland to Hamburg, thus connecting a large portion of northwestern Europe. Likewise, in the early 18th century, Paris had commenced semi-weekly mail service to several towns in the French interior. By the time the Industrial Revolution was underway in the third quarter of the 18th century, improved roads and routes had cut in half the delivery time of mail. However, rapid and consistent movement of mail and improved communication required a massive effort to upgrade roads and develop other forms of transportation, a trend that did not begin until the late 18th century. In the early 1700s, Great Britain's roads were no better than they had been in Roman times some 1500 years earlier. The wet climate meant that for much of the year they were a muddy quagmire and impossible for any form of wheeled vehicle to traverse.[3] Indeed, in 1731 John Metcalf raced a Colonel Liddell from London to Harrogate in the county of Yorkshire. Although he was blind and on foot, Metcalf completed the journey in six days and arrived two full days before Colonel Liddell, who had travelled by coach. Stories also circulated that men at times drowned in the large potholes in East Anglia. And, the city of Lincoln constructed an inland lighthouse to guide night travelers over the surrounding plain because the roads near the city were virtually impassable after dark. These conditions would prevail until the development of improved roadbeds, the construction of canals, and the arrival of the railway and telegraph systems.[4]

Below the middle class came the artisans and shopkeepers who, in the early 18th century, still organized themselves in a guild system over much of Europe. Below these groups were the servants and laborers. As many as four out of five poor women might become a domestic servant in the city until they married. At the bottom of the scale was the unemployed poor who became homeless when work became infrequent. The poor were easily identifiable in their drab, meager garments. Poor women in Paris wore poorly fitting woolen skirts, dark blouses, caps, stockings, and a pair of shoes that often did not fit properly. The poor often found themselves on the dark edge of society, just beyond the more comfortable neighborhoods of the upper and middle classes. They usually gathered in cramped quarters on narrow, dark, dirty, and damp streets teeming with humidity and foul odors or sleeping under bridges or in abandoned homes like animals, with no consideration of age or gender.

To be sure, until the advent of the Industrial Revolution, life for the vast majority of Europeans was a hardship that focused on survival and remained concentrated in rural areas that had witnessed little change since the collapse of the Roman Empire a thousand years earlier. People adhered to traditional economic patterns that had been handed down orally from one generation to the next. The essential unit of society was the village community, with its inherent conservative nature. Agriculture was the dominant livelihood, and little real modification in farming practices had occurred until the Agricultural Revolution on the eve of the Industrial Revolution. The three field system still employed the use of manure, rotation of crops, and letting a field lay fallow as the primary means to enrich the soil. Cattle served as the primary source of meat for humans and fertilizer for the crops. The traditional and patriarchal family continued to be the basis of European society throughout this period and retained its ancient focus on the welfare of the collective whole rather than the individual. Childcare remained an important responsibility, but many children died in childbirth or at an early age. In the 17th century perhaps as many as 20% to 25% of all children died within the first year of birth. Of those children surviving the first year, it is estimated that half died by the age of 20. As the Industrial Revolution approached, the average number of children per household declined. However, peasant families often tended to have more children than their urban counterparts because of the necessity for additional hands to do the work on the farm. From 1650 to 1700, upper class families usually averaged six children. That number dipped to three in the first half of the 18th century and averaged two in the period 1750 to 1800. Later marriages contributed to this trend as men deferred marital age until 27 to 28 and women until 25 to 27. This development came about as breadwinners waited to establish their economic independence and resulted in a self-imposed means of birth control. Illegitimacy also remained relatively low for a large portion of the 18th century. Estimates for France are 1% and Great Britain 5% until 1750. In the German states the rate was about 2% in 1700 but increased five times over the course of the century. Rates for other countries increased to perhaps 20% by the end of the 18th century as the traditional family structure strained under the beginning throes of industrialization and as the old rural communities experienced the loss of population to the urban areas.

In the lower classes, rearing children created much more anxiety than in the upper classes. During the 17th century, approximately 10% of women died in childbirth. Children remained a health risk, not only for themselves but also for the mothers, and a burden on the family at large during hard times if there were many mouths to feed. Indeed, infanticide by what was claimed to be accidental suffocation was not uncommon. As the 18th century progressed, some steps were taken to protect children. In the Austrian Empire, for example, a 1784 law forbade children under five from sleeping in bed with parents. Furthermore, foundling homes sprang up across Europe and became depositories and hospitals for unwanted children. It is estimated that perhaps one-third of all children born in Paris on the eve of the French Revolution ended up in such an institution. With little regulation of their operations, it is not surprising that the mortality rate for children in foundling houses could be as high as 50% to 80%.

Even as conditions improved by the mid 18th century, life on the margin remained exceedingly difficult. The better economic times of the 18th century did not translate immediately into any improvement in the lower classes. Food production increased, but that did not eliminate sporadic shortages. Wages rose throughout the 18th century, although the rise in prices diluted its positive impact. With the increasing demand for food and manufactured goods by the 18th century, peasants who could sell their agricultural surplus at city and town markets and artisans who could successfully peddle their wares fared much better than peasants with meager holdings or city day laborers. These unfortunate souls often lost their land and livelihoods and wandered in the countryside seeking food, or ended up in the cities boosting the number of urban poor.

The upper and middle classes worried constantly about the number of poor in their midst. Throughout the 18th century, for instance, it is estimated that France had as many as 200,000 seasonal workers who migrated throughout the country. The numbers of beggars and vagabonds put an added financial stress on European governments. At times ten percent of Europe's urban population was on public welfare. One solution was to put these persons into workhouses that served as workshops, hospitals, and, on occasion, prisons. These institutions rarely achieved their stated purpose of finding individuals some measure of work because many of those entering the overcrowded workhouses were sick and died within a few months. The cost to governments could be staggering. Great Britain witnessed a 60% rise in the cost of its workhouses in the period 1760 to 1785. Even American cities such as New York, Boston, and Philadelphia sponsored similar institutions in the later 18th century to deal with the problem of the growing number of urban poor.[5]

The cities on the eve of industrialization remained dangerous, filthy, and experienced to a lesser degree the social woes that would attract efforts for reform in the nineteenth century. As the number of physicians grew, they found themselves having not only to convince a skeptical public of their value but also to fend off the likes of bloodletters, midwives, and charlatans who advocated unscientific remedies to a variety of ailments. Professional societies, government sponsored licensing, and widespread vaccination did not occur until the late 18th century. Thus, city dwellers, particularly the lower classes, continued to die in large numbers from following unsanitary practices, wearing dirty clothes, constant exposure to human and animal excrement, taking home remedies, and not understanding the basic health benefits of cleanliness. Bathing, for example, actually declined until after the Industrial Revolution began. Public baths were viewed as sources of disease, and private bathing was associated with making contact with impure water. Even the upper classes refrained from bathing for a great part of the 18th century, choosing instead to change bed linen and clothes and use cosmetics to mask the horrific stench and smell of daily living. Death therefore was always at the doorstep as influenza, typhus, smallpox, and dysentery continued to take their toll on the population throughout the 18th century.

The Role of Science and Technology

Until the 18th century, technology generally remained tied to agriculture. But at that point change occurred rapidly with the acceptance of new ideas and approaches in technology that would play key roles in the transition to the Industrial Revolution. Beginning in the early modern era, the number of works that focused on machines and technological subjects proliferated in Europe, emphasizing such subjects as weapon-making, iron working, metallurgy, etc. In addition, the spirit of rational inquiry that fueled the Scientific Revolution in the 16th and 17th centuries found practical application in the proliferation of technology that began to emerge in the 18th century. The old medieval practice of separating science and technology disappeared as the new approach was one of cooperation and collaboration between the two fields. The struggle took place in the 17th century between those seeking a grip on the old ways and the visionaries of the future. The latter would win. It became increasingly apparent that nature could be understood and manipulated, a realization that spurred a belief that change was positive and encouraged technical experimentation.

The growing number of scientific studies had the effect of focusing increased attention on the manufacturing field. Moreover, the growth of scientific societies across Europe joined in discussion and debate, those persons who conducted research on the theoretical aspects of technology with individuals such as merchants and manufacturers who had more interest in practical applications, solutions to specific technical problems, and the financial rewards that might be gained. For example, chemists married their discoveries with manufacturers who sought a better glaze coating for their pottery pieces. Likewise, studies in the properties of gases actually led to 17th century developments such as Otto von Guericke dabbling with the properties of atmospheric pressure and the first extremely primitive steam engine by Denis Papin—one designed to use water vapor to drive a piston in a cylinder. At the same time, other scientists advanced the idea that steam power might propel a boat. Thus, economic necessity stimulated innovation and invention and converted older techniques to more modern ones which could be utilized to build successful commercial enterprises. Indeed, even failed inventions often had the asymmetrical result of stimulating different inventions, even perhaps in unrelated fields. As a result, by the 18th century, technological advancements proved capable of solving heretofore perplexing problems in the two important industries of mining and cloth production, setting the stage for the acceleration of industrial development.[6]

Capitalism and Consumerism

Between the 16th and 18th centuries, major developments associated with economic growth had taken place across Europe in response to the emergence of a burgeoning overseas trade network. These trends became the foundation for the birth of modern capitalism. Previous medieval trade and commercial arrangements were too restrained by the guild system, remained local in orientation and adhered to inadequate financial procedures to handle the distance, scope, and scale of a growing world-wide economy. Fierce competition resulted in the creation of new communities across the Atlantic as the British, Dutch, and French gained a toehold in North America and the Caribbean and European ships dominated international trade and commerce. A complex hierarchy and trade network sent European manufacturers to Africa for slaves, who in turn were taken to the Caribbean and North America as a source of labor. Raw materials from the New World traveled to Europe and were exchanged for its manufactured goods that colonial subjects desired to acquire. The importance of the colonies cannot be underestimated. For example, colonial exports from Great Britain increased nine times in the period 1699 to 1774; French exports to its West Indies and North American colonies increased eight times in the 1700s. Colonial exports also represented the close economic relationship with Europe. Moreover, as the British textile industry blossomed in the early stages of the Industrial Revolution, American cotton exports to Great Britain outpaced its former main suppliers of India and Asia. These large-scale trade arrangements, often referred to as the Atlantic System, stimulated a major commercial revolution in Europe and resulted in a large accumulation of capital. Profits from these overseas ventures flowed into European agricultural development, mining, and the manufacturing enterprises in the early stage of the Industrial Revolution. In response, private interests experimented with new ideas in business, commerce, and technology and in many instances joined forces with governments to develop more complex and less constrained economic arrangements to increase profits, reduce risk, and sustain growth.

These trends included the breakdown of old family arrangements and its replacement with new organizations, fresh approaches in legal systems, adoption of new business practices and standards such as banking procedures, bills of exchange, a guarantee of insurance, and more sophisticated tax collection. In many cases, former family kinship business arrangements shifted to the idea of a firm around which individual working lives revolved and separated private family property and business interests. In the legal arena, Europe witnessed the emergence of sophisticated commercial law and court systems specifically designated to adjudicate disputes in trade and commerce. In the case of Great Britain, by the late 18th century this trend had resulted in the recognition that even foreign merchants should be provided a fair and impartial hearing in British courts.[7] In 1694, the Bank of

England was founded with an initial capital of 1.2 million pounds. Following the previous developments of the creation of a stock exchange in London in the 1660s and the establishment of rates of exchange for European countries, the Bank of England developed innovative financial instruments and facilitated the creation of a number of new regional or country banks over the next century. The growth of the banking system was a critical component in marshalling capital resources across the nation and stimulating private investment in transportation and new industrial infrastructure. The Bank of England, in the minds of some scholars, became an extension of the British constitution because it brought together men of property with the government—men who as members of the political system now also served as the watchdogs of government borrowing. Thus, wealthy and political interests joined forces in ways never before possible in the country. Trust between the borrower and the lender was the essential ingredient in the increasing sophisticated financial transactions. As a result there was a reduction in interest rates on bills of exchange or the money lent to the government from the pre-Bank of England rates of 12% to 20% to an average of 8%. In addition, the adoption of bills of exchange reduced the requirement to have huge sums of money on hand to conduct business. These monetary policies stimulated a financial revolution in the early 1700s.[8]

This practice began to find increasing utility in the growing number of complex international and regional transactions and resulted in the eventual appearance of deposit banking, which operated similarly to the process by which banks facilitate the transfer of large sums of money today. The country banks accumulated a ready money supply for the working capital that could be used by the growing number of entrepreneurs. Finally, Great Britain and the Netherlands became the first nations in northwestern Europe to adopt a more stable and rational system of taxation. By the 17th century, these nations had moved away from the old feudal approach of arbitrary confiscation and had adopted a stronger parliamentary or representative voice in the area of taxation. In fact, the merchant classes dominated the seats in their respective parliaments and thus guided tax policy to improve their respective position regarding wealth and investment. Thus, those men of means who had the ability to accumulate wealth were provided greater security to do so. The creation of a rational tax system meant that these individuals had identifiable collection rates and times and provided them the ability to accumulate wealth to pour back into a variety of investment ventures such as real estate, commerce, or manufacturing enterprises that emerged in the early days of the Industrial Revolution.[9]

These important trends contributed to the growth of a large consumer-oriented society in the 18th century, one that would only increase in size and consumption levels as the Industrial Revolution progressed. The expansion in population in the 18th century also resulted in the creation of a large number of new family and household arrangements and thus a stimulus for more goods and products. In many cases the former family enterprises began to shift from producing goods that it consumed itself to the production of goods that others might purchase. The ensuing consumer revolution occurred because the desire to acquire such goods and products became a prerogative not only of the wealthy but of all classes of society. It appeared in Great Britain first because the class lines of that nation were more blurred and social mobility was more possible than in other countries of Europe. Furthermore, the growth of literacy and the ability to be influenced by advertising and the printed word made more of an impression at an earlier date in Great Britain. Women and children began to find employment opportunities less tied to agriculture as the economy expanded in the 18th century, and more discretionary income became available. While it is true that necessities continued to dominate purchasing habits, there is evidence that income was increasingly available for the purchase of wants in addition to needs. As one example, the growing number of trade catalogues by the 18th century illustrates the variety of new and improved products from the booming British textile industry. Clothing certainly was a prime commodity, but apparel also stimulated accessory items such as buttons, belts, hats, shoes, handkerchiefs, gloves, etc. Not only did a variety of items appear for the first time, but they also began to be marketed by such distinctions as for women or men and by size, color, etc. In addition, the rise in demand created a corresponding increase in producer goods as manufacturers and businessmen purchased items such as machinery, tools, engines, and other forms of equipment for their firms and enterprises and, as a result, stimulated the growth of associated and subsidiary industries and enterprises. In this regard, the acquisition of producer goods increased the production and quality of consumer goods and also fueled growth in consumer demand.

Another example of the growth of consumerism was the increasing consumption of luxury items such as tobacco, sugar, tea, chocolate, and coffee. In 1660, the American colonies shipped 9 million pounds of tobacco to Europe. That number had risen to 225 million pounds on the eve of the American Revolution. In the last quarter of the 17th century, tobacco imports into Great Britain doubled. Sugar trade imports to France doubled in the years 1698 to 1733. In the 1770s, sugar made up 60% of Great Britain's imports from the American colonies and nearly half of France's imports. In the 1670s, almost no tea was imported into Great Britain, but a half century later it was 9 million pounds and by 1750 amounted to 37 million pounds.[10] These commodities created an insatiable demand in the European populace and changed social habits and patterns. For example, in the early 1700s England had an estimated 2,000 coffee houses, and within four decades almost every country town boasted at least two coffee houses. The first cafes appeared in Paris at the turn of the 18th century, the first coffee house in Berlin in 1714, and eight Leipzig establishments in 1725. Coffee houses became the local spots for men to gather, smoke, read the latest newspapers, imbibe, and converse on important topics of the day. The public sphere now gained greater visibility and acceptance and attracted the attention of an ever broadening spectrum of society.

Conclusion

At the dawning of the 18th century, Europe was in a position to embrace and exploit the rapid changes that had prepared for the coming Industrial Revolution. The dark days of the early modern era, ones that had been filled with death, uncertainty, and dislocation, had become a distant memory. Although life for many persons at the lower end of the economic and social spectrum remained a significant struggle, Europeans were poised to move from a rural society and economic foundation that had long been characterized by want and survival on the margin to one that was more urban and industrial and offered growth and hope for the future. Population had surpassed its 14th century levels and surged rapidly by the 18th century because of increased food supplies, healthier diets, and declining death rates from disease and plague. The increase in population brought about the beginning of a sustained shift of people from rural areas to the cities. These urban areas grew in size and composition, particularly in northern and Western Europe. New and complex economic and social organizations occurred as the upper, middle, and lower classes evolved and developed fresh and distinctive characteristics. The cities, to be sure, were challenging and often dirty and dangerous places to live and work, but the energy and opportunity that awaited its residents promised unlimited potential. At the same time, Europe experienced an intellectual revolution that broke down ancient thought patterns about the purpose and utility of science and technology and emphasized a cooperative relationship between the two disciplines. The growth of new scientific inquiry and its growing partnership with technology ensured that the spirit of innovation and inventiveness became key ingredients that fueled the Industrial Revolution after 1750. The explosion of overseas trade and commerce led to the quest for colonies, raw materials, and worldwide markets and in turn created new national and local financial institutions and relationships that provided the capital investment opportunities for the enterprises that arose during the Industrial Revolution. The cumulative result of these dynamic changes was the growth of a consumer society that developed an insatiable appetite for new products and behaviors that enhanced the lifestyle and standard of living of the peoples of Europe. The rapidly advancing tempo of economic development convinced many entrepreneurs and inventors that past ways and old technology did not meet the demands of this new environment. The stage was now set for the Industrial Revolution, that momentous era that would accelerate these trends to levels heretofore not seen.

Notes

1. C. M. Cipolla, *Before the Industrial Revolution: European Society and Economy, 1000–1700* (New York: W. W. Norton and Co. Inc., 1976), 256.

2. S. M. Beaudoin, *Problems in European Civilization: The Industrial Revolution* (New York: Houghton Mifflin Company, 203), 71–77; L. Hunt. T. R. Martin, & B. H. Rosenwein, *The Making of the West: Peoples and Cultures*, 2 vols. (Boston: Bedford/St. Martin's), 2: 581–585.

3. Beaudoin, *Problems in European Civilization*, 73.

4. *Pulse of Enterprise*, 51.

5. Hunt, Martin, & Rosenwein, *The Making of the West*, 2: 621–629.

6. U. Eco and G. B. Zorzoli, *The Picture History of Inventions* (New York: MacMillan Company, 1963), 195–196; P. Stearns, *The Industrial Revolution in World History* (Boulder, CO: Westview Press, 1993), 17–19.

7. Beaudoin, *Problems in European Civilization*, 75–76.

8. P. Deane, *The First Industrial Revolution*, 183–185, 191.

9. C. Hill, *Reformation to Industrial Revolution: The Making of Modern English Society, 1530–1780*, 2 vols. (New York: Pantheon Books, 1965), 1: 146–148.

10. Beaudoin, *Problems in European Civilization*, 75–76.

CHAPTER 3

THE AGRICULTURAL REVOLUTION IN GREAT BRITAIN

The "Agricultural Revolution" as a stimulus to the Industrial Revolution remains a much-debated topic. Some historians consider the label a misnomer that contributes to the myth that dramatic and far-reaching agricultural changes in the 18th century influenced to no small degree the launching of the Industrial Revolution. Other scholars have argued that the agrarian developments beginning in the 16th and 17th centuries and reaching fruition in the mid-1700s did indeed provide a solid foundation upon which industrial growth could be sustained until the late 19th century. This debate essentially is centered on whether one supports an evolutionary or revolutionary interpretation of the relationship of agricultural developments to the onset of industrialization. Despite the persistence of criticisms over the use of the term Agricultural Revolution, the fact remains that by 1750 significant political, economic, and social changes and the adoption of new farming techniques related to crops and livestock significantly boosted agricultural production, fed Great Britain's growing population with a smaller agrarian work force, and helped in some degree to prepare the way for the Industrial Revolution.

Until the middle of the 18th century, agriculture was the most basic technology of Western society, and on its success rested the survival and continuity of the communities that it supported. The landscape had long been characterized by fields that lay open and uniform all the way to the horizon broken only intermittently by hedges, stone walls, fences, or clusters of trees. The typical scene at the turn of the 18th century revealed several groups attempting to survive off the land. There was a patchwork of small plots marked out by small boundary stones. Larger holdings were usually not continuous but rather scattered around the agricultural district. The small tenant farmers and cottagers who worked such land more often than not had the right to graze their few animals and gather firewood on the large expanse of common land throughout the countryside. Below these groups were the poorest families owning no land but who eked out a living by farming whatever parcel they could work in the commons where they built their shacks. By its very nature, agriculture had remained a very conservative endeavor, rarely entertaining changes that might create risk to traditional practices and thereby reduce yields. Thus, for more than a millennium following the fall of the Roman Empire, basic agricultural practices had remained virtually unchanged and provided little more than subsistence for the population. The important modifications to agricultural techniques that did appear in the Middle Ages such as the iron-tipped plow, the three-field system, the use of heavy manure for fertilizer, and the cultivation of narrow, rectangular strips had indeed increased yields, but these changes generally remained within the scope of the long-established cooperative village community.

Beginning in the 17th century, several major developments paved the way for the agricultural transformation that occurred in Great Britain. Europe once again experienced favorable climatic conditions that persisted well into the 18th century, a trend that proved beneficial to the newly emerging farming practices and techniques that greatly enhanced agricultural productivity. Furthermore, political developments occurred in Great Britain that, after the Restoration of Charles II in 1660, gave impetus to agricultural changes that appeared over the next century. Parliament took action to free larger landowners from their previous heavy dependence on the monarchy, allowing them to gain absolute ownership of their estates. The last feudal tenures were abolished, and the government began to rely on revenues from excise taxes rather than taxes on land, a burden that fell increasingly on the poor. These shifts in land tenure and revenue collection served to free up capital so that larger landowners could make long-term planning and investment the cornerstone of their estate management. As a result, many of the historical agrarian relationships between landowners and their tenants, already in the throes of a long, visible change, eventually evaporated and the market place emerged as a major impetus for growth and prosperity.[1]

The changes on the land occurred slowly and gradually until the middle of the 18th century. Because of the fixed amount of British land, the only means to provide larger returns from the farms was to squeeze additional output from the existing land or to cultivate land previously seen as inadequate for agriculture. The classical economists of the 18th century—Adam Smith, David Ricardo, and Thomas Malthus—all concluded that sustained growth was not possible, as the state of agricultural productivity was static because the land needed to feed a growing population would eventually run out. This view centered on the notion that the food supply of a nation was directly proportionate to the amount of available arable land. It is understandable that this opinion was arguable in their eyes in the late 18th and early 19th centuries. However, it did not materialize because the massive changes wrought by the transformation of British agriculture proved more than sufficient to nourish its booming population.

What new approaches and practices stimulated these significant changes to British agriculture? It should be emphasized that during the late 18th and early 19th century, no radical agricultural inventions set the stage for the transition. The improvements that did occur were merely within the scope of existing technology, such as a modification of the moldboard on the plow to bury weeds, the introduction of the all-iron plow by the end of the 1700s, and then, shortly thereafter, interchangeable parts for plows. Rather, the significant development was that British landowners employed aggressive management and investment techniques. British farmers increased the land acreage under cultivation by reclaiming wetlands and cultivating lands previously not farmed. The British were certainly influenced by the Dutch example in the 17th century but took the approach to significantly greater heights. Many powerful and influential landowners aggressively pursued the consolidation of smaller, dispersed plots into larger ones. In many cases, livestock raising and the growing of crops became intertwined pursuits. Grain production more than doubled in the period 1600 to 1800 and new fodder crops appeared, and both trends meshed to support livestock through the winter months. The survival of additional livestock resulted in more manure for fertilizer and thus more enriched land and higher yields. In addition, selective animal breeding became an obsession, and the size and quality of herds increased significantly and provided further nutritional advances for the populace. These advances in agriculture found their impetus in the changing organization and ownership of the land brought about by a trend known as the Enclosure Movement.

The Enclosure Movement

This enclosure movement, or the consolidation of smaller agrarian holdings into larger estates, was not a new phenomenon in the 18th century. Some enclosures had occurred in the 1200s and again in the 16th century. In fact, Sir Anthony Fitzherbert's 1523 work *Boke of Husbandrie* observed that the latest agrarian trends were better suited to consolidation of larger tracts of land rather than the smaller farm estates common in his day. These earlier enclosures involved a relatively small number of land holdings and had little relationship to meeting the subsistence needs of the populace but rather focused on the production of wool for the growing textile and leather industries. However, in the 17th and 18th centuries, the pace of enclosures quickened and the ancient pattern of small land holdings began to wane rapidly as more acreage fell into the hands of larger landowners. This group comprised a successful and confident class of individuals who had become wealthy through trade or political office and desired the social status that came from the ownership of land and the old landed aristocracy which had begun to reassert itself by the first half of the 18th century. In reality, these landowners had formed a successful marriage of agrarian and urban means and were a secure and enterprising agricultural capitalist class. These men sought profits by increasing production for the growing agricultural market. A substantial amount of capital was required to meet the demands being placed on farm production through the use of new agricultural techniques and practices. Thus, these groups took advantage of low interest rates and on occasion mortgaged their estates to acquire the capital to purchase additional land, an approach that was beyond the means of the smaller land owners.[2]

Until the late 18th century, enclosures generally consisted of private contractual agreements between proprietors. If one or more larger landowners obtained property rights in an area, substantial pressure might be placed on the many small land holders to sell their property. Enclosures accelerated in the period 1730 to 1750 as cheaper food prices encouraged some of the yeomen farmers to sell their small holdings to those large landowners and use the profit to set up leasehold farms or become involved in the growing manufacturing enterprises. By 1770, the situation had become increasingly difficult for the poorer cottagers who farmed only a few strips of land in the open fields and supplemented their income by working part-time as laborers for their wealthy neighbors. They might be granted some tiny plot as the land was restructured. But their previous ability to graze cattle in common areas or to gather wood for fuel disappeared as waste lands increasingly became the property of larger land owners. On the fringe of these groups were the squatters who secured their livelihoods through wage earning, poaching, begging, and at times thieving. As the enclosure movement gained momentum, particularly after 1770, this group found their rickety abodes torn down to place more land under cultivation, and they ended up on the periphery of society, unskilled, and frequently unemployed and relying on the government to provide minimal subsistence through poor law administration. Many contemporary observers who chronicled the enclosure movement in the 18th century praised the trend because, in their opinion, it further subordinated the lower agrarian classes, forced them into perpetual labor, and denied their economic independence. For example, In 1732 Robert Walpole advocated a tax on salt, not candles, because such a levy would force the poor to work since they made their own candles. Such a view, while difficult to comprehend today, was the acceptable norm for the elites of the 18th century, who had little sympathy for the plight of the lower classes and looked how best to meet their interests of personal and national wealth.

After 1640, the government did not attempt to check the trend to enclose the land. All questions regarding enclosure fell to the interpretation of property rights under the provisions of common law. Naturally, this development led to a weakening of the position of the small and tenant farmers in relation to the more influential large land holders. Beginning in the early 18th century, more aggressive parliamentary action spurred on the enclosure movement. From 1727 to 1844, Parliament passed 4,000 acts approving the enclosure of 7 million acres of land. Over the next half century an additional 1,000 parliamentary acts enclosed 1 million acres more.[3]

During the early period of parliamentary involvement, Parliament generally did not work out the specific details of an enclosure act but rather left those provisions to the sponsors once it had passed. However, the large number of enclosure requests that occurred in the 18th century forced Parliament to pass the first Public General Act in 1801 in order to refine the procedures and save that body's time. Later the General Enclosure Acts of 1836 and 1840 permitted landowners to enclose land without referring the proposal to Parliament as long as a majority (consisting of both numbers and value of the land) opted to do so. The last major act in 1845 amended the earlier ones in order to protect the interests of smaller landholders. For the most part, each enclosure act appointed commissioners whose role was to administer the process. This General Enclosure Act of 1845 appointed permanent commissioners who drew a salary. These commissioners had the authority to award enclosures without submitting legislation to Parliament and to allocate plots deemed as fair equivalents of the previous open lands and common rights.[4]

That is not to say that those affected, the small farmers, cottagers, and the like, had no recourse. For example, in the period 1730 to 1839 in Surrey County, 101 enclosure bills were sent to Parliament and only fifty gained passage. While this is a higher percentage of failed legislation than found in most other counties, the statistics highlight that opposition did exist and was not necessarily meek. Some persons sought to modify only portions of the legislation to gain personal advantage in the bill, while the more serious opponents filed counter petitions. In Surrey County, some twenty-five counter petitions were filed against the enclosure proposals. These tactics might cause a new bill to be introduced or delay a decision on the original proposal, perhaps for years. Such opposition potentially was fraught with several challenges. At least one person amongst the group would have to be literate enough to read and understand the bill and explain it to fellow dissenters. Such opposition might lead to the hiring of a lawyer to represent their views. In addition, someone might be required to travel to London and spend perhaps weeks in the capital while the bill was being debated, an expensive and sometimes fruitless endeavor requiring substantial sacrifices for the group of farmers opposing the bill. So, in theory the small farmers and cottagers might have a free decision to make when the pressure arose to enclose lands in their community. However, it is obvious that no matter the outcome of legislation or persuasion, opposition might incur the ire of those powerful landlords who sought enclosure in the first place and result in the loss of common rights, increased expenses for rents and fertilizer, and perhaps even a voluntary departure from the village. In the end, 21% of British land had been affected by enclosures, two-thirds of the total arable land and one-third waste or common land.[5]

New Farming Techniques

The enclosure movement made a dramatic impact on British agriculture. The enclosures resulted in a period of land reclamation that opened up thousands of new acres for the growing of crops. This reclamation included the draining of wetlands, the opening up of wastelands and moorland for cultivation (perhaps as much as 30% of arable area of Great Britain from 1650 to 1800), and continuing deforestation, a trend that reduced British woodlands, although differently from county to county, from 10% of the land in the 14th century to just 5% in the early 1800s. The enclosure movement also introduced new crop rotation practices, stimulated regional specialization, and resulted in an increase in agricultural output. The real impetus for many of the agricultural changes came about as a result of the wave of agricultural techniques and advances led by energetic large landowners. Of particular importance were the innovations in Norfolk. The so-called Norfolk

System entailed applying a series of interrelated measures on the enclosed farm. These included the use of sandy soils of marl and clay to aerate the land and improve drainage, a four-crop rotation: turnips, barley, clover, and wheat, a shift from sheep production to grain and cattle, and the employment of tenants under long leases on the larger scale holdings. The 18th century witnessed the spread of the Norfolk approach to other parts of Great Britain and the old three-crop rotation cycle of winter crop, spring crop, and fallow withered away. The result was a tenfold increase in the land values in Norfolk in the period 1730 to 1760.[6]

Traditionally, several individuals have been associated with the forward-thinking and new techniques associated with the changes in British agriculture in the 18th century. More recent interpretation has downplayed their role significantly, but their names are worthy of mention, even if they merely represent the collective trend that had begun to modernize British agriculture. One such figure was Jethro Tull. He was educated at Cambridge and studied law in London. However, for health reasons he left his study of law and collaborated in agriculture with his father, who was a member of the landed gentry. In the early 18th century seeds were distributed (or drilled) into furrows by hand. Tull observed that the usual heavy sowing densities were not efficient, so he instructed his farm laborers to drill at somewhat precise low densities. He held the theory that plants obtained their nutrition through tiny particles that he named atoms. Tull believed that the persistent pulverizing of the soil through working it to greater depths would bring on better nutrition of plants. His agrarian laborers apparently did not follow his instructions to his satisfaction, so out of necessity he invented a machine to standardize the work. Although he was not the first person to dabble with a mechanized approach to planting seeds, his device was sophisticated enough to distribute the seeds evenly and at the precise depth required and then cover them with soil. The key aspect of his apparatus was to eliminate a major portion of the waste inherent in the previous seeding technique and to make the crop easier to weed.

After relocating and traveling in Europe to study techniques on the continent, he revised his machine and approach. He believed that he had eliminated the need for a heavy manure application and supposedly grew wheat in the same area for more than a dozen years without using manure as fertilizer. Skeptics believe that the soil remained fertile and productive because the device prevented weeds from taking control. His ideas did not take immediate root. In 1731 he published *Horse Holding Husbandry*, a work that provided specifics regarding his discoveries, although most observers believe that he overstated its importance. His difficult personality and the controversy generated by his book delayed widespread adoption of his approach until the 19th century. By that time, several other seed drill inventions and improvements had appeared. Nonetheless, his name has remained affixed to the development of the seed drill in generations of textbooks.[7]

Another important agrarian pioneer was Robert Bakewell. Born into a tenant farmer family in Leicestershire, he obtained enough means to travel in Europe to study farming methods. After his father's death in 1760, Bakewell inherited the family farm, which consisted of one quarter arable land and the remainder for grasses and grazing. Tradition states that he began experiments with manure fertilization in the grassland portion and conducted a major effort to irrigate the area by diverting river water and using canals to bring water to these fields. However, it was his interest in stock breeding that brought him notoriety. Until this time, farmers kept livestock of both sexes together in the same fields, a practice that resulted in random breeding and the creation of a variety of breeds possessing unique but often random traits. Bakewell decided to separate the males from the females and then forced the mating to occur deliberately and specifically. This approach known as the "in and in" or inbreeding meant that he obtained livestock that generally possessed both fixed and exaggerated characteristics that he deemed desirable. His first experiments were with an established Lincolnshire breed of sheep that he transformed into the New Leicester. This larger breed possessed delicate bones, a high quality fleece, and fatty fore-quarters. This latter trait was important as the British had a taste for fatty shoulder mutton to grace their tables. Bakewell also hired out his best rams to other farmers so that they might improve their stock. He also founded the Dishley Society, an organization with the mission to maintain the standards of the New Leicester sheep breed he had developed. The result was highly visible. In 1710 the average sheep sold at the major London market weighed approximately forty pounds. By the end of the century the weight had doubled.[8] Unfortunately, following his death, the taste in meat changed and his New Leicester sheep died out, although the later breeds maintained a lineage founded in his sheep. "Just as Boulton produced buttons for the people, not the nobility, so Bakewell said he did not breed sheep for gentlemen's tables but for the masses."[9] Bakewell's interests turned to cattle breeding. He observed that the Longhorn breed ate less and put on more weight and thus were the best meat producers. He applied the "in and in" technique to cattle with success but only for a short while. As with the New Leicester sheep, the fashion in meat consumption changed, and Charles Colling and his brother developed the Shorthorn breed that supplanted Bakewell's Longhorn cattle. Some critics have claimed that Bakewell has received more credit than he was due, because his new breeds barely survived his lifetime. Other commentators, while conceding that point, emphasize that his innovations in stock breeding influenced later practices and led to more meat for consumption by the general public.

Arthur Young (see Document 13) is also considered a controversial 18th century agriculture reformer. In 1759 he inherited his father's estate in Suffolk and began a series of agricultural experiments in order to increase cultivation. His real contribution was not in any specific improvements but rather in his keen observation and analysis of changes taking place around him in agriculture in the late 18th and early 19th centuries. He traveled widely in Great Britain and France and commented on developments in these countries. Beginning in 1770, Young wrote extensively for the next four decades, publishing works on experimental agriculture, agrarian developments in British counties and Ireland, and interesting commentaries on the state of French agriculture on the eve of the Revolution.[10] His writings were very popular, quickly ran through many editions, and were translated into several continental languages. His forty-five-volume *Annals of Agriculture* was in print from 1784 until the early 19th century. Young had a staunch belief in individual property rights, but he also possessed an open mind. He originally was a supporter of the enclosure movement but later lamented that it had put great stress on the agrarian lower classes. In one account he wrote about the wretched circumstances of one of the families dispossessed of its land. The scene he described was one of a poor, ill, and starving mother, lying uncomfortably on a bed too small for her frame, and her dead infant in a cradle beside her. His works are also laced with pithy quotes that speak of his close attachment to the land. For example, "Great farmers are the soul of the Norfolk culture."[11] After returning from France, his reputation led to his appointment as the Secretary of the Board of Agriculture in Great Britain. In this role he supervised the collection and preparation of agricultural surveys of the British counties. Unfortunately, in later life he experienced blindness brought about by cataracts and worsened by an unsuccessful operation to cure the ailment. Some critics have questioned the data he collected and the conclusions that he drew from his analysis, often referring to him as a charlatan or a mere scribbler. However, despite the flaws and inaccuracies found in his works, Young's importance rests in his insistence on keen observation of the conditions of the rural countryside and the collection of a compendium of data related to cultivation practices, livestock, and productivity of the land. These methods provided an early model for the application of statistical analysis to the changing nature of agriculture over time.[12]

The increase in arable land had several important impacts. Over the space of several decades, an increasing variety of crops such as asparagus, artichokes, and fruits spread across the landscape. That development, coupled with falling food prices, ensured that even the average person could afford a more diverse and healthy diet and contributed to the rapid growth in population. In addition, the new forage crops of alfalfa (lucerne), turnips, and clover supplemented the raising of hay and resulted in higher yields and the reclamation of former marginal pasture lands for productive farming. The turnip was the most important crop in this system. The turnip reduced the fallow land that formerly had been used to clear the land of weeds by plowing. However, crops of turnips planted in rows could be hoed to remove weeds while growing. In 1700 fallow land was 20% of arable land, but that percentage dropped to about 4% over the space of the next two centuries. Fallow land had been used in the past to allow time for the soil to replenish itself and to control perennial weeds. Fallows began to be replaced using crops such as turnips and clover, which accomplished the same end and provided additional nitrogen-rich fodder crops. Manure produced by the animals grazing on these crops returned a better fertilizer to the soil. In addition, higher yield crops, such as wheat and barley, replaced the lower yielding rye. In the 18th century, British wheat yields increased by a quarter and were 40% greater per acre than that of the French. An important contribution to the improvement of cereal yields was nitrogen, a property that farmers certainly did not know about until later in the 19th century. However, their practices indicate a growing feeding of nitrogen to the soil. The collection of manure from animal stalls and its application to needed areas was one means to increase nitrogen. The long-held practice of growing legumes continued to contribute to nitrogen enrichment. And, the introduction of red and white clover in the 17th century improved the amount of nitrogen in the soils used for cereal crops. It is estimated that in Norfolk the use of legumes and introduction of clover may have tripled the rate of nitrogen found in the soil from 1700 to 1850. The significance of this new approach was that it was sustainable, and thus the increase in food output could be maintained almost indefinitely, one key reason why Britain's burgeoning population could be easily fed even though the agrarian work force had dwindled.[13]

Agrarian Worker Productivity

New agricultural techniques and practices are one explanation for the increase in agricultural productivity and crop yields in Great Britain in the 18th and 19th centuries. A second was the phenomenal increase in worker productivity during the same era. The agricultural worker in Great Britain produced more food, allowing the proportion of workers devoted to agriculture to fall. By the 18th century, Great Britain had experienced an increased output per person engaged in agriculture. This feature of British growth is striking because the population more than doubled in that period, but the number of persons engaged in farming increased only moderately from 2.78 million in 1700 to 3.84 million in 1850. The actual proportion of the workforce engaged in agriculture actually had declined for several centuries, but the country nonetheless had achieved self-sufficiency in food production. This fact is even more remarkable when one considers that Britain's output per agricultural worker was double that of the rest of Europe in the period. By 1800, four in ten adult males in Great Britain made their livelihood by farming while the corresponding ratio on the continent was six to eight out of every ten persons, a number not seen by the British since Elizabethan times. By 1850, only 22% of the British worked in agriculture. Viewed another way, in 1600 the average farmer in Great Britain had produced enough food to support his family and half an additional one. By 1800 that same farmer could feed his own family and one and one-half more. By the mid-19th century, Great Britain had the lowest proportion of its workforce in agriculture than any other country in the entire world. Thus, the majority of the British agrarian workforce was not only providing food for their family but also farmed for the market.[14]

This ability of the British farmer to produce well beyond the subsistence level had an additional component. By the 19th century the agrarian worker harvested enough fodder to sustain a large draught animal force that contributed to increased productivity not only for the farms but also provided labor for the mines, growing manufacturing enterprises, and transportation. Scholars have estimated that an individual can produce only 1/10th the foot-pounds per hour as the horse, and that three oxen provide the equivalent work of two horses. There were approximately 19 million acres under cultivation in Great Britain in 1820. Just ten years prior, figures point to about 1.2 million horses in the nation of which 0.8 million were used in agriculture. By the turn of the 20th century those numbers had increased to roughly 3.21 million and 1.51 million, respectively. Using these numbers, it is estimated that almost six horses existed for every 100 acres of British arable land in 1820. Comparing the French animal numbers in a corresponding period underscores the greater productivity of the British. In 1820 France had an estimated 52 million acres under cultivation and 1.87 horse equivalents (horses and oxen), resulting in 3.6 horses per 100 acres of arable land or nearly 40% less than Great Britain. Draught animals also had an important uses well beyond the normal tempo of planting and harvesting the land. A large number of draught animals also produced additional manure and promoted higher cereal yields and in no small way contributed to a healthy diet. Furthermore, considerable animal labor was used in clearing land and transporting marl, lime, shells, chalk, and organic manure to the fields for application, sometimes at a distance of several miles from their supply points such as pits or stalls. It is estimated that 100 to 150 tons of marl had to be applied per acre. Thus, an estate of 100 acres required repeated trips back and forth, resulting in thousands of ton-miles of transport. This level of agricultural productivity resulted in an overall 43% increase in British farm output in the 18th century, and productivity improved further in the next century. Although there were exceptions, by 1800 the general nature of the English agricultural workforce had evolved gradually over the course of 200 years and consisted of the large landowners, tenant farmers, and a class of landless wage laborers.[15]

Conclusion

Despite the debates that historians engage in regarding the relationship and impact of the Agricultural Revolution to the Industrial Revolution, there can be little disagreement that significant agrarian changes were underway in the 18th century. This Agricultural Revolution consisted of a myriad of parliamentary and informal land tenure changes, the introduction of new crops and livestock breeding practices, and the adoption of innovative farming techniques. Led by enterprising and dedicated men, the agricultural developments increased the productivity of a smaller rural labor force that sustained a growing population, one that could be released from subsistence farm labor and shifted to other opportunities for work in the growing manufacturing enterprises of the nation. Thus, by the 19th century Great Britain's rural economy and society had experienced a dramatic transformation in large part fueled by the changes in the nation's approach to agriculture. The appearance of Britain's laboring folk, formerly reflected in their weather-worn and creased faces from toiling in the fields, now increasingly became that of the working men, women, and children in the mills and factories of the nation's booming industrial towns.

Notes

1. Hill, *Reformation to Industrial Revolution*, 1: 115–117.
2. T. Williams, *The History of Inventions* (New York: Facts on File Publications, 1987), 179; T. S. Ashton, *The Industrial Revolution* (Oxford: Oxford University Press, 1971), 18–19.

3. Williams, *The History of Inventions*, 199.
4. http://www.surreycc.gov.uk.
5. Ibid.
6. Hill, *Reformation to Industrial Revolution*, 222.
7. http://www.bbc.uk.history/historic_figures/tull_jethro.shtml; Ashton, *The Industrial Revolution*, 20–21.
8. http://www.bbc.uk.history/historic_figures/bakewell_robert.shtml; *Pulse of Enterprise*, 51.
9. Quoted in Hill, *Reformation to Industrial Revolution*, 1: 222.
10. For a detailed review of Arthur Young's travels and observations regarding French agricultural life, see M. Bentham, ed., *Arthur Young's Travels in France during the Years 1787, 1788, 1789* (London: George Bell and Sons, 1909).
11. Quoted in *Pulse of Enterprise*, 52.
12. http://www.econlib.org/library/YPDBooks/Young/yngTFO.html.
13. http://www.bbc.co.uk/history/british/empire_seapower/agricultural_revolution_03.shtml.
14. Ibid.
15. E. A. Wrigley, *Continuity, Chance and Change: The Character of the Industrial Revolution in England* (Cambridge: Cambridge University Press, 1988), 34–43.

CHAPTER 4

THE INDUSTRIAL REVOLUTION IN GREAT BRITAIN

The Industrial Revolution that began in Great Britain marked a distinct break with the continuity of economic life that had dominated the Western world for centuries. In the early 18th century, Great Britain's economy was similar to that of other nations in Europe, characterized by a heavy reliance on an agricultural system supplemented by basic handicrafts and localized commerce and mercantile activity. Spurred by a combination of favorable conditions, within the space of one century (1750–1850), Great Britain had erased the long-standing era of agrarian dominance and replaced it with a modern industrial and urban society. By 1850 Great Britain had become the wealthiest nation on earth and achieved a position of power and influence that no other country could rival. The booming cotton textiles, mining, and iron-producing industries brought about the transition, and new energy sources of coal and steam powered machines that were increasingly sophisticated replaced the age-old reliance on man, animal, wind, and water power. Great Britain's labor-intensive agrarian society gave way to a capital-intensive economy that was dominated by machine manufacturing, new arrangements to perform labor, and industry characterized by the factory system. These changes had enormous consequences and not only fundamentally altered the way the British people worked and sustained themselves but also changed Great Britain's physical landscape, political and social institutions, and the nation's outlook and relationship with the wider world. Indeed, the Great Britain of the mid-19th century had developed its own special setting and bore little resemblance to the nation of just a few generations earlier.

Causes of the Industrial Revolution in Great Britain

Historians have long debated the causes of Great Britain's emergence as the world's first industrial nation. These discussions notwithstanding, it is apparent that a number of factors had coalesced by the late 18th century to put Great Britain in the position to experience its "take off" moment on the road to embrace industrialization. These include Great Britain's geographical location in Europe, rich natural resources, the marriage of science and technology and inspired inventors, revised thinking about national economics, a ready supply of capital for investment and risk-taking entrepreneurs, government support for innovation and economic growth, an available labor supply, the rapid development of a commercial economy, and an ever expanding worldwide trade network to secure raw materials and markets.[1]

Geography

The luck of geography played directly to Great Britain's advantage. The relatively small and consolidated terrain coupled with rich farm land, a good river and improving road network, and an excellent coastline with sufficient ports linking Great Britain to the wider world ensured that the nation was knitted together economically on a far more efficient basis than its European counterparts. Long before their rivals on the continent, these advantages helped the British to reduce and then eliminate internal barriers to commerce. France, by comparison, had three times as many people as Great Britain in the 18th century. However, that nation retained much of its regional distinctiveness until and even after the French Revolution. A poor road network and many internal and local tolls and customs duties prevented France from adopting a new commercial attitude prior to the disruption of the revolutionary and Napoleonic eras. As an island fortress, Great Britain's separation from Europe allowed it to avoid on its home soil the ravages of warfare (other than the Civil War of the 1640s) that had devastated continental Europe during the 17th century and the international conflicts of the 18th century. Thus, Great Britain invested less in defense and retained more of its young, talented, and energetic citizens who in ever increasing numbers turned their attention to economic matters. Even during the upheavals of the Napoleonic Wars, Great Britain did not resort to burdensome taxation and military conscription. After the defeat of Napoleon's fleet in 1805 at the Battle of Trafalgar, little disruption occurred in Britain's trade network. Furthermore, Napoleon's heralded Continental System, which had as its purpose the boycotting of British goods and stifling of its economic clout, collapsed under the weight of Britain's cheaper and higher quality products.

Resources

Great Britain also had a readily available treasure trove of coal and iron ore, key ingredients needed in the manufacturing enterprises. Coal had early replaced Great Britain's rapidly dwindling supply of wood as a source of heating, but the Industrial Revolution brought new applications such as the generation of steam power. Great Britain sat atop a large seam of coal that stretched from the British Isles through Belgium and France and across northwestern Europe. It is noteworthy that the most advanced industrial development in Europe occurred along this rich seam of coal. Great Britain mined an ever increasing amount of coal: in 1700, 3 million tons a year (six times the rest of the world combined); in 1800, 11 million tons; in 1830, 22 million tons; in 1845, 44 million tons; and in 1870, more than 100 million tons.[2] The existence of such large deposits of coal provided Great Britain's growing industrial base with sufficient fuel to power rapid and widespread expansion. During the 17th century, small scale manufacturers had discovered how to produce coke from coal through the use of special ovens that heated and concentrated the coal. This coke was then used in place of the former wood-derived charcoal to smelt iron ore. This process became more proficient as sophisticated furnace designs appeared and steam blasting made the process more efficient. The growth of the iron industry had other major impacts. It stimulated the mining industry so that sufficient coal could be harvested for the iron smelting process and the production of steam power. It also introduced the production of iron rails to move carts of coal and other materials from the mines to the manufacturing enterprises. Lastly, the growing availability of cheaper, usable iron found utility in the production of steam engines, spinning, and other machines at an ever increasing pace.

Inventive Spirit

Another key aspect of the Great Britain's industrial progress was the impact of the inventors who developed new machines and techniques to solve problems of productivity and save labor. It seems reasonable to conclude that in the 18th century, Great Britain enjoyed a greater degree of technical skill and fascination with machine operations than that found on the continent. One assumption is that the rigid influence of the guild system and the heavy-handed mercantilism of the other nations of Europe fixed attention on solutions of the past and thus stifled imagination and new thinking. This approach likely explains why, as Great Britain moved into the throes of industrialization, the other countries of Europe did not hasten to copy the British model until much later. Although all scholars do not agree, some have speculated that this somewhat unique characteristic of the British to seek new solutions may have its roots in the Scientific Revolution of the 16th and 17th centuries. It is impossible to understand completely the mind and motivation of the important inventors who forever modified the direction of British technology in 18th and 19th centuries. However, the developments in science probably persuaded some that nature had a rational explanation and potentially could be controlled for productive purposes. Carried a step further, the implication was that beneficial change was possible, and the result was a wider interest in developing and utilizing new technical experiments.

A brief survey of the background of a few of the major inventors dispels any notion that they were merely uneducated tinkerers who plodded by trial and error. While social advancement often remained tied to aristocratic means, Great Britain had moved further than any other nation in Europe to recognize and appreciate talent that opted to pursue other livelihoods to achieve financial success. Manual labor and technical skill were not viewed as negative attributes. Some inventors had a measure of education, particularly backgrounds in the mathematical principles of arithmetic and geometry. Captain Thomas Savery ("Miner's Friend" steam engine) was from a notable Devonshire family; John Kay (flying shuttle) was from a substantial yeoman family; Samuel Crompton's (mule) father worked in agriculture but gained a comfortable living from producing cloth as a second source of income; Edmund Cartwright's (power loom) father was an aristocrat, and he himself graduated from Oxford. Furthermore, the breadth and depth of such knowledge sprinkled itself throughout the realm as the industrializing areas of Lancashire, for example, recruited craftsman from across the country and used their skills to perform tasks required of the new industrial enterprises.

Economic Theory

The 18th century also witnessed a new intellectual approach to explain and harness the economic dynamics of the era. The most influential thinker was Adam Smith (1723–1790), who became the notable proponent of *laissez-faire* economics. His significance is more surprising because of his provincial upbringing. Smith was born in a rural

Scottish village where iron nails rather than minted coins were used for money. He experienced an unhappy childhood. His father died six months before his birth, and at a young age he was kidnapped by gypsies. Only the strong-willed perseverance of his uncle resulted in the reunion of Adam with his family. He grew up to be a near-sighted but inquisitive, brilliant scholar who also had eccentricities such as absent-mindedness and having lengthy conversations with himself or falling into trance-like states. In 1759 he published *The Theory of Moral Sentiments*, a work that explored the motives, self-interest, and impartiality of society. He became a professor at Glasgow University in Scotland and spent two years traveling throughout Europe, where he conversed with David Hume, Voltaire, and Benjamin Franklin. Smith's seminal work was the 1,000 page *The Wealth of Nations*, published in 1776, the year of the outbreak of the American Revolution. Smith attempted to put complicated economic theories into a narrative that the common man could comprehend. This work was so influential that it appeared in Danish, French, German, Italian, and Spanish within just a few years. Smith is often referred to as the world's first economist, although he did not view himself as a revolutionary. He set out to describe his version of how an economy should move from agriculture to mechanization. He proposed three key principles of economics, and in so doing argued against the state-directed mercantilism, the prevailing economic theory of the day. His main focus was the advocacy of free trade. He first attacked the idea of protective tariffs, proposing that if one nation could sell its product to another more cheaply than the latter could produce it, that nation should purchase the product rather than make it.

Smith's second major principle was the labor theory of value. He did not see the soil, gold, or silver as the basis for a nation's wealth but rather the combined labor of agrarian workers, artisans, and merchants as the natural wealth of a country. He viewed the new factory system as one in which each worker performed a specific task in the process of production, an approach that was essential to the development of a thriving economy. Finally, Smith argued that the state should not interfere in economic affairs but rather focus only on its defense, law, and order and infrastructure (roads, canals, etc.). Smith advocated letting the consumer, not the government, determine the price of goods and asserted that institutions were not responsible and did not contribute to more efficient production. His belief in letting the forces of the marketplace dictate the nation's economic tempo came to be referred to as the "invisible hand" theory. He believed the sum of individual economic interests, even those motivated by greed, were compatible with the interests of the nation at large. These ideas may seem somewhat elementary today but in the late 18th century they were revolutionary, a clear statement opposing the medieval idea of wealth as sinful. His view, known as economic liberalism, meshed neatly with the interests of the growing manufacturing sector of Great Britain by the beginning of the 19th century and in turn was embraced by those same classes that emerged in other nations as the Industrial Revolution spread.[3]

Capital Investment and Entrepreneurship

Great Britain also had a sufficient supply of capital available to invest in machinery and large industrial facilities needed to house them. Much of the capital for industrial investment was derived from Great Britain's favorable trade balance created by its burgeoning colonial empire in the 17th and 18th centuries and the profits from the domestic sale of agricultural and cottage industry goods. Furthermore, members of the British aristocracy did not have a bias against commercial activities, and many engaged in establishing manufacturing and mining operations. And, while aristocratic bloodlines remained relatively pure, the marriage of wealth and entrepreneurship through investment opportunities provided real stimulus for industrial growth. Great Britain's central bank and the regional banks that had emerged by the 18th century facilitated a flexible credit system that relied on paper instruments to make capital transactions (see Chapter 2). New partnership arrangements, not specifically tied to family, arose to pool capital and establish borrowing terms aimed to keep interest rates low. Banks frequently extended credit for three months for commercial transactions and echoed more modern versions of revolving or open credit accounts and overdraft protection. These factors produced a highly favorable business climate where working capital had a much greater impact than fixed capital.

The impact of these new financial opportunities can be seen in the early transition of British industrial enterprises. In the first part of the 18th century, the craft shop continued to dominate industry at the local level with its organization of master craftsman, journeyman, and apprentice. The artisan had his livelihood inextricably linked to the merchant who supplied him with the necessary raw materials for production and then peddled the completed work often outside of the local area as he had an understanding of the interests of customers in far distant places. Farmers in the off season and women and children with free time on their hands were also a ready-made work force. Merchants saw the cheap labor supply in the countryside as a boon to their financial success. This cottage industry format proved successful in certain industries. For example, the wool industry remained in this mode for the greater part of the 18th century and grew from producing 6 million pounds in 1700 to 9 million pounds a century later.

However, beginning in the 18th century, a number of entrepreneurs and inventors began to realize that this domestic arrangement was insufficient for the new economic challenges and opportunities. The growing population and demand for consumer goods began to outstretch the production capability of the cottage craft industries. Inventors allied with the early manufacturers who generally were merchants experienced with selling finished goods from Great Britain's thriving cottage industry. Because these men were attuned to the ongoing changes, many realized the possibilities for increased profit inherent in larger manufacturing entities using the machines being constructed by the inventors. For example, between 1769 and 1800, some 110 cotton spinning mills operated in an area known as the Midlands. Of this number, 62 had been established by merchants and entrepreneurs who had made a profit in some aspect of the cottage textile industry.[4] The new machines were generally rather easy to construct and, although more costly than previous devices, remained inexpensive enough for substantial investment opportunities. For example, as late as 1792 a typical spinning jenny with 40 spindles cost only 6 pounds and a carding machine only 1 pound per inch of roller width. Mill owners might also save expenses by picking up advertised used items for a cheaper price. The real capital investment was in the buildings for the factories and the growing reliance on new power sources to run the machines. In reality, until the 19th century the large factory was not the common sight in the industrial districts, as most mills were essentially just more sophisticated workshops of the past. The typical cotton textile mill in the late 18th century consisted of less than a dozen workers, one or two spinning jennies or mules, and a carding machine with the power supplied by the men or women working the equipment. But the growing demand soon led to the realization that the emerging large factory environment required a small bureaucracy. The new tasks required to run the operation—purchasing raw materials, supervision of the work force, and the selling of the goods produced—could not remain the purview of one man as in the old cottage industry. Thus, the old family firms broadened their scope and brought in entrepreneurs to earn the potentially large profits. There continued to be a fine line between success and failure, as a bad harvest or economic disruption from war, etc. might spell doom for even the most efficient entrepreneur. However, the constant flow of capital into these new and growing ventures ensured the long-term success of the Industrial Revolution in Great Britain.

Government Support

The British government provided substantial support for the Industrial Revolution both in its overt actions to stimulate growth and also by its willingness to allow the new economic forces to gain momentum with little political interference. The revolutions of the 17th century created in Great Britain a climate of power that rested in the hands of forward-thinking individuals who saw the opportunities inherent in economic change. The more conservative absolutist governments on the continent based their power on tradition and the status quo, whereas in Great Britain the government encouraged economic innovation and change. For example, tough tariff restrictions in the 18th century had banned the importation of cotton cloth from India and therefore supported new industry. In addition, the British government forbade the export of industrial technology, in order to prevent other countries from latching onto and imitating British developments. Parliamentary law facilitated the organization of new companies and enterprises and restricted the ability of workers to form combinations or unions. Local governments also had much more of a free hand in supporting industrial growth in their areas by assisting in the funding of roads and later canals and ultimately railroads.

This infrastructure meant a faster transportation of raw materials and finished goods and ultimately reduced costs. Furthermore, there was little government regulation of manufacturing activities unlike on the continent, where rules dictated the quality, technology, and working conditions of the workshops. Even the nature of British urban life as the industrial revolution began differed significantly from the rest of Europe. Cities on the continent such as Paris and Madrid served as administrative, judicial, and religious centers and were dominated by bureaucrats, military men, shopkeepers, artisans, and domestic workers to support these groups. These political and cultural centers pulled in revenues and rents from the rural areas. The German states were fractured into rural areas dominated by local capitals. Great Britain, on the other hand, had its national seat of power in London, but the overall size of its political structure was smaller than its European counterparts and not all the fruits of economic activity flowed to the center. By the 18th century the older urban centers such as York, Chester, Stafford, etc. were in decline, and already the new industrial entities in the northern and western parts of Great Britain such as Manchester, Birmingham, Leeds, Glasgow, etc. had revealed their emerging economic power. In addition, a growing number of industrial villages sprang up connecting the rural areas to the nearby growing industrial centers and ensured a steady and smooth flow of goods and raw materials.

Labor and the Factory System

After 1760, Great Britain experienced a visible shift in the workplace from the artisan's shop and cottage industries to the factory. The dramatic changes in agriculture, rapid increase in population, immigration, rise in consumerism, relaxing of legal restrictions related to the poor, and rapid innovation and the entrepreneurial spirit created conditions favorable for a supply of labor to work in the larger factory enterprises by the time of Richard Arkwright (see Document 4).

The transition had begun in the late 17th century. As an example, some farmers in Yorkshire had combined agriculture with wool cloth production in order to supplement their income. Within the space of just several decades some of these farmers had purchased additional wool and hired others to produce the cloth for them. Within a generation, these families had separated themselves from the others and begun to form their own class, hiring and firing workers as disposable pieces in their enterprises and viewing themselves as socially superior. The primitive model for factory work and organization had begun. By the 1730s this new approach became more commonplace as the population began to grow rapidly. The impact of agricultural changes brought about by the consolidation of land holdings and new efficient techniques reduced the opportunities related to farming. While the overall agrarian population increased during the 18th century, its percentage of the workforce actually declined. Thus, businesses and entrepreneurs turned to hiring wage earners to perform labor for them.

Technology also played a major role in the establishment of the new workforce profile. While the more primitive handcrafts remained viable well into the 19th century, it became increasingly apparent that mechanization served as a magnet to draw workers into the new factory organizations. These workers could be unskilled or require only rudimentary training to operate devices associated with manufacturing. As the process of spinning and weaving in the cotton industry became wedded with the power of steam, factory centers grew rapidly near energy sources or where a large pool of workers was available. The result was a significant demographic change in Great Britain between the late 18th and middle of the 19th centuries. Of the ten largest cities in Great Britain in 1851, six were factory towns, of which only three were of any national importance before 1700. Indeed, two of the factory towns—Birmingham and Leeds—were unincorporated until the 1830s. Manchester, the cotton capital of Great Britain by 1830, grew from a population of 25,000 in 1777 to more than 300,000 in 1851.[5] Glasgow and Bradford's population leaped four times in the first half of the 19th century. The important centers of textile manufacturing and metal working, Birmingham, Leeds, and Sheffield, increased in population by more than 40% in the period 1821 to 1851.[6] During this era a majority of British families moved and saw their livelihood shift from a reliance on agriculture to one associated directly or indirectly with industrial activity.

The demographic shift had to overcome some impediments. The 18th century transportation infrastructure had to improve before the mobility of the population could be affected. The road network, although often unsafe due to banditry or kidnapping, was sufficient for foot traffic but often unsuitable for heavy transport. It would take the appearance of improvements such as the macadam roadbed, the canal system, and later the railroads to speed the transformation. Another restraint was the administration of the Poor Law. In the 18th century the law stipulated that if a person left his parish and remained in another for a year he lost his relief privileges in the former and could apply for such in his new domicile. For this reason, many parishes frowned upon accepting newcomers. As a result, business owners in dire need of workers often resorted to hiring laborers for short periods of time. Workers who fell on hard times were forced to return to their original homes in order not to lose their relief subsidies. In addition, it took some time for earlier work practices to adjust to the new economic realities. In certain corporate towns, it had long been illegal to earn a skill without first becoming an apprentice for six or seven years. While this deterrent withered away fairly quickly as the process of industrialization gained pace, employers also faced the difficult task of selecting those persons who seemed capable of quickly learning and adapting to the new form of industry and at the same time prevent them from accepting some better wage offer. The Watt-Boulton enterprise, for example, required men who constructed their steam engines to enter into either a three or five year labor agreement. Other individual factory owners had arrangements that might range from twenty-five years to life. One might assume that where labor arrangements were not specific, there might have been a rash of "labor raiding." However, other natural forces were at work. If an employer sought to entice a worker from another area, he often found that he might be unable to offer work to other members of the worker's family. Thus, some employers developed creative solutions such as diversifying their operations by starting a textile mill near their iron works to provide women and children employment opportunities or ensuring agricultural work for the men where female and child factory labor was the aim.

Other factors also arose to ensure that the labor supply for the factories grew to meet the need. As the pace of industrialization quickened in the late 18th century, large numbers of unemployed and unskilled persons who fell under the Poor Law relief provisions were encouraged to move from London and the south to the textile factories in the northern and western portions of Great Britain. As word spread of higher wages being paid in manufacturing and in the face of famines of 1782 to 1784 and 1821 to 1823, large numbers of Irish men and women poured into Britain, a substantial portion taking up occupations in the mining and textile industries. Some of these labor gains were offset by the departure of Englishmen and Scots for overseas locations, although the British government expressly prohibited the emigration of individuals in certain positions in order to prevent the loss of industrial secrets to competitors. These restrictions were lifted by a series of statutes between the years 1815 and 1824, and afterwards British labor could move freely to any country.

Thus, in the first half of the 19th century, Great Britain had accumulated a large body of wage-earners who now toiled in the factories, occasionally peddled their labor by moving from place to place, and found their pay closely tied to the overall economic dynamics at work in the country at large. The details of the 1851 census reveal the depth of the transition for the British working classes. Approximately 4 million persons (43% of the workforce) were engaged in manufacturing and mining industries, while 2.1 million persons (22% of the workforce) were tied to agriculture.[7] The cities also supported a large domestic work force and artisans and crafts people continued to have viable trades for a time, but the latter's inability to compete with the cheaply produced factory goods spelled eventual doom. Women and children also sought employment in factories and mines. The former economic system of local markets that operated in a less than perfect manner now had evolved into a national economy where wages in one industry were tied to those in others, to include even farm laborers. This change in the lifework of individuals marked a far cry from the agricultural economy that had dominated Great Britain prior to the 18th century. While it was truly a significant event in the long-term, it did not occur evenly or quickly throughout Great Britain.

The Cotton Stimulus

The cotton textile industry, rather than wool, became the major agent for the Industrial Revolution in Great Britain. The cotton plant is subtropical in its origin. Its light, durable characteristics made it very popular with the British public, a trend that was facilitated by its importation from the Middle East, particularly Egypt, through Great Britain's thriving overseas trade.[8] In 1700, British cotton imports totaled about 1 million pounds and wool approximately 40 million pounds, a difference that remained similar for half a century. Most cotton manufacturing in the first half of the 18th century took place in small workshops and on farms in Lancashire, and by the 1760s cotton increasingly had become the nation's major manufacturing enterprise. The change came about despite laws that lingered on the books and supported the older wool industry. One such provision was the requirement that all burials would use woolen shrouds and restrictions on the importation of competing fabrics such as cotton. Despite these laws, cotton could not be denied its new role and the timing could not have been better. Great Britain found the growing American cotton supply a boon to the increased demand for the fabric as the supply rose significantly, particularly after the invention of the cotton gin, and the price fell markedly. In 1760 Great Britain's raw cotton imports had risen to two and a half million pounds. A generation later that number had increased nearly ten times and by the 1830s had grown to 366 million pounds. Perhaps most significantly, by 1860 the cost of cotton imports was no different that it had been in 1700. In the mid 19th century Great Britain had 1,800 cotton mills generating 53,000 kilowatts of steam power and employing 328,000 workers who produced 1.75 billion yards of cloth.[9] One factor that contributed to this phenomenal growth was the fact that the fabric was better suited to the new mechanization processes sweeping Great Britain. Wool fiber is less substantial and consistent than cotton, which has a tough plant fiber and proved more adaptable to the unpredictable and sometimes awkward operations of the early machine devices. Even the adaptation of wool production to machinery could not compete with the speed and quality of cotton production. Finally, cotton found an eager and expanding market, as the taste for this more comfortable and easy to wash and maintain fabric had a revolutionary impact on work and everyday dress. Cotton allowed for the dying of vibrant colors and generated new fashion styles for the upper classes. But more significantly the wearing of cotton undergarments by the common person became commonplace. While production of woolen goods did grow throughout the 18th century, an insatiable appetite for cotton goods arose not only in Great Britain's prime markets but also in temperate climes such as the Mediterranean, the Americas, West Indies, Africa, and Southeast Asia. British cotton exports to the American and West Indies colonies, for example, increased from 10% of its national total at the turn of the 18th century to 37% on the eve of the American Revolution and to nearly 60% by the late 1790s.

In addition to the availability of cotton, technology became another driving factor for the industry. Textile manufacturing took place in four steps: cleaning/combing, spinning, weaving, and finishing. In 1700, little mechanization was available. One issue was providing the weavers with a sufficient amount of yarn. Necessity and demand drove the new developments. In the span of six decades a number of machines appeared that would undermine the old cottage industry approach and solve the problem of matching production capability with demand. John Kay's flying shuttle (1733) provided weavers with increased speed, and Edmund Cartwright's power loom (1787) replaced the individual weaver at each loom with a number of looms capable of being powered by steam or water; a variety of spinning frames in the 1750s; Hargreaves's spinning jenny in the 1760s, which provided the single spinner the ability to spin multiple threads simultaneously; Richard Arkwright's water frame (1769) and Samuel Crompton's "mule" (1779), a hybrid of the water frame and jenny, combined to facilitate the process through mechanization. These devices, primitive by later models, provided advantages of six to twenty-four to one for a typical spinning jenny and perhaps 200 to one for the frame, a ratio that made the old spinning wheel obsolete. Yet even the most sophisticated eighty-spindle spinning jenny soon became incapable of competing with the steam power-driven mule that could operate 200 to 300 spindles.[10] James Watt's steam engine was first applied to cotton manufacture in 1785, and the boom began. The quantity of yarn produced increased 12-fold by 1800 and stimulated enhancements in the weaving process.

Ironically, despite the appearance of steam power driven machinery, the prosperity and wages of spinners and hand-weavers actually rose in the last two decades of the 18th century because of the insatiable demand for cotton goods. The trend to mechanization, however, became a substantial threat and sounded the eventual death knell for this occupation. The power loom was the catalyst. The device operated on par with the hand loom for several decades and had to overcome the problem of breaking threads. Although a solution was found, the disruption of the Napoleonic Wars and the trade restrictions placed on Great Britain delayed its widespread adoption until the 1820s. By that time one young boy operating two power looms could equal the output of 15 hand weavers. A decade later, one man and one boy assistant operating four looms produced twenty times that of the hand weaver. The number of power looms proliferated in Great Britain: 2400 in 1813, 14,000 in 1820, 55,000 in 1829 100,000 in 1833, 250,000 in 1850, and 369,000 by 1857.[11] The number of hand weavers naturally declined although not without great resistance. It is estimated that some 250,000 hand weavers remained at work between the years 1810 and 1820, although the number fell dramatically to roughly 3,000 by 1850. Furthermore, the preliminary tasks in cotton textile production, such as cleaning, carding, and roving, also lent themselves to mechanization and thus added to the speed of the overall process.

That is not to say that the entire transition went smoothly. Lack of uniformity in machines and the frequent early breakdowns in equipment forced restarts and meant that much trial and error had to occur before success could be assured. Once the flaws had been corrected, British cotton production increased and exports soared. In 1800 Great Britain's export ratio to domestic consumption of cotton cloth stood at four to three. By the late 1840s cotton made up about 50% of all British exports. Initially, the continent was the main market for British cotton, taking in one third of Britain's exports, but increasingly Great Britain cast a wider net for its export market. After the 1820s, Latin America purchased one fourth as much cotton from Great Britain as Europe, but that percentage rose to one half by the 1840s. As the British advantage in machine production advanced steadily, it virtually destroyed India and Southeast Asia's hand labor ability to compete and resulted in a 1,500% increase of British cotton exports to those areas in the 1820s and 1830s. For example, in 1813 Great Britain imported more than 2 million pounds of cotton cloth from Calcutta, India, but by 1830 Britain was exporting that same amount *to* Calcutta. Africa also felt the effect to a lesser degree, and only China resisted the British juggernaut until after the Opium Wars.

The British cotton industry experienced a major transition from 1750 to 1860 because of a number of factors. A growing consumer market placed a new and rising demand for cotton textiles. A thriving inventive spirit solved a number of problems that had created a bottleneck in the spinning and weaving processes. Entrepreneurs seized upon these developments and with few constraints standing in the way pushed for ever greater productivity using water and then steam power. Thus, the older, more primitive small-scale cottage industries could not compete with the new bustling factory enterprises emerging in areas such as Lancashire. By 1857 the once idyllic rural landscape had been transformed by the smoke belching from more than 2,200 cotton mills operating 33.5 million spindles and the growing number of workers herded into factory towns.[12] These images became the testimony to the fact that the cotton industry had achieved dominant status and paved the way for the Industrial Revolution in Great Britain.

Iron Industry

The 18th century also witnessed a revolution in technology associated with iron production. Although this industry did not challenge the dominance of the cotton industry, the advances in the smelting and refining processes nonetheless did increase significantly the supply of cheaper and more usable metal for a variety of purposes during the Industrial Revolution. The developments in the chemical process of metallurgy moved steadily to reduce iron in a compound form to a pure form. Carbon and heat are required to achieve this end. Before the 18th century, charcoal derived from wood had been used for smelting iron ore. However, the cost of wood had risen as Great Britain's forests became depleted. Great Britain's seemingly endless abundance of coal had been used for heating since the late Middle Ages, but the coke produced from coal had more impurities than the charcoal produced from wood. In 1709 Abraham Darby succeeded in coke-blasting iron and began a long but steady process that resulted in the production of wrought iron that had the malleable characteristics needed in industry. For six decades after Darby's breakthrough, coke supplies increased as blast furnace design improved and size increased until steam blasting brought the process to new heights. Because blast furnaces produced pig iron, which was too hard to work with, it had to be poured into cast molds to remove the remaining impurities. For decades this process required the heating and reheating of the metal in charcoal fires to get a workable metal, a long and expensive endeavor. Beginning in the 1730s new innovations appeared that ultimately led to Henry Cort's famous "puddling" process in 1784 that saved fuel and ensured faster production and increased the amount of usable iron by nearly 1,500%. Steam power rolled the metal and quickly replaced hammering by hand. As a result, Great Britain's production of pig iron accelerated: 25,000 tons by the 1720s, 125,000 tons by 1740, 250,000 tons by 1804, 581,000 tons by 1825, and 2,700,000 tons by 1852.[13] Similar to the developments in the cotton industry, the iron industry had its own fits and starts with small gains at times and significant leaps at others. The dramatic shift of fortunes can be demonstrated in other ways. In the middle of the 18th century, Great Britain imported double the iron it produced, but by the end of the Napoleonic Wars the nation exported five times the amount imported. Britain's exports of iron ore increased twenty times from 57,000 tons in 1814 to more than one million tons in 1852.

    The improvement in iron production stimulated developments in other industries such as beer-brewing, pottery making, glazing, printing, commercial baking, but most significantly mining. The growing demand for coal to be used in the smelting process created the need to mine deeper as the surface veins became depleted. The penetration of the water table then led to the problem of flooding of the mine shafts similar to the dilemma faced by the tin, copper, and lead mines in the early 18th century. The first response was the use of horsepower to raise the water in buckets. In Warwickshire some 500 horses did the labor, but fatigue and costs associated with food and housing the animals were a consideration. Captain Thomas Savery introduced steam power to solve the problem with his device known as the "Miner's Friend" in the late 18th century. His engine was a tireless machine that operated more efficiently than the horses and used a small amount of the bountiful supply of coal being mined. His original patent lasted 14 years. Once it expired, a number of inventors seized the opportunity to improve his original machine as the depletion of surface veins forced mine shafts to go deeper for mineral resources. In 1800 Great Britain used 11 million tons of coal annually. That amount increased two times by 1830, doubled again by 1845, and doubled once more by 1870. The mining industry also employed iron rails to facilitate carts of coal pulled by horses or people and after 1800 by steam powered devices. In addition, iron producers shared knowledge with textile and other industries regarding machine building and steam power. Again, a lag occurred. For example, a dozen years passed from the appearance of Watt's steam engine in the mid-1760s to the construction of more standardized cylinders for the engine.

Great Britain's Transportation Revolution: Canals, Roads, and Railroads

It is difficult to imagine an era before modern transportation moved people and goods unimpeded at a steady pace over long distances. Prior to the late 18th century, only the royal court, aristocrats, soldiers, sailors, political adventurers, missionaries, and merchants traveled freely. A sedentary society had a local orientation and for the most part was held in check by physical impediments. Great Britain experienced three important transportation developments in the first century of the Industrial Revolution: canal construction, improvements in road-building, and the appearance of the railroad.

The first leap in transportation came in the form of artificial waterways or canals. In 1692 the French constructed the first modern canal, the Canal du Midi, connecting the Atlantic and Mediterranean. Originally built as part of Louis XIV's grand military strategy, it soon led to further canal building and boosted commerce. The implications of the French canals did not escape the British. During the middle of the 18th century, the Duke of Bridgewater traveled to France and Italy, where canal construction had also begun. His experience led him to encourage the introduction of canals into Lancashire in order to move coal quickly from mines to the growing industrial town of Manchester. The result was the Bridgewater Canal, which opened in 1761. The effort required river improvements. The duke's dedicated approach ensured that a marriage of public and private efforts succeeded in the canal's construction. Parliamentary legislation specified the routes, and private companies purchased the land. The first canals were a product of an economy of engineering, lined in clay to create a watertight seal, and could only support very narrow boats. Unlike later versions, the first canals generally followed the contours of the landscape to avoid tunneling wherever possible. Brick and masonry aqueducts were constructed to cross rivers.

The men who designed and built the canals were truly remarkable and inspired the development of modern engineering technology in Great Britain. For example, the Duke of Bridgewater hired James Brindley, a millwright, for three shillings a day to build a canal. Brindley employed navies (a term referring to navigators or men who used shovels and wheelbarrows to excavate earth). He was noted for his tough, tenacious work ethic and possessed few social graces. Brindley was articulate enough, however, to convince Parliament of the worthiness of his projects. This initial effort resulted in a canal eighteen feet wide, four and a half feet deep, and 10 miles long, which sliced in half the expense of transporting coal to Manchester. The cost of the canal is unknown, but its profits financed the duke's next venture—a canal linking the port city of Liverpool with Manchester. Brindley constructed the canal along a valley to keep it level and then gently let it slope down using a series of 10 locks. The canal is estimated to have cost about 225,000 pounds, but it also cut in half the cost of freight charges between Liverpool and Manchester. The economics were simple. Eight horses formerly were needed to haul a wagon weighing six and a half tons, whereas a single horse walking along a towpath could move with little effort a loaded barge weighing almost thirty tons.[14] Adam Smith observed the success of the canal system and urged its expansion. Josiah Wedgewood believed that Smith was correct, and he as well joined the canal building craze. Previously Wedgewood had employed pack horses to bring in raw materials to his potteries and to transport the fragile finished product.

The canal provided a cheaper and more reliable mode of transportation. In less than a decade, between the years 1764 and 1772, private enterprises pooled capital and financed the construction of canals linking Great Britain's major rivers. In 1790 alone nearly three million pounds was spent on canals. By the 1830s the investment had swelled to twenty million pounds. In 1800 some forty-two canals consisting of 1400 miles of waterways crisscrossed Great Britain. The result was a boost in employment opportunities for the working classes. Josiah Wedgewood's potteries, for example, flourished with the construction of the canals and increased his work force from 7,000 in 1760 to more than 21,000 in 1786. As canal building increased, older canals were enhanced through tunneling and improved embanking to straighten the routes. By 1858 Great Britain had constructed 4250 miles of canals. Napoleon's campaigns forced the British to pour resources into military channels and resulted in an interruption of canal building. At the conclusion of the Napoleonic Wars, railroad construction was set to commence, a sign that the canal age was ending.[15]

Road building also garnered additional interest in the late 18th century. However, this endeavor had to overcome significant obstacles. Overland transportation was extremely difficult, as road arteries had improved only slightly over Roman times. Much of the year roads were streams of mud and frequently impassable for wheeled traffic. The resources for road building and improvement differed from the canals. The effort was initially sporadic and uneven because local areas had the responsibility for construction and upkeep. In the first half of the 18th century, Parliament passed an average of eight turnpike acts a year. However, the growing demand placed on transportation infrastructure to keep pace with the nation's economic growth soon led to further road developments. These efforts were boosted with the creation of turnpike trusts that were joint enterprises of landowners and entrepreneurs who could pool their capital for infrastructure improvements. The initial efforts were small but steady and gained momentum with the efforts of several men who changed the actual complexion of the roadbeds. The Scotsman Thomas Telford (see Biographies) developed a heavy foundation roadbed using seven inches of crushed stone over a sublayer of soft soil and covering it with a two-inch layer of gravel. As wheeled vehicles traveled over the road they solidified the base layer so that the road became even more viable over time. His most important road project was the 300-mile thoroughfare linking London and Holyhead, Wales, which lessened the travel time between the two cities by 32% from 41 to 28 days.

However, Telford's approach proved more expensive than some turnpike trusts could afford. Thus, the next major enhancement in Great Britain's roads occurred with the work of another Scotsman, John L. McAdam, whose approach was simpler and less expensive than Telford's heavy foundation. McAdam, working in conjunction with his three sons, devised a method to ensure that the subsoil drained readily so that the surface would remain dry and firm and thus eliminate the need for Telford's deep foundation. He placed a thin layer of fine gravel over a carefully surveyed and well-drained foundation. The elastic surface became tightly packed as vehicles passed over it and did not deteriorate or have potholes or ruts appear as quickly as the Telford model. It is estimated that by the early 1820s several thousand miles of roads had been constructed according to the macadam method. The improved road standards in the 18th and 19th centuries reduced travel time significantly. In 1745 the trip from London to Edinburgh took almost two weeks. Fifty years later that same journey had been reduced to less than three days. By 1830 it had been trimmed almost in half again. The journey from London to Bristol, formerly two days by coach, was only 19 hours by the 1780s. In 1756 only one stagecoach a day made the journey from London to Brighton. By 1811 that number had increased to eleven. And, in 1820, 1500 stagecoaches departed London daily pointed in all directions in the country. The replication of these "macadamized" roads eventually became the goal of all European nations and the United States.[16]

Safety in travel also improved, and more frequent and comfortable inn accommodations sprang up along Great Britain's growing road network. More people were on the move and doing so more frequently. However, the cost of transporting people and goods overland by roads remained an expensive and time-consuming endeavor. Mule trains continued to be the principal means for moving cargo and were a common sight in the late 18th and early 19th centuries. The real revolution came with the appearance of the railroads.

Although the railroads were a 19th-century innovation, in some respects they were not new. The Romans had used grooves or ruts in their roads to fit a common wheelbase, and the Chinese had employed a similar technique in the 3rd century BC. By the 16th century the mining industry in Great Britain and areas on the continent such as Transylvania had developed wooden tramways over which trucks pulled by horses would haul ore. Wood quickly rotted. By the 18th century iron rails, some covering distance up to ten miles, had appeared at several mining areas in Great Britain. By the early 19th century Richard Trevithick (see Biographies) had developed a device or locomotive powered by steam to carry passengers or cargo at a pace of five miles per hour. Several independent efforts began to appear simultaneously, but it took the work of George Stephenson (see Biographies) to bring the railroad into the forefront of British transportation. Stephenson's improvements included strengthening the tracks, adopting the latest developments in steam power for his locomotive, and establishing a standard gauge for the tracks. After his successful Stockton to Darlington run in 1825 and win over the competition in 1829 for the rights to the Liverpool to Manchester railway line (see Document 2), passenger and freight service began on a regular basis, marking the onset of the railroad age in Great Britain.[17] Mainline construction began immediately in the 1830s. By 1847 a quarter of a million navies were employed in railroad construction, and more than 2400 miles of railway were in operation carrying 30 million passengers at a dizzying pace of 60 miles per hour across the country. That mileage had climbed to 6,800 miles in 1851. The railroads required constant attention to ensure that proper signaling devices and safety regulations kept pace with more efficient and powerful locomotives. Professional organizations for mechanical and civil engineers appeared, and constant training in maintenance and railroad operations became essential for all employees. This model was adopted later by other transportation industries such as automobile and airplane manufacturing. The appetite for railroad expansion was insatiable. The railways not only moved people but also reduced transport time for goods, thereby lowering transport costs and thus stimulating investment. Other benefits arose from the railway age. Postal service received a real stimulus. In addition, reduced travel time compressed the nation and changed the concept of time and turned people's attention from being exclusively local to an understanding and appreciation for larger national concerns. As more and more railway lines crisscrossed the nation, the old concept of local time evaporated. The development of strict timetables and regularly scheduled service by the railroads led to successful lobbying of Parliament to abolish local times and establish a national concept of time in 1845. In 1851 a large percentage of the nearly 6 million people who visited the Great Exhibition traveled to the event by rail. Queen Victoria first traveled by train in June 1841 and was a frequent passenger on the railroad. It not only provided a fast and efficient means to travel but also provided additional opportunities for the royal family to be seen by the British people. Between the years 1861 and 1868 mileage increased more than 80% and passenger traffic moved 180%.[18] The railway age also resulted in more people taking excursions and the concept of the vacation, heretofore an impossible thought in the lives of ordinary folk, became a reality for millions. The first holiday package offered by a railroad occurred in 1841. The initial fear of railway travel soon became a thing of the past. Statistics for the years 1870 to 1873 indicate that 397 million journeys were taken in Great Britain. The total number of railway accidents from all causes in that period was 59, with an annual fatality rate of 35 or one death per every 11 million trips.[19] Henry Booth perhaps captured the spirit of this dramatic change best: "What was slow is now quick; what was distant is now near; and this change in our ideas pervades society at large."[20]

The Price of Industrialization

The Industrial Revolution had a dramatic impact on the life of Great Britain. Although evidence of industrialization had appeared on a wide scale, it should be remembered that Great Britain was still basically a rural country in 1800. Agriculture dominated the economic life of the nation, and the fastest thing one could observe was a galloping horse, which at best could cover 30 to 100 miles a day. London was a faraway place for most of the British people, and even the concept of time was irregular as people relied on when the sun rose and set in their particular locality to judge the progress of the day. Yet, if one had been born in the early 1800s, that world had disappeared almost entirely by the end of the century. The country manners of Jane Austen's novels in the early 19th century had given way to the harsh urban realities of Charles Dickens characters in the mid-19th century and finally the wild notion of time travel in the work of H. G. Wells by the end of the century.

The forces that had begun to churn in the late 18th century—agricultural reform, population increase, and the emergence of machines powered by steam—set the stage for rapid industrialization. In 1801 British population stood at 9 million, increased to 21 million in 1851, and stood at 37 million at the turn of the 20th century. The age of the city and the factory had arrived. In the late 18th century a typical textile mill might be valued at three to four thousand pounds, while a basic hand loom might cost twenty-five pounds. In 1788 the first recorded multi-story factory enterprise had a value of 13,000 pounds and its steam engine alone cost 1,500. Operations related to mining and metallurgy had even higher values. In order to operate on this grand scale, partnerships formed to accumulate greater sums of capital and bargain for new credit arrangements to facilitate investment. These larger entities required a new organization to ensure the highest degree of productivity. In many respects, however, the pace of industrialization progressed slowly and unevenly. The typical cotton mill in 1850 had 50 workers, most of whom did not operate machinery, although some enterprises boasted 1,000 or more employees.[21] Thus, much manufacturing remained on a small scale, and family firms financed through personal loans outnumbered large partnerships that drew upon the resources of banks and financial institutions. This mixed nature of industrialization should not lead one to surmise that the impact of the new economy was neither dramatic nor far-reaching. Indeed, by the middle of the 19th century, Great Britain had more than lived up to its moniker as "the workshop of the world."

Almost from its inception, the factory or mill required a new work ethic from its employees. Life on the farm had been a family and community endeavor. However, the hum of activity in the factory demanded a discipline and behavior that operated at a tempo and speed not previously experienced by the ordinary working man. In the initial stages, this regimentation was foreign to individuals who were used to the more irregular and leisurely pace on the farm. Even those workers who engaged in cottage industry pursuits of weaving and spinning in their domiciles could perform their tasks on a surge basis and then have time off. The machines operated by the workers, however, were expensive and could not remain inactive. Factory owners had to dictate a strict system of time-work in which employees labored in shifts for set hours and performed a specified number of tasks in a repetitive manner to obtain maximum output from the machines. Some owners sought shortcuts by hiring orphans from London and other cities and bringing them to the northern textile mills with the promise of wages, food, and housing. Women and children appeared in greater numbers in the factories, not a new phenomenon as they had worked on the farm, but their presence held down overall factory wages at times. The old practice of St. Monday when no work was done gave way to a week in which work of twelve to sixteen hours a day stopped at either midday or the end of the day on Saturday. Over time this distinct break between work and leisure time would change the nature and style of activities pursued by the working classes. By the later 19th century some of these new interests became spectator sports, such as cricket and football, and music hall entertainment. The comfort of the former rural, close-knit community no longer existed. Even the church could not fill the vacuum. Church attendance declined rapidly as evidenced by the 1851 Census Sunday Report that only 50% of the population attended a church service. The Anglican Church with its ritual and formalism suffered the most from the changing social dynamics in Great Britain. Methodism, on the other hand, took heartily to the new spirit of the age that the Lord watched over those persons who take care of themselves. Methodism's emphasis on honest, hard work and self-discipline meshed neatly with the mores of the era.

Mature workers faced a litany of fines and punishments if they did not perform according to the factory owner's standards. These shortcomings might include tardiness or slovenly behavior such as drunkenness, an extremely serious infraction that employers viewed as having a negative influence on the work force. Adults might be given a reduction in pay or outright dismissal. Children, often prized by factory owners because they could be easily disciplined for the arduous work, often received beatings to enforce the rules. At times the conditions under which the labor force toiled played havoc with the workers. The many physical dangers inherent in the early factories might include working in mills with temperatures of more than 80 degrees, inhaling dust from the textile fibers, and injury or death from fast-moving, unsafe machinery. The mines might have cave-ins, explosions, or poisonous fumes. Furthermore, working in mines with damp crawl spaces of only three or four feet in height resulted in twisted bodies and lung disease. Although not attractive places to work, the necessity for the booming population to find work drove many workers into the mines, factories, and mills. Pauper apprentices, orphans in the community under the control of local parishes, were another source of workers. The parishes often put the children to work in the local factory for low wages and little food. Until child labor reform appeared later in the 19th century, these unfortunate children were easy prey for profit-driven factory owners who possessed no moral pangs about abusing these children. However, as long as the population growth remained steady, there were always new workers to replace those whose productivity fell short of expectations. By the second and third generations of the factory system, the majority of British workers had accepted the new regimentation of factory life, a development that helped to sustain British industrial growth throughout the 19th century.

The larger impact of the early period of industrialization has fueled much debate. The standard of living did drop for many rural workers, and many rural women lost their jobs as spinning moved to the factories. As stated earlier, the hand weavers suffered a dramatic decline in wages and numbers throughout the first half of the 19th century. Factory and mining wages remained more stable for unskilled workers, and those persons with skills associated with constructing or maintaining machines fared even better. The annual average wages for a man working in a factory rose from roughly 25 pounds in 1750 to 44 pounds in 1860. Yet, in comparison to productivity of the workers, wages remained low for several decades and allowed the factory owners to invest in new equipment and often times expand operations. But workers had no safety net to catch them if times turned difficult. Employers made no provisions for workers who became ill or too elderly to perform their duties. Few options existed to affect change. In the past, workers always could turn back to the land, but that option no longer existed. In the early years, as will be discussed later, workers did conduct mostly unsuccessful heated verbal protests against reduction in pay or increases in the price of food at company commissaries. At times such acts became more violent.

Life in the Industrial City

In 1800 London was the only British city with a population of a million residents, and a half a dozen other cities had populations of between 50,000 and 100,000 persons. By 1830, London's population had more than doubled and was nine times larger than other British urban areas. Nine additional cities had more than 100,000 residents, and 18 other cities had populations of 50,000 to 100,000. These twenty-seven cities accounted for nearly 6 million, or one fifth, of the population of Great Britain. When urban areas of under 50,000 are included, the census of 1851 indicated that approximately half of Great Britain's population resided in cities and towns, the first time any society in history had a ratio where urban population had achieved parity with that of rural. In 1830 approximately 14% of British people lived in cities of 50,000 or larger. That percentage had increased three times by 1900. The reasons for this growth of cities have already been discussed. What is noteworthy is the impact that such a transition had on the lives of people living in the cities. Certainly, the cities and towns offered a chance for employment and wage earning that was more often than not better than that in the countryside. However, there was a bleak side to the opportunity. In the 1820s a person living in a British urban area with a population of 100,000 had a life expectancy of 35 years. Ten years later that number had declined to 29. Some areas had more dire statistics. In 1851 a boy born in Liverpool would generally live to be 26, but his counterpart in nearby rural areas might live more than twice as long. Twenty percent of all children born in a city in 1820 would lose a parent before the age of 15. During the majority of the 19th century, the very nature of urbanity not only played havoc with life expectancy but also made the existence of those years extremely difficult. Crammed living arrangements, pollution, unsanitary conditions, high incidence of disease, and little effort by political authorities to seek solutions meant that until the late 19th century death rates in the larger cities rivaled those of the period of the Black Death. Indeed, Queen Victoria's consort, Prince Albert, died of typhoid fever in December 1861. Finally, while still a teenager, Princess Victoria made a trip into North Wales and witnessed the stark contrast between her life and that of her subjects. From the security of her carriage, she peered into the blackness of the sky and on the faces of her future subjects who toiled in the growing number of factories that poured flame and smoke into the countryside.[22]

By the late 19th century London was a megalopolis. The city consisted of 7,000 miles of streets. A birth occurred every four minutes, and London newspapers recorded an average of 300 births and deaths a day. The rate of consumption of food and drink staggered the mind. It was estimated that the population of Britain's capital consumed 200 million quarts of beer, 50 million quarts of wine, and 10 million quarts of rum annually.[23] It is little wonder than some Londoners mourned the encroachment of modernity in the city. As one account stated, "The suburbs of the metropolis... are fast losing, with their fields and woods, the old and distinctive flavor. Kensington (the site of the Great Exhibition of 1851) has long since been built over...what was country a year ago is now an integral part of the city, and the old manor house, with its glory unimpaired has suddenly become an anachronism."[24]

In the beginning of the 19th century most cities had governing entities dominated by elites and little sense of civic pride or responsibility existed. City-dwellers often refused to pay taxes to these bodies, and even after parliamentary statutes appeared in 1835 to reform local municipalities, little change occurred, a situation satirized by writers such as Charles Dickens and magazines such as *Punch*.[25] The intolerable situation in the cities began to improve slowly after the expansion of the electorate with the passage of the second Reform Act of 1867. The result was a political pact that developed between the workers and the industrialists to address the cleanliness and efficiency of the cities through public taxation and spending. With a more enlightened political mood, the voices of reformers such as Edwin Chadwick (see Biographies) and the words of Victorian novelists helped to popularize reform efforts.

One event that prodded British political leaders to action was London's "Great Stink" of 1858. Great Britain had experienced its first major outbreak of cholera in 1831, a ravage that took its toll regardless of financial status. More members of the wealthy classes in London began to adopt the use of water closets rather than the privies or cess pits that the poorer classes relied upon. The storm drains intended to carry rain water into the Thames River ended up also transporting raw sewage to the river. Thus, the drinking water taken from the Thames had high contamination levels, and people of both a high and low social status fell sick and many died. In 1858 the smell emanating from the polluted Thames River was so revolting that the curtains of the House of Commons were soaked in chlorine in order to prevent its members from fainting. It is little wonder that Parliament rushed a bill through in less than three weeks to build a brand new sewer system for London.[26]

Despite the reaction to the "Great Stink" of 1858, urban reform was sporadic for the next two decades. Rather than opening new terrain to better housing arrangements, the working class areas became more densely crowded with no adequate thoroughfares and dark, dirty, and foul alleyways. For example, in the 1840s at least 25% of London's residents lived in open yards and another 10% lived in cellars. In 1847 a four-room house in London had fifty people from eight families living together, with an additional eleven lodgers sleeping in the basement. In 1854, officials in Newcastle-upon-Tyne discovered that at least 50% of its families lived in single room dwellings that often oozed liquid filth through the walls and left individuals breathing noxious fumes through their few windows. The American writer Herman Melville, who visited Liverpool in 1839, was horrified to observe the endless poverty of the working classes who howled a sickening wail and were represented by rigid figures on the streets that left him wondering whether they were dead or alive.[27]

It became increasingly apparent that these dreadful working class living areas bred not only disease but also challenges to moral order. The lack of planning for housing and streets led not only to problems such as poor ventilation but also to the inability of police forces to stem criminal behavior and prostitution. Indeed, it has been pointed out that in the 1860s the city of Liverpool had 9,000 prostitutes, and of these nearly a quarter were not yet 15 years of age. Great Britain was deemed the prostitution capital of the Western world because the enclosure movement and attraction of factory work had lured many women from rural areas. The stigma of divorce and the growing idea of the "cult of domesticity," which placed middle- and upper-class wives on a pedestal, led to men frequenting brothels and bringing home venereal disease to their wives.

The Example of Manchester

Located in Lancashire, Manchester is a prime model of how the new industrial city attempted to cope with the conditions for its working classes. By 1830, Lancashire boasted 550 cotton textile factories employing more than 100,000 workers, of which a third were children, some as young as six years old. Children's wages were nearly nonexistent, at times only one tenth that of adult workers. In the employers' minds it made sense to hire as many young people as possible in order to have a larger return on their investment. Unscrupulous factory and mine owners placed harsh and dangerous demands on these young workers, such as crawling underneath unsafe equipment to loosen cotton that might impede operation of the equipment.

For the most part, Manchester workers lived near the factory or mine in the inner city, whereas the owners and other wealthy citizens might dwell in the suburbs in a more posh lifestyle. Workers homes were often built by the factory owner but normally they were small, of poor construction, and crammed with as many persons as possible. The houses were damp, and rainwater and moisture seeped through the thin walls. The only escape from these conditions might be in the basements of buildings, but even these cellars became residences for subtenants as the population grew. Mold was everywhere and

The Industrial Revolution in Great Britain

contributed to the ill health of inhabitants. Privacy was nonexistent. People worked in shifts and shared beds. It was not unusual for a dozen persons to sleep in one room. Fresh water was not readily available. Perhaps up to 100 people might share the same privy or toilet, often a large, deep hole dug in the courtyard or a "midden" or heap against the wall. In one district of the city more than 7,000 persons shared 33 privies.[28] Conditions were appalling at every turn. Streets became sewers and open drains and were often littered with animal and vegetable wastes, and the stench of such conditions was unbearable.

Manchester's working classes often had a difficult time surviving. As late as 1889 a report based on interviews with working men stated that 40% of this group had irregular employment and that more than 60% could be described as very poor or having wages below the subsistence level. A main problem was the large number of workers who performed casual and seasonal labor. The majority of workers in these categories were warehousemen, general laborers, and transport men. Manchester also had a high percentage of immigrant labor. By the mid-19th century at least 15% of the city's population was Irish, with some of the poorer sections having nearly half. Italians also migrated to Manchester. One area of the city was known as "Little Italy." The residents there formed the largest portion of the city's casual work force—street vendors, construction workers, and domestic servants—laboring long hours in good times but being the first laid off when economic conditions deteriorated.

Besides the hygiene problems found in the workers living areas, other poor health conditions existed in the early history of industrial Manchester. The workers burnt coal to stay warm, and the smoke from these domestic fires combined with the belching smoke from factory chimneys to create a stagnant air mass, which in turn resulted in acid rain. A plethora of respiratory illnesses often swept over the city—bronchitis, asthma, and pneumonia. The elimination of sewage did not make great strides until later in the 19th century. The communal cesspits and ash pits often overflowed and ran freely during rainy periods. City regulations required that these pits be emptied and the contents carted away, but the task was so overwhelming that it was infrequently accomplished. There were numerous accounts of middens overflowing into the basements where people resided, and little effort was made to resolve the problem. Even after the turn of the 20th century, Manchester had only about one third of its privies as water closets, and those that existed prior to that date ran directly into the river system used to obtain drinking water, often resulting in summer outbreaks of cholera (many decades after London's "Great Stink"). Contemporary observers noted that the height and weight of middle-class family members was visibly greater than the scrawny and thinner bodies of the working class. While not necessarily the norm, as late as the 1870s the life expectancy of some working men might be as little as 17 years. These same observers lamented that such less than desirable living conditions ultimately led many poor people to seek outlets such as crime, prostitution, drunkenness, and sexual misconduct.

Manchester officials did not totally ignore these obvious ills that plagued the city. More hospitals opened their doors after 1850 and approaches, such as isolation, attempted to eliminate the more serious infectious diseases such as small pox and scarlet fever that had particularly ravaged the working classes. In the 1850s, Manchester initiated a sanitary commission devoted to public health and sanitary reform. A dedicated effort was made to educate the populace through the publication of pamphlets (although many of the poor people were illiterate) and the delivery of public lectures. Progress was slow, particularly in the city areas where the poor formed the heart of the population. Between the 1850s and the 1890s, more reservoir water became the norm for drinking purposes and the incidence of cholera and typhoid declined precipitously, although people often had to wait in long lines at street standpipes to obtain fresh water. Tuberculosis and other respiratory ailments continued to be a serious health problem into the 20th century, as no adequate air filtration systems appeared in the factories until much later. A high infant mortality rate persisted, and the chief cause of death in young children was diarrhea caused by the slow transition to better sanitation facilities and poor diet. The initial sewer systems appeared in the late 1860s, when the city's first appointed medical officer closed most of the cellar residences and established public bath houses. In addition, new housing standards appeared that mandated a certain number of windows for ventilation and attempted to create litter-free backyards and alleys. The city provided funds to overhaul 500 poor dwellings a year between the years 1885 and 1900, and that number grew to 2000 annually afterwards. By 1900 Manchester, long considered the black spot of British urban and industrial life, finally began to shed that negative label.[29]

The Rise of the Industrial Middle Class

The growth of industrial capitalism in the 19th century created a new group within the middle class. Of course, the middle class had existed since the growth of towns during the Middle Ages and originally consisted of townsmen who were craftsmen and artisans engaged in mercantile activity or held a professional position such as a lawyer or scholar. The designation evolved to include a wider variety of individuals who participated in commercial activities, banking, medicine, and government. By the late 18th century the new industrial entrepreneurs were those who actually built the factories and mills, controlled the mines, bought the new machine technology, and determined the scope of markets. These men displayed traits such as forward-thinking, determination, ambition, sense of purpose, and naturally a certain lust for money. In the initial phase of the Industrial Revolution, the tasks were not well delineated and the industrialists tended to have a hand in every aspect of their operations—raising money, building factories, supervising labor, and training managers. Nonetheless, this growing class of industrial capitalists did not engage directly in labor themselves, and their workers, unknown to them, by name became mere cogs in the operation. The ancient relationship of master to worker disappeared, as making money became the overarching goal. Because competition was fierce, these men tended to be hard-nosed and ruthless in order to expand their interests. At times, success was only marginal, and the difference between making a profit and going bankrupt was not significant. Most industrial firms remained relatively small until the 1840s, with only about 10% employing more than 5,000 workers and less than half fewer than 100 workers.

The industrial entrepreneurs emerged from a wide variety of social backgrounds. Of course many had mercantile origins, but there was also a marriage of land and industrial interests. Sheep farmers might earn enough capital to establish working looms on their estates. Other prominent aristocratic families began mining operations, constructed mills, supported canal building efforts, developed ports, and often leased properties for building purposes. Rarely did all sons survive until adulthood, and thus the transition of large numbers of landed families into these new industrial enterprises was small but steady and influential. In addition, religious minority groups such as the Quakers and others that were prohibited by law from entering public office, channeled their energies into enterprises such as banking, mining, brewing, etc. Finally, there were numerous examples of persons with pluck who saw the new opportunities, saved money from agriculture and domestic spinning, and set out to establish their own larger scale businesses. This intercourse between landed interests and industrial enterprise was distinctly a British characteristic attendant with few barriers. The noted British traveler, Arthur Young (see Document 13), observed while traveling in France in the late 18th century that such contact and exchange between economic interests was virtually nonexistent, whereas in Great Britain representatives of the nobility and bourgeoisie frequently dined together formally in order to transact business.

For nearly a century the rise of these industrial entrepreneurs sustained the dramatic economic growth in Great Britain. By the 1830s and 1840s, the roles of these men shifted as a business aristocracy began to emerge as sons inherited their fathers' mills and mines and moved into larger banking and commercial enterprises. As they accumulated great wealth, these capitalists slowly gained a measure of political control of local and municipal governments and as a result had an increasing influence on local and regional policy. While the aristocratic land-owning classes still dominated the government at the national level, these men began to exert pressure for local social and political reform, which eventually resulted in the passage of new poor law legislation, suffrage extension, and the establishment of free trade. These wealthy industrialists set the stage for the emergence of large-scale corporate capitalism by the end of the 19th century.

The Politics of Industrialization

The Industrial Revolution changed the nature of politics in Great Britain. Even though the number of workers in British factories and mines remained less than half the work force through the early 1850s, it had become increasingly apparent that the working class was simultaneously responsible for new sources of both wealth and poverty. The famous French aristocratic traveler, Alexis de Tocqueville, visited Manchester in the 1830s and observed that the filth and hard labor of the workers produced riches as valuable as gold yet they were brutalized in the process. The increasing numbers of persons in the working classes and the difficult working and living conditions that they faced eventually forced the political leaders in Great Britain to embrace reform. The movement for reform took decades to reach fruition, and along the way British authorities faced brief moments of strife and confrontation. However, unlike the frequent bloody clashes that occurred on the continent, Great Britain weathered the potential storm and gradually adopted political and social change that averted revolution.

In the early 19th century Adam Smith's emphasis on *laissez-faire* economics had taken root in the growing industrial and business community of Great Britain. These men opposed any government interference in their economic endeavors such as the establishment of working conditions, hours, and wages. In addition, they supported free trade and the elimination of tariff barriers which impeded their conduct of business. In reality the British government supported this approach in most areas by passing little reform legislation and only permitting the existence of relatively few monopolies. In addition, the appearance of Thomas Malthus's *Essay on the Principles of Population*, published in 1798, had raised the specter of a rapidly expanding population that would outstrip the ability of a nation to feed itself and that the natural consequences of war, famine, poverty, and murder would ultimately restore equilibrium. Therefore, no reform should be proposed as that approach would upset the cycle, an idea that allowed the wealthy industrial classes to justify ignoring pleas for reform.

Malthus's work appeared at the end of the French Revolution. The specter of the unruly French working classes convinced the British government to enact a series of laws known as the Combination Acts in 1799 and 1800 to prohibit the formation of workers' associations. These measures did not prevent workers from organizing local trade unions similar to the craft guild organizations of earlier times. Thus, cotton spinners, weavers, miners, etc. had their own bodies aimed to protect their respective livelihoods and restrict entry to their trades. On a few occasions workers even resorted to strikes to achieve their limited objectives. For example, in 1810 cotton spinners in Manchester went on strike, and their trade union association paid out 1,500 pounds a week for strike money.[30] The British government responded by repealing the Combination Acts in the 1820s but passed additional laws that allowed supervision of their activities. By the 1830s, some trade unions began to appeal for the creation of national organizations. This movement gained momentum and received an endorsement from Robert Owen, a noted cotton magnate and advocate of social reform, who believed cooperation was the key approach. Under his auspices, a national trade union organization emerged calling for a general strike to support an eight-hour workday. Widespread worker support for such a bold endeavor did not materialize, and although several other efforts to organize more strident action occurred, real reform remained years in the future.

Despite the failure of the early trade union movement, the lower classes did not remain entirely silent. One example was reaction to the Corn Law. During the wars with Napoleon and the War of 1812, the importation of cheap European corn virtually ended, and the price of British home grown corn soared. The result was a hefty profit for British farmers and landlords. Once the conflicts ended in 1815, Parliament passed the Corn Law to place a tariff on imported grain at a rate high enough not to undersell domestic grain. To be sure, many of the parliamentary seats were in the hands of the landlords and farmers who did not want to see their profits evaporate in the face of cheaper grain. Riots broke out immediately. In London, some members of

Parliament were roughed up by an angry crowd. In Sheffield, protesters marched through the streets with bread dipped in blood skewered on the tops of poles.

The Luddites

As the industrial workplace shifted from the home to the textile mill, cottage weavers became the first industrial saboteurs. The domestic textile worker was independent and self-sufficient, and the arrival of the factory system placed this livelihood in peril. Once it became apparent that one boy operating two steam looms could produce the three and a half pieces of cloth to a single piece by a man operating a hand loom, the resentment could not be contained. Often workers saw the factory owners living in an opulent style that was built on their backs. The Luddite movement got its name from the perhaps mythical Ned Ludd who in 1799 allegedly smashed a machine. During the Napoleonic Wars, stocking weavers began to feel the pain of the transition to machine-made stockings. The British government turned to purchasing the lesser quality but cheaper machine-made stockings, and the stocking weavers could not compete with the new market reality. In 1811, after a poor harvest pushed the price of bread to unbearable levels, the stocking weavers banded together in a secret society with the goal to destroy machines. The British government issued statutes to make the offense of machine breaking punishable by death. These laws did not deter the stocking weavers, who raced north and began to smash power looms and burn down mills. In one week during November 1813 the movement destroyed 90 stocking frames in Nottinghamshire. Although the local populace remained mute about the culprits, the British government nonetheless nabbed, tried, and hung 13 Luddites. Government troops remained in the area, and the Luddite movement died away.[31]

In addition to the Luddite movement, the most significant confrontation took place in Manchester in 1819. For several years radical members of the press had argued for a reform that would transform Great Britain along the political path of the new American republic. One of the most popular voices was William Cobbett, editor of the *Political Register*, a periodical that had a circulation of 50,000 in 1816. Cobbett's appeals for reform resulted in his imprisonment on several occasions and a brief self-imposed exile to Long Island, New York. The discontent over the Corn Law resulted in a flash-point in August 1819 when a crowd of 30,000 marched to St. Peter's Field in Manchester carrying banners protesting the Corn Law and advocating equal representation in Parliament. A leading reformer, Orator Hunt, addressed the throng and called for increased voting privileges and parliamentary reform. The size of the crowd worried the city leaders and factory owners and the militia was summoned. As the mounted troops approached the crowd to arrest Hunt, the people blocked their progress. Suddenly a bugle blared and the troops rode forward with sabers flailing. Within the space of 15 minutes, 11 people were dead and more than 400 lay injured. The event was soon described as the "Peterloo Massacre," a pun directly aimed at the British victory over Napoleon at Waterloo in 1815. Members of the royal family who supported the repression at Waterloo found themselves booed and pelted with stones and eggs when they appeared in public in London.

The Peterloo Massacre became a watershed moment for reform, although the next major step was over a decade away. Indeed, some observers believed that a bloody confrontation between rich and poor was a potential calamity that could happen at a moment's notice. Two British monarchs died in the space of ten years, the long-ruling but insane monarch George III in 1820 and the extravagant and immoral George IV in 1830. He was succeeded by the liberal-thinking, middle-aged William IV. Parliament at this time was dominated by the aristocratic landlords and a small number of industrialists and merchants who were not paid for their political duties and could only run for office if they owned property valued at 300 pounds. Two political parties dominated Parliament: the majority conservatives or Tories who wanted to protect their own economic interests, and the minority Whigs who viewed reform as essential to keep British society stable. The Whigs proposed a reform of the British boroughs and an extension of voting privileges to bring about more equal representation. An intense political debate ensued. The Tory majority stopped the measure, and rioting occurred in several British cities. In Bristol, the town hall and bishop's residence were burned and prisoners were freed by the mobs. The king dissolved Parliament, and the Whigs worked to gain additional support. In 1832 the Great Reform Bill passed after the king announced his support. The measure reformed local governments, stripped away certain patronage positions, and extended voting rights to additional members of the middle class. Roughly one in seven British males could now vote, although workers, women, and paupers remained ineligible to cast ballots. Other reforms followed in the 1830s as religious discrimination virtually disappeared. However, the improvement in the status of the working classes had to wait another decade.[32]

The status of the growing working class became a major focus of reform by the 1840s. In 1844 the German Friedrich Engels visited his father's cotton export office in Manchester. He observed the glitz associated with the progress of industrialization in Great Britain—the impressive railway station, the fine homes of the factory owners, and the opulent opera house. He also witnessed the gloom of the working classes—dirty laborers, dark and flimsy houses, squalor and filth, disease, and crowding and stench and soot everywhere. Troubled by what he had seen, Engels published his famous work, *The Conditions of the Working Class in England*, a book that exposed not only for the British but also for Europeans in general the undesirable results of industrialization in Great Britain. Consequently, many citizens appealed to the government to improve the plight of the workers. Reformers published additional reports of the destitute state of many of the factory workers and their families. However, suggested remedies such as the elimination of cesspools, better drainage, and a pure drinking water system found little support in government circles.

In the 1830s the British government revised the parameters of the Poor Law. As stated previously, the Poor Law had been originally administered by the church parishes with small sums of money tied to the cost of bread paid to poor families. The revenues came from property taxes levied on local landowners. In many respects, landowners and factory owners kept wages low because they realized that the church would make up the difference. However, as the price of bread rose substantially in the first three decades of the 19th century, the taxpayers successfully pressured Parliament to pass a new law in 1834. This statute required the establishment of workhouses to house and feed the poor in return for labor service. The workhouses were very austere and uncomfortable in order to discourage laziness. Common vices such as alcohol and tobacco were forbidden, and males and females had separate domiciles. The Poor Law of 1834 was very unpopular with the lower classes but played into the prejudices of the upper and middle classes who viewed the poor as morally weak and believed harsh conditions would motivate the poor to improve their situation. As living and working conditions worsened for the working class and as the number of abandoned and orphaned children increased, the workhouse at times became the only available alternative to the ugliness of the slums.

By the late 1830s, new calls for reform came not only from liberal political and social thinkers but also from writers such as Charles Dickens. Dickens himself was engaging, generous, and humorous. He had a boundless energy, not only writing novels but also editing newspapers and magazines; penning, producing, and performing in plays; and traveling extensively. His characters reflected the realities of British industrial society in both their positive and negative aspects. Dickens' novels captured the face of the poor, destitute, hopeless, and exploited lower classes and orphans. It is likely that no other single person influenced the middle and upper classes to stare more directly at the dark underside of British society than Charles Dickens. A number of members of Parliament read his works, and as a result many were moved to acknowledge the harsh realities of British industrial society and take political action on behalf of the lower classes.

In reality, the progress for reform had its roots in the early 19th century. A series of parliamentary inquiries and reports of civic-minded private citizens had convinced Parliament to enact measures to place restrictions on child labor in the factories. Children under nine were not permitted to work, and older children could labor only twelve hours a day. In addition, all children were to receive a rudimentary education during working hours. While these measures seemed enlightened for the time, their real impact was limited. They applied only to cotton mills, not to mining enterprises where some of the worst conditions for children existed. In addition, Parliament did not dictate any specific reporting or inspection system that would enforce compliance with the laws. In the wake of the Reform Bill of 1832 new laws appeared. The Factory Act of 1833 (see Document 15), Ten Hours Act of 1847, and Factory Act of 1850 provided for additional protections for children, incorporated women into its provisions, and appointed inspectors who had the authority to levy fines on violators. These measures established the length of the workday first at twelve hours a day, then the work week at sixty hours, and began the weekend at 2 P.M. By the middle of the 19th century the standard of living for the lower classes was visibly higher than a century earlier. Industry provided more frequent work, the prices of goods had declined, real wages had continued to rise, and productivity per worker was twice that of 1800.[33]

One of the most visible efforts for reform came from the Chartist Movement, the first major political ground swell of the working classes in the 19th century. As Parliament had begun the reform of factory working conditions, some reformers believed it was time to extend political rights to the lower classes. The term chartist derives from the 1838 document known as the People's Charter. The London Working Men's Association prepared the charter that included six demands: (1) the right of all men to vote, or universal suffrage; (2) annual elections and sessions for Parliament; (3) revision of electoral districts; (4) elimination of property qualification for voting; (5) payment for those elected to Parliament so that all classes might run for office; (6) adoption of the secret ballot. In reality the charter was a national petition with millions of signatures presented on two occasions to Parliament in 1839 and 1842. The reluctance of Parliament to act on the charter led organizers to call for a general strike, but it had little impact.

Parliament, fearful of the consequences of the provisions, rejected the charter. While the Chartist Movement did not achieve its goals in the short term, it did educate the working people, provided a sense of class cohesion, and laid the groundwork for the ultimate adoption of its provisions in subsequent reform bills in 1867 and 1884.

The impact of the reforms of the 1830s, the Chartist Movement, and the factory and working hour limitation acts of the 1840s began early in the reign of Queen Victoria (1837–1901), at the time when Great Britain enjoyed its era of greatest power and prosperity. She and her consort, Prince Albert, urged a new spirit of reform and public responsibility on the part of their subjects. Good works as well as healthy profits became their focus. Their popularity and the ongoing movement for change merged to create an atmosphere favorable for further reform. By the early 1840s the mining industry sought accommodation with its workers and improved working conditions. No longer did these enterprises send women and children underground into dark, damp and cramped mine shafts. In addition, reformers such as Edwin Chadwick (see Biographies) published disturbing reports related to public health and sanitation, and the result became the formation of a Board of Health. Another significant development was the repeal of the Corn Law. Manufacturers who argued for free trade saw the repeal of the tariff on grain as a means to feed the workers more cheaply and eliminate cost-of-living wage increases. Aristocratic landlords wanted to keep the tariff to maintain high profits on domestic grain. In the middle of the 1840s, economic forces beyond the control of Parliament forced the change. The Irish potato blight pushed a tidal wave of immigration into Great Britain. Furthermore, a banking crisis and recession on the continent stirred revolutionary activity. Members of Parliament, fearful that the unrest might spread to British working classes, ultimately decided to repeal the Corn Law in 1846, thus bringing together Adam Smith's vision of free trade and Queen Victoria's interest in good works.

The Great Exhibition of 1851

No single event represents Great Britain's supremacy as an industrial nation more than the Great Exhibition of 1851. Prince Albert and a group of prominent businessmen convinced skeptical members of the government of the worthiness of the project, one that would highlight the industrial and technical developments of all participating nations. The effort to create a venue for the exhibition was immense. Joseph Paxton, the chief architect, had to prove that his modern and different design for the exhibition building would be substantial enough for the ambitious venture. It consisted of 2,300 cast iron girders, 3,300 pillars, and more than 900,000 feet of glass and resulted in a structure in Kensington Park that covered more than 19 acres or approximately three times the length of St. Paul's Cathedral in London. It took several thousand workers nine months to construct the edifice, with a skeletal framework of more than 202 miles to hold it together, its roof arching majestically over the trees of Hyde Park. Critics complained that it resembled an oversized greenhouse. In the end, the Great Exhibition, also dubbed the Crystal Palace Exhibition, was a huge financial success. The nearly 17,000 contributors set up more than 100,000 exhibits. Half of the exhibits came from Great Britain or its colonies. Many of the displays showed current British industrial expertise, although futuristic items such as an early submarine and a steam powered brewery attracted much attention. Charlotte Bronte, the British poet, upon observing the exhibition wrote, "Whatever human industry has created, you will find there."[34] Six million visitors, approximately one-third of the population of Great Britain, arrived mostly by train to visit the exhibition during its 141-day showcase. The Queen herself visited the Crystal Palace on thirty occasions. The Great Exhibition served as a breath-taking, visible testimony to the ideal of progress and the genius of literally hundreds of inventors and entrepreneurs. The Great Exhibition netted a profit of 750,000 pounds from its ticket sales and concessions, an amount that provided enough money to purchase land in Kensington for additional museums. Following the conclusion of the Great Exhibition, the Crystal Palace was dismantled and moved to South London where it became a popular venue for a number of events until it burned down in 1936.[35]

Conclusion

By the mid-19th century, Great Britain sat alone atop the industrialized world. In the short span of one century the nation had transformed itself from a rural agrarian and cottage industry society to a modern urban and manufacturing giant. A unique set of circumstances set Great Britain on this course. Geography, sufficient resources, capital, and manpower contributed to this development. In addition, Great Britain also possessed a more liberal political establishment that supported industrial growth. That is not to say that Great Britain did not experience significant stress in making the transition. Massive demographic shifts, rapid urbanization, and its attendant ills of health and sanitation vexed the nation for a number of decades. However, over time the nation marshaled resources to solve the political, economic, and social problems inherent in industrialization that might have led to disruption or even revolution. In addition, enterprising and imaginative entrepreneurs and inventors combined forces to create new enterprises capable of achieving levels of wealth and prosperity never before experienced in the Western world. The nation produced two-thirds of the world's coal and half of its cotton and iron. Britain's per capita income was markedly higher than that of any of its neighbors. British products saturated world markets and virtually smothered the competition. Although every Western nation wanted to imitate Britain's success, it seemed inconceivable that Britain's role as an industrial goliath could be matched. As the afterglow of the successful Great Exhibition of 1851 waned, however, Great Britain found its role as the industrial pace-setter challenged in the late 19th century by the United States and the countries of Western Europe. These nations at first embraced Great Britain's basic practices and then developed their own innovative approaches to become rival industrialized societies.

Notes

1. B. Stalcup, ed., *The Industrial Revolution* (San Diego, CA: Greenhaven Press, 2002), 29–34; Stearns, *The Industrial Revolution in World History*, 34–39. These two works provide an excellent summary of the multi-causal aspect of Great Britain's rapid rise as an industrial nation.

2. Landes, *The Unbound Prometheus*, 97.

3. C. Bland, *The Mechanical Age: The Industrial Revolution in England* (New York: Facts on File, 1995), 4–8.

4. Landes, *The Unbound Prometheus*, 66.

5. http://www.manchester2002-uk.com

6. http://www.bbc.uk/history/british/victorians/speed_01.shtml

7. http://www.bbc.uk.history/trail/victorian_britain/earning_a_living/working_life_census_03.shtml

8. R. A. Buchanan, *The Power of the Machine: The Impact of Technology from 1700 to the Present* (London: Penguin, 1992), 93.

9. *Pulse of Enterprise*, 73.

10. Buchanan, *The Power of the Machine*, 94; Landes, *The Unbound Prometheus*, 80, 84–85.

11. Landes, *The Unbound Prometheus*, 86; *Scientific American*, Vol. 12, No. 36 (May 16, 1857), 286.

12. *Scientific American*, Vol 12, No. 36 (May 16, 1857), 286.

13. Landes, *The Unbound Prometheus*, 96.

14. Buchanan, *The Power of the Machine*, 123–126.

15. Deane, *The First Industrial Revolution*, 79–80; Bland, *Mechanical Age*, 41–43.

16. Deane, *The First Industrial Revolution*, 75.

17. Williams, *History of Inventions*, 175–177; Deane, *The First Industrial Revolution*, 74–75.

18. http://www.bbc.co.uk/history/british/victorians/victorian_technology_01.shtml

19. *Manufacturer and Builder*, Vol. 8, No. 7 (July 1876), 166.

20. As quoted in Williams, *History of Inventions*, 177; http://www.pbs.org/empires/victoria/history

21. http://www.bbc.co.uk/history/british/victorians/workshop_of_the_world_02.shtml

22. *Pulse of Enterprise*, 65; http://www.pbs.org/empires/victoria/empire/experts.html

23. *Manufacturer and Builder*, Vol. 22, No. 3 (March 1890), 66.

24. *Harper's New Monthly Magazine*, Vol. 67, No. 398 (July 1883), 165.

25. http://www.punch.co.uk/historyofpunch.html. The first edition was published in 1841 with the aim of being a more sophisticated journal than other acerbic British publications of the era. In the early days its celebrated cartoons became classic visual statements and provided biting commentary on social ills brought about by industrialization and at times an unsympathetic political establishment. *Punch* always struggled with circulation and was bought and sold on several occasions, closing briefly in the 1990s and then finally in 2002.

26. http://www.bbc.uk/history/trail/victorian_britain/social_conditions/victorian_urban-plan.shtml

27. *Pulse of Enterprise*, 70.

28. Ibid., 64.

29. http://www.manchester2002-uk.com/history/victorian/victorian1.html

30. *Pulse of Enterprise*, 61.

31. Ibid., 54–57.

32. Bland, *Mechanical Age*, 56–60.

33. Deane, *The First Industrial Revolution*, 266–267, 270, 287–288.

34. As quoted in http://www.pbs.org/empires/victoria/history

35. Bland, *Mechanical Age*, 111–112; http://www.victoriastation.com/palace.html

CHAPTER 5

THE INDUSTRIAL REVOLUTION IN AMERICA

The Industrial Revolution and the American Revolution occurred simultaneously. During the quarter of a century between the end of the French and Indian War (1763) and the adoption of the United States Constitution (1787), British developments in industrialization gained unstoppable momentum. The collaboration of Watt–Boulton, the culmination of the work of Hargreaves, Crompton, Cartwright, and Arkwright, the digging of the first canals, the beginnings of the modernization of the iron industry, and the plying of the waters by the first primitive steamboat happened during this era. Thus, the new American republic was a fortunate heir to the advances in Britain's technology and the growth of modern industrial organizations already underway in the late 1700s. In addition, the stable and flexible nature of the nation's political system, an almost unlimited supply of natural resources, and a growing, energetic, and enterprising population set the stage for industrial and economic expansion that would eventually surpass even that of Great Britain by the late 19th century.

The Colonial Experience

During Colonial times, the new settlers and their families lived off the land as had their ancestors in the Old World, raising and consuming their own food, making most of their garments by spinning their own yarn, weaving their own cloth and sewing their own clothes, and using simple hand tools to construct their homes and furnishings. Even the light in their homes was created by candles they had dipped by hand. Colonists with more than modest means who desired expensive luxury items such as fine china, cloth, or furniture purchased them from England. Indeed, many of the raw materials used to create these finished items originated in the colonies. Yet, the outward appearance of a slow and methodical existence was actually building the foundation for dramatic change. In reality, the colonies experienced rapid growth in the 17th and 18th centuries. For example, Virginia had approximately 350 settlers in 1610, whereas by 1650 that number had soared to 20,000. Fifty years later the population had tripled to 60,000 and, on the eve of the Revolution, Virginia boasted a population of one half million. Although forty percent of Virginia's population was black, having arrived through the African slave trade, the meteoric pace of growth attests to the richness of the land and the hardiness and ability of the settlers to subdue their environment to sustain such growth. Even the small number of early urban centers grew at impressive rates. In the early 18th century Baltimore had only seven houses, but by the time of the Declaration of Independence the city had 70,000 residents. Philadelphia's population numbered 4,000 in 1690 and grew nearly nine times by 1776. Put in aggregate terms, all the colonies from Maine to Jamestown had 50,000 people in 1650. The number swelled to 250,000 in 1700 and was estimated at 1.2 million in 1750. In 1650 a trip between New York and Boston was not only a frightening adventure, it was an expedition. There were few roads, and those that did exist were barely passable and dangerous as the Native Americans were a constant threat along the journey. Two generations later the same trip could be accomplished in approximately two weeks and the few Native Americans that appeared did so infrequently. Associated with the population increase was a slow but steady rising tide of trade and industry. Between the years 1700 and 1775 the value of colonial shipments to Great Britain in pound sterling grew from 395,000 pounds to 1.9 million pounds, the vast majority in agriculture and related areas such as tobacco and timber. However, the faint din of manufacturing could also be heard in America. Philadelphia distilleries produced 200,000 gallons of rum per year for export by the Revolution. In addition, the Chesapeake Bay was home to the most modern flour mills, and the thirteen colonies had more forges and blast furnaces for iron production than England and Wales combined by 1776.[1]

The potential for growth was inevitable as the colonies were not actually underdeveloped as much as they were undeveloped. The climate was similar to that of Great Britain, and the land was plentiful, rich, and full of natural resources. Furthermore, the umbilical cord that linked Great Britain and America provided sustaining life juices that stimulated change, new opportunity, the spirit of adventure, and expansion and abhorred apathy. These traits created a special relationship that was unlike any other in the long period of European colonization. The often-cited Puritan ethic of hard work and discipline brought to the New World by many of the early settlers also gave an undeniable boost to the desire for unfettered enterprise in the colonies. Even the lack of an abundant, ready supply of capital comparable to Great Britain was not a huge detriment as the colonies could fall back on the mother country for support in terms of British investors, entrepreneurs, equipment (tools, machines, and supplies), and shipping (80% of the Atlantic trade was carried on British ships on the eve of the Revolution).

In spite of the importance of the linkage between the colonies and Great Britain, the mother country in the first half of the 18th century on occasion attempted to stifle the growth of certain infant American industries. In fact one of the main grievances of the colonists against the British government was its restrictions on manufacturing by Americans. In most cases the pressure to ban certain colonial manufacturing came from competing enterprises in Great Britain. For example, in 1699 parliament forbade the export of woolen fabrics between the colonies. Furthermore, in 1732 London declared that the colonies could not export hats. Finally, in 1750 a Parliamentary act attempted to prevent the colonies from constructing mills or engine devices for the purpose of slitting or rolling iron or furnaces for making steel. In reality, the distance and effort in monitoring these acts proved too difficult for Parliament and most prohibitions were ignored.

The Impact of the American Revolution

Eventually, the American Revolution eliminated the long-standing connections and set the new nation on its own course. Indeed, the Revolution foreshadowed the importance that manufacturing would assume in the nation in the years ahead. Some industry grew out of the war effort. Smelting iron in small charcoal furnaces helped to produce items for the colonial army. George Washington's winter encampment in 1777 to 1778, for instance, was at Valley Forge near metal workshops. The army also required shoes, caps, uniform items, firearms, and powder, but the demand surpassed the production capability of small and fledgling colonial industries. In addition, America no longer provided Great Britain with raw materials and served as the focal point for its finished products. The new nation found markets for timber, tobacco, cotton, and other raw materials in far distant ports from Spain to the Indian Ocean. After the Treaty of Paris in 1783, the United States and Great Britain gradually restored their economic ties. This relationship ultimately prevailed in spite of the renewed tensions with Great Britain during the Napoleonic era and the War of 1812. However, the development and growth of a national economy was not assured and at times seemed to advance at only a snail's pace. Manufacturing was present but not highly visible and in the early 19th century lagged well behind that of Great Britain, as only one of thirteen males worked in the trade or manufacturing sectors. In some respects this disparity was misleading because a number of farmers continued to serve as rural artisans and produced manufacturing wares such as soaps, candles, cloth, and simple tools at the local level. The larger industrial enterprises were centered in the towns and cities. In 1787, Philadelphia, for instance, had some 60 examples of manufacturing but their scale remained small. Iron foundries did outpace Great Britain but produced only 30,000 tons a year, an amount about equal to lesser developed countries today. Nails were so scarce that restless pioneers who moved often burned down their old houses in order to gather the nails for use in constructing their new homes. The up-to-date flour mills exported only 250 tons a year and shoemakers in New England produced only 60,000 pairs a year or one pair for every forty persons in America's white population.

Despite this small hint of the potential for manufacturing, the interest in industry that had been piqued by the Revolution waned and the new nation returned to an emphasis on agriculture and the trade of foodstuffs and related products. Even such leading figures as George Washington, Benjamin Franklin, and John Adams advocated that the country revert to its pre-war practices. The United States had not adopted or developed the necessary industrial techniques to compete with Great Britain, which in the first few years following the Revolution forbade export of technology and impeded access to its markets. This situation changed with the arrival of Samuel Slater in the United States in 1789. Slater had been employed by Richard Arkwright. He labored to create efficient cotton mills and collaborated with Moses Brown, a Rhode Island textile pioneer who had previously failed in his effort to establish a working mill. Within two years the pair had built a successful machine that had 72 spindles. After several missteps, Slater and Brown had a mill in operation at Pawtucket, Rhode Island that employed nearly 100 children under the watchful eye of adult overseers. Over the next several years more than two dozen mills of the Slater–Brown type sprang up, although almost all of these factories failed soon after beginning operations. Furthermore, until the second decade of the 19th century, manufacturing developments in the United States remained haphazard at best because of a series of bounties, an awkward patent application process, claims and counter-claims, little investment of public funds, and the paucity of technical publications to assist in standardization of machines and processes.[2]

Jefferson versus Hamilton

The early republic had a significant debate between two of its most prominent statesmen on the future of manufacturing and the prospects for industry in the nation. Thomas Jefferson and Alexander Hamilton took opposing views and saw a different outcome if the United States introduced industrial enterprises. Their only area of agreement was that manufacturing would not occur unless the federal government and local leaders lent support and encouragement. While their difference of opinion was real, it should be remembered that neither Jefferson nor Hamilton understood completely the transformation of Western economies that was occurring right before their eyes. They did not have the luxury of looking back in time at the British industrial model since it had only gained momentum in their lifetime.

Thomas Jefferson had traveled in Great Britain, and he objected to what he had observed in the early stages of its industrial growth: poverty, the filthy and overcrowded cities, and a working class with few rights and no political voice. Jefferson seriously questioned whether such a society could foster democratic principles. It should be emphasized that Jefferson was a firm believer in science and technology. He experimented frequently at Monticello, his Virginia estate, and even attempted to supplement his income with the manufacture and selling of nails. Thus, he did encourage the continued use of home-based manufacturing, similar to the American enterprises in the colonial period. However, he remained suspicious of larger-scale factories because he believed such enterprises tended to dominate the cities and subject the working classes to corrupt influences. Jefferson also observed that because Europe had cultivated all of its available land, it seemed only natural that the Europeans had turned to manufacturing out of necessity rather than choice as the only alternative livelihood for its people. Jefferson opined that the United States' situation was markedly different because of the infinite amount of land stretching west. This abundant land was ripe for agricultural development, and it would take nearly the entire population to subdue and improve it for the benefit of the nation at large. He favored a country populated by landowners and farmers, persons who tilled the soil and were favored by God. He considered them proud, highly valued citizens who had exhibited the admirable traits of vigor, independence, and liberty. Jefferson saw those same cultivators as honest and not easily corruptible, whereas those involved in manufacturing depended on the capriciousness of the buying public and acted in concert with blind ambition, a characteristic that he claimed led to subservience and the abandonment of virtue. His creed was that the land, not the workshop, was the key to the value of work. Agricultural, not mercantile, interests should dominate the nation's economic life. A man who had unlimited freedom of action should live on his land and plan and manage it without any outside or governmental influence. If, for some reason, the available land had been cultivated over time and the nation had a surplus of farmers, the excess people should turn their economic pursuits to the sea rather than manufacturing. A national government, while essential, must not usurp the authority and power of the states, political entities that could best safeguard his vision of democracy.[3]

Alexander Hamilton had a distinctly different perspective. He had an urban background and believed that the federal government should manage the country's economy as a whole. Did Hamilton have an inkling that something important (we now know it was the Industrial Revolution) was beginning, even in its early stages during his lifetime? It seems he possessed just such an intuition and appeared willing to embrace and encourage it. He rejected Jefferson's purely democratic emphasis, stating that such an approach had the potential to break up the union, an unacceptable outcome that only a strong national government could prevent. He saw the U.S. and British industrial interests as intertwined, but if Great Britain failed to see the value of such an economic alliance, America should warm to the French. Yet he also viewed the United States as a potential rival to Great Britain. Immediately upon becoming Washington's Secretary of the Treasury, Hamilton became a charter member of the New York Manufacturing Society. He also encouraged his Assistant Secretary of the Treasury, Tench Coxe, to obtain British industrial techniques by luring textile managers to the United States to teach their secrets, a venture that proved successful over time despite a Parliamentary act levying a fine of 500 pounds and one year in prison for any British subject committing such a transgression. On one occasion, a man was sent to Great Britain to snoop around textile mills and make models of machinery to smuggle back to the United States, and on another Coxe gave a British subject a U.S. patent for a flax mill that would use Arkwright's design.[4]

Hamilton conducted exhaustive research on the state of U.S. manufacturing enterprises. He surveyed a number of revenue collectors and early U.S. cotton, wool, and other industries in the Northeast to obtain information on the volume of production and prices and quality of goods. He even set up a trade fair in a committee room of the House of Representatives with samples of the wares he had gathered in an effort to sway members of Congress to see the utility of federal support for manufacturing. In 1791 Hamilton published his *Report on the Subject of Manufacturers* and submitted it to Congress. In this work, Hamilton recommended that the federal government take an active role in the promotion of manufacturing and that it should enact import tariffs to protect native goods. Hamilton's work aimed to rebut the widely-held Jeffersonian view that agriculture and trade were the heart and soul of the nation's economy as they alone provided subsistence to the people. Hamilton conceded that while these pursuits were indeed important, manufacturing would provide a positive impact on American society and that the productivity and revenue of the nation from such enterprises would be higher than without such a capacity. He argued that the nation possessed the capacity to accumulate enough capital for development across the country. He also wrote that factories would surpass local handicraft production because of the division and specialization of labor. His report implied that factory-produced goods would find markets abroad and further stimulate the economy. Furthermore, Hamilton believed that his program offered employment to segments of society not otherwise engaged in business practices and emphasized that manufacturing served as a magnet for immigrants, a necessary additional labor component of any economy. In his opinion, manufacturing also encouraged the development of a variety of talents, and the resulting increased production would ultimately enlarge the market for agricultural products. Members of Congress, many of them landowners themselves, ignored Hamilton's report, believing his ideas were too far-fetched for them to embrace.[5]

In the same year as Hamilton's report to Congress, the New Jersey state legislature created the Society for Establishing Useful Manufactures (Hamilton himself was one of the sponsors). This organization had the authority to raise $1 million in shares and had the mission to support the manufacture of a wide range of items. The Society showed early promise and had visible support. It was not required to pay local taxes and was exempted for a decade from paying state taxes. The state granted the society a large parcel of land near present day Paterson, New Jersey. Major Pierre-Charles L'Enfant, the individual who planned the nation's capital, was hired to lay out the town and its mills. The state made an initial investment of $10,000, and many local officials and citizens soon boosted the total to $100,000. The society did not realize its vision. In truth, none of the individuals engaged in the enterprise had any manufacturing experience, much of the initial investment was spent on construction costs, and the early articles produced could not compete with those from Great Britain. Within five years the endeavor failed, although the Society remained in existence until after World War II when it was purchased by the city of Paterson. It had survived such a long time by selling land for factory locations and because it controlled the important sources of water in the area.[6]

Thus, the industrial opportunities that arose in America in the late 18th century failed to gain momentum. Even enterprises such as the Slater mill projects and the Society for Establishing Useful Manufactures had only temporary success because the nation seemed content to rely on agricultural exports to finance the purchase of European manufactured goods. Nonetheless, Hamilton's vision eventually was validated although in the near term the prejudice for agriculture remained strong; the country lacked both infrastructure, and an adequate supply of skilled labor and persons with sufficient capital to invest shied away from the risk. However, the trend toward industrial development in the long term was unstoppable. The transition occurred, albeit slowly, for several reasons. First, a few manufacturing enterprises such as cotton goods, arms making, and flour milling emerged to match British competitors. Second, proponents of manufacturing argued that sufficient labor existed in the form of women and children and that men could remain employed on the farm. Finally, the shortage of capital for investment could be supplied by the state through the extension of credit and enhanced by a strong currency. These developments supported Hamilton's viewpoint. Even Thomas Jefferson, after witnessing the stress that the War of 1812 had placed on the country, conceded before his death in 1826 that manufacturing was a worthy partner with agriculture and trade to ensure the health of the nation's economy and maintenance of its liberty.

The 19th Century

Beginning in 1800 the pace of change quickened in the United States. By the late 19th century, the United States would grow to rival Great Britain as the most powerful industrial nation in the world. The rate of change was dramatic. On the eve of the 19th century, the United States had roughly 4 million people and the nation was still predominantly rural, with approximately 3.7 million persons employed in agricultural pursuits. The nation's population was divided half and half between the North and South, although some 700,000 slaves were included in the latter. Urban living was a rarity. There were no cities with a population in excess of 50,000 persons, only two with a population more than 25,000, three with 10,000 to 25,000 persons, seven with 5,000, and only a dozen with 2,500. On the eve of the Civil War, the United States had acquired a different complexion. Although a majority of workers still toiled on the land, the population had increased six times to over 30 million. Whereas in 1790 relatively few people lived west of the Appalachian Mountains, in 1860 half of the nation's

The Industrial Revolution in America

population resided there. The shift in population from rural to urban began to accelerate. The nation began the new century with a birthrate of 55 per 1000, an incredibly healthy rate that reflected the push west for land and the necessity of farming families to have as many hands as possible for labor.[7] In 1820 one person in twenty lived in a city of 8,000 or more persons, in 1840 it was one in twelve, and in 1850 it was one in seven. The old cities of New York, Boston, and Philadelphia had new rivals such as Pittsburgh, Cincinnati, St. Louis, and Louisville springing up along the Ohio and Mississippi Rivers. Nine American cities had populations in excess of 100,000 persons. Furthermore, the population increase and westward expansion resulted in an increase in the number of states from 16 to 39 on the eve of the Civil War.[8]

The economic relationship that had been restored between the United States and Great Britain following the American Revolution experienced fundamental challenges as a result of warfare in the first two decades of the 19th century. The Napoleonic Wars changed the dynamic as Napoleon's Continental System attempted to strangle Great Britain by preventing British goods from entering Europe. In retaliation, Britain aggressively attempted to sever the lines of raw materials headed for France. As the contest evolved, each side vied for advantage by stopping and searching all ships, even from neutral nations. President Jefferson countered with the Embargo Act of 1807 that halted all American vessels from departing the country for foreign destinations. The embargo had two different outcomes. Those individuals and firms engaged in the export business suffered terrific losses of revenue as the demand for United States' exports declined precipitously from $108 million to just $22 million in the first year. On the other hand, manufacturers who could make articles formerly bought abroad found a brief but profitable niche. Before 1808 only fifteen cotton mills existed in the United States. By 1809 more than one hundred cotton mills were in operation, and more continued to be built for the next three years. A report issued during the middle of the war recorded that there were 76 cotton factories containing more than 50,000 spindles in operation within a thirty-mile radius of Providence, Rhode Island.[9]

However, after 1812 the situation reversed itself. An unfettered wave of British goods flowed into the country and undermined the infant industries that had emerged just several years prior. Furthermore, the imposition of additional tariffs after the War of 1812 ended merely accumulated additional revenues and did little to stimulate growth of America's young industries. Even the major tariff passed in 1828, referred to as the "Tariff of Abominations" by Southern agricultural interests because it increased the cost of imported manufactured goods, was in reality a resurrection of the anti-Hamilton economic views and brought the nation to the brink of a political crisis in the early 1830s.

At that moment, however, the nation was poised to take its next step in the industrialization process, one that took the form of new factory enterprise approaches and the creation of a transportation network that stimulated a market revolution. On the surface, the United States potential for industrial growth in 1815 seemed to be no stronger than the situation in 1800. The nation was still one of farmers. Only ten percent of the population lived in urban areas, defined as communities with 2,500 or more residents. In the American South the number was half that amount. The dominant economic pursuits in these cities still revolved around merchant business, sea trade, simple handicrafts, or service activities that supported these endeavors. It is estimated that the total number of factory workers in textile, iron, saw mills, paper mills, and flour mills numbered no more than 15,000 persons.

In 1815 the nation faced several challenges if it was to realize any ambition for industrial development. First, the geographical magnitude of the United States posed an impediment to industrialization, especially since the country expanded and consolidated so rapidly after 1815. Great Britain, with its relatively compact size, an intricate port, river, and canal network, and short distances between natural resources and industrial centers, did not have to contend with constructing an infrastructure to overcome the obstacle of the sheer breadth of a nation like the United States. Indeed, no town in Great Britain was situated farther than 70 miles from the sea, and by the early 19th century the country had approximately 20,000 miles of roads and an important network of canals. In many respects the United States remained a rough and primitive country. In 1815 it took a yoke of three oxen three days to make a round trip between New York and Boston. Furthermore, the overland transport of items such as iron or corn might be greater than transatlantic shipment and could only sustain a profit by moving them only a few miles from their source. Second, the shortage of labor was also a key hurdle. As a result of the enclosures, Great Britain had experienced a long, steady transition of its labor supply (men, women, and children) from the rural areas to the factories in the cities. The situation in the United States was similar in that a population boom was underway, but there was also an abundance of land to occupy and own. Third, despite some flashes of individual technical ingenuity such as the invention of the cotton gin and the perfection of steam powered transportation on waterways, the United States lacked sufficient capital investment to finance the construction of machines necessary for the factory system to operate profitably. During the last three decades before the Civil War, these three obstacles would be overcome through the creation of a vast transportation network, the employment of women, children, and immigrants in the mills, and the growth of technological capabilities to support new transportation and factory organizations.

Transportation—Roads

The impetus for the creation of a wide-ranging transportation network began in the early days of the new nation. The turnpike system, a combined effort of private investors with state support, began in the 1780s. The first turnpike was constructed in Virginia in 1785, and the Philadelphia to Lancaster, Pennsylvania turnpike was completed a decade later.[10] During Thomas Jefferson's second administration, serious discussions took place about linking the nation together north–south and east–west through the construction of roads and canals. The proposal ran into partisan and sectional bickering and did not move forward beyond the national government's building of one major overland turnpike, the National Road or Cumberland Road. The construction for this road took place from 1811 to 1839. Originating in Cumberland, Maryland, the road ran initially through what is now Wheeling, West Virginia on the Ohio River and eventually through Columbus, Ohio and Indianapolis, Indiana to its termination at Vandalia, Illinois, the original capital of the state of Illinois. Until the 20th century and the appearance of a federal highway program, the National Road was the only endeavor of this type constructed under the auspices of the national government. Congress mandated that the road have proper grading and be sixty-six feet wide with its surface of stone covered by gravel. All bridges were also constructed of stone. The original portion of the road opened in 1818, and soon a steady stream of wagons, people, and animals poured westward. By the time the final phase of construction reached Vandalia, much of the earlier portions had fallen into disrepair. The last segments of the road also presented problems because of improper leveling and the failure to remove even tree stumps from the road.[11]

Besides the National Road, private and state interests became involved in road construction. Between 1800 and 1810 the number of state governments and private enterprises seeking to make a profit in turnpike construction swelled from 72 into the thousands. New York had almost 400 toll roads, although many were difficult to traverse. The significant consideration in road construction was its cost, not the benefits offered by more rapid or efficient transit, as evidenced by the fact that the roads built took a direct route between points rather than the longer but less obstructed passage over flat terrain and through valleys. The utility of the early roads also suffered from the ravages of the weather, which often left them as streams of mud, or legal provisions that permitted stumps or obstacles to remain on the thoroughfares. By 1840 substantial private investment had been made in turnpike construction: more than $6 million in New England and a similar amount of combined public and private money in Pennsylvania alone. This impressive investment must be tempered by consideration that nearly half of the turnpikes had failed either partially or wholly by this time because of lack of proper planning or poor supervision and construction. Nonetheless, the steady carving out of routes for travel helped the economic growth in America and set the stage for the next developments in transportation.[12]

Transportation—The Erie Canal

Turnpike construction waned not only because of the heavy investment and physical effort required but also because of a new venture—canal construction. Of course, the British had engaged in canal construction and proved its worth since the 1760s. The U.S. government had in fact considered the viability of canals during the debate surrounding the construction of the National Road. However, the serious impediment involving canals was the exorbitant cost when compared with building roads. Turnpikes cost between $5,000 to $10,000 per mile to construct, and in most cases took only several years to complete. Canals, on the other hand, cost between $8,000 to $25,000 per mile, depending on the terrain, and took a decade or longer to construct. The United States only had about 100 miles of canals in operation in 1816, and most of them were only several miles in length.

Canal construction hit its zenith with the Erie Canal. The idea for such a project arose in the late 1760s with a proposal to connect the Hudson River with Lake Ontario near Oswego, New York. In 1792 the New York state legislature chartered the Western Inland Lock Company to construct such a water route by linking the Mohawk and Oneida Rivers and Oneida Lake. The project faced insurmountable problems in financing and construction, and thus the company constructed only a one-mile bypass around the Little Falls of the Mohawk River. The company's toll collections barely kept the canal in operation. The work of the company did inspire other political and business officials to expand their vision and push for the construction of a canal that would link the Hudson River and Lake Erie. The most prominent voice for such an endeavor was DeWitt Clinton, former mayor of New York City and a nephew of George Clinton, the governor of New York (see Document 16). In 1808 a survey was conducted to determine the most appropriate route. Work began officially when the then-Governor DeWitt Clinton broke ground on July 4, 1817 near Rome, New York. Few of those in attendance at this ceremony had any idea of the daunting task awaiting those who designed and labored to construct the canal. In the early days of its construction, the canal obtained the not so flattering sobriquet of "Clinton's Big Ditch."

The Erie Canal was an engineering marvel. It stretched 363 miles from Albany to Buffalo and required innovative construction techniques to overcome swamps, rivers, and hills. The canal was cut to a uniform depth of four feet with a width at the bottom of twenty-eight feet and at the top of seventy feet. The length of canal descended and ascended 675 feet, a hindrance that was overcome through the use of eighty-three locks. This entire feat was accomplished despite the fact that there was no official civil engineering school in the United States. Therefore, the men who presided over the construction basically learned while undertaking the project. Many of these individuals later built other canals, bridges, and railroads and contributed to other related areas such as the creation of water supplies for the nation's growing cities. In addition, a 3,000-man, mostly immigrant, labor force did the difficult spade work and was paid an average eighty cents per hour for back-breaking ten- to twelve-hour work days. The workers constructed eighteen aqueducts to transport water over rivers and streams and numerous bridges to provide the roads and farms cutoff by the canal access to the wider world.

Work on the Erie Canal ended officially on November 4, 1825. Governor Clinton presided over a ceremony in which he poured water from Lake Erie into New York Harbor. The reduction of transportation costs was immediate. Prior to the Erie Canal, the precarious overland shipment of wheat, corn, and oats from western New York State to New York City cost between three and ten times the value of the crops. In financial terms it had cost between $90 to $125 a ton to ship cargo between Buffalo and New York City. By 1835 the canal alternative had reduced that amount to $4 a ton. As another point of comparison, before 1820 it cost about 20 cents a ton-mile to ship goods from Buffalo to New York. By 1855 the canal had dramatically reduced the cost by more than 90% to just shy of one cent a ton-mile. Boats initially hauled a maximum of thirty tons of freight, moved along by draught animals (horses, mules, or oxen) being led by a person walking along the towpath on the bank of the canal. In the first year of the canal's operation, an army of 2,000 boats, 9,000 horses, and 8,000 men conducted the business of transporting goods along the route. Passengers seeking a picturesque experience along the canal paid 4 cents per mile for the journey.

Even though the canal reached its potential just as the railway age appeared in America, it continued to enjoy success. As the rush of New England and immigrant farmers flowed westward, the canal provided a cheaper means to send farm products eastward and receive manufactured goods from factories in return. The huge volume of traffic on the canal resulted in two major enlargement projects. The first occurred between the years 1836 and 1872. This expansion widened the original canal to seventy feet, increased its depth to seven feet, reduced the number of locks to seventy-two, and allowed boats to haul 250 tons of cargo. The amount of tonnage moving along the canal increased from 58,000 tons in 1836 to 1.6 million tons on the eve of the Civil War to more than 3 million tons in 1868. The second enlargement took place beginning in 1903 and resulted in a canal of 120 to 200 feet in width, twelve to fourteen feet in depth, and meant that boats hauling 3,000 tons of cargo could pass safely along the canal. In addition, beginning in the late 19th century, several canal branches were dug, the tolls along the canal disappeared, steam and diesel powered boats replaced animal power to push and pull traffic along the route, and electricity operated the locks. Even though the Erie Canal's last commercial traffic ended in 1994, the federal and New York state governments designated millions of dollars to maintain the canal system for recreational purposes.

The Erie Canal provided a great boost to the canal building enterprises in the United States. In 1826 more than one hundred canal projects were underway. By 1840 the mileage of canals in operation in the United States measured more than the distance from the Atlantic to Pacific Oceans. In the two decades from 1820 to 1840, approximately $125 million in public and private cooperative ventures was spent on canal construction. By 1859 the total tonnage shipped along the nation's canals totaled nearly 2 billion, in spite of the booming rate of railroad expansion. However, the profitability of the canal projects was never a certainty, and few canals enjoyed the long-term financial success of the Erie Canal. In the long run, however, in addition to revenues, the canal age provided important intangible benefits that added to the economic strength of the nation. The canals stimulated related industries in the areas through which they passed, helped to funnel a booming U.S. population westward, and ensured that the agricultural products of the Midwest found a profitable conduit to the nation's factory population in the east and the Atlantic port cities for shipment abroad.[13]

Transportation—Steamboats

At the same time that interest in canal building was growing, the prospect of improved waterway transportation also arose. During the 1780s John Fitch (see Biographies) and James Rumsey had proved the value of steam as a source of power for boats on the Delaware and Potomac Rivers, respectively. Other experiments continued in the United States and Great Britain throughout the 1790s. However, Robert Fulton brought the new era of steam-powered water transportation to fruition in the early 19th century. Fulton was born in Pennsylvania and from an early age showed an interest in both artistic and technical endeavors. At age thirteen he developed a special paddlewheel concept for fishing boats. While residing in Philadelphia, he painted portraits and landscapes, made mechanical and architectural drawings, and met and received instruction from Benjamin Franklin. He traveled to Great Britain and became an apprentice to the Duke of Bridgewater, who had been instrumental in canal construction. He continued his experiments and obtained patents for several devices associated with water transport. In the mid-1790s he traveled to Paris. After further tinkering, in 1801 he showed the French government an invention for submarine navigation that would employ torpedoes for military purposes. It failed, and he returned to Great Britain to seek that nation's support for his project. After several additional miscues, Great Britain rejected the submarine concept but remained somewhat intrigued by the torpedo, although the nation did not pursue further development at that time. Fulton eventually returned to the United States and attempted to convince Congress of the efficacy of his maritime proposal. Congress appropriated funds for testing but never adopted his idea. At the same time, Fulton developed plans for surface steam navigation. He gained financial backing, but several efforts on the Seine River achieved only partial success. Fulton, encouraged by his progress, purchased a Watt–Boulton engine and returned to the United States to place it in a steam paddle-wheeled boat. In August 1807, Fulton's *Clermont* (see Document 14) made a methodical thirty-two–hour trip up the Hudson River from New York City to Albany, covering a distance of 150 miles at the rate of five miles per hour. By the fall of that year, Fulton's steamboat began making regular trips between the two cities. Fulton's success generated a number of challenges by competitors who claimed that he should not receive exclusive patent rights for his invention.[14] But the advent of more rapid water transportation was now a reality and became even more important as the United States entered the canal age. The situation would be reversed only after railroad expansion began in the 1840s, at the very moment canal construction had peaked. However, despite the transition to railroads by mid-century, steamboat travel continued to be important. This is clearly evident from the record of steamboat accidents. In 1858, for example, the United States had 75 steamboat accidents (47 sunk, 19 fires, and 9 explosions) resulting in 259 deaths and property losses of $1,924,000.[15]

Transportation—Railroads

The arrival of the railway system provided the final ingredient to the rapidly expanding U.S. transportation system in the 19th century. In 1809 a survey map highlighted a "tramroad" or rail of wooden tracks that employed horsepower to pull a wagonload. This technique remained in use for some time and gave little indication that a major change was about to occur in overland transportation. James Watt's improved steam engine and efforts to apply steam power to water transportation that culminated in Robert Fulton's *Clermont's* sail on the Hudson River in 1807 prepared the way for the adoption of steam power to the railroad, the key component in the emergence of a railroad system in America.

Events gained momentum in the 1820s. John Stevens is considered to be the father of American railroads. He showed the potential of steam locomotion on an experimental iron rail circuit he constructed in Hoboken, New Jersey in 1826, three years before George Stephenson demonstrated his steam powered locomotive in Great Britain. Stevens obtained grants for railroad construction, and others soon followed suit. Serious efforts began in 1830 as surveying, mapping, and construction commenced on the Baltimore and Ohio line. By the end of the year, fourteen miles of track had been laid, although that line continued to use horsepower for another year. Over the next two years the United States had put only 73 miles of rail lines in existence. It took substantial effort and persuasion to continue railroad construction in the face of real and perceived obstacles. The foundation bed for the tracks often caused the rails to shift and loosen the spikes, and sparks from the locomotives set the surrounding grasses on fire. In addition, the locomotives frequently jumped the tracks and, for a time, a fearful public viewed the ever-increasing speed of the locomotives as dangerous and unhealthy.

The path was not always an easy one. In this early period railroads remained in competition with turnpikes and canals, which still attracted financial backers who viewed those older endeavors as safer vehicles for capital investment. Furthermore, the economic depression that swept the nation beginning in 1837 tightened the monetary supply

The Industrial Revolution in America

and slowed railroad construction until the early 1840s. However, the foundation for long-term change occurred when Peter Cooper's *Tom Thumb* became the country's first steam powered locomotive and carried passengers and cargo along a thirteen mile route from Baltimore to Ellicott Mills, Maryland in the same year. New lines appeared in rapid succession: the Mohawk and Hudson in the fall of 1830; the Saratoga in July 1832; and the South Carolina Canal and Railroad Company which boasted 136 miles of track in 1833, the longest steam powered railroad line in the world at that time. It was only a matter of time before the railroads supplanted canal era. In 1830 the country had 3,326 miles of canals and 3,328 miles of track. During the next decade the amount of railway lines increased nearly three times.[16] By 1851 the United States had 10,600 miles of track, including a 1,497 mile leg connecting New York and New Orleans. In 1852 an additional 2,000 miles were constructed, and the pride in America's achievement was clear as "no country in the world could equal ours (U.S.) for the number of railroads."[17] By the Civil War the amount of track had more than doubled to 27,000 miles.

Investment capital began to surge into railroads. In the 1840s, $200 million was spent on railroad construction. That sum is greater than the amount of investment in turnpikes, canals, and steamboats in the previous forty years. Foreign investment also flowed into the American railroad industry. In 1853 nearly one fourth of all railroad bonds in the United States were foreign owned. By 1860 the railroads represented the first $1 billion industry in the United States. Railroads, like canals, quickened the tempo of the country's economic development by reducing transportation costs even more than canals. In addition, the construction of locomotives and rail lines energized the nation's iron, then steel, metal working, and other manufacturing enterprises so necessary to the expanding rail network. That growth was varied depending on the section of the nation. By 1860 New England had twice as much railroad mileage as the Old Northwest and four times that of the South. Speed of transit became the ultimate goal. The early railroads quickly provided transport at three to four times that of the most efficient steamboats. The rapid growth of rail transportation also generated wild ideas about how to deal with the environmental disruption that had occurred. For example, one such proposal advocated the planting of shade trees on each side of the tracks to provide shade, screen dust, and strengthen the embankments along the tracks. Supporters of this plan conceded that it might take ten to fifteen years to have trees mature to the point of achieving these goals, a concession that ended any further serious discussion.[18] Another idea came from an individual who traveled between Baltimore and Washington and had to move forward several passenger cars to escape the thick dust that filled his car. He advocated the opening of railroad-company owned farms along the railroad routes that would utilize crops as ground cover and grasses along the railroad embankments to reduce or eliminate the clouds of dust enveloping the trains. His theory was that this would generate additional income for the railroads to encourage investment and also provide employment for agrarian laborers.[19]

The acceleration of railroad construction by the mid-1830s stimulated a demand for surveys and mapping, an activity that aided in the planning and construction of lines. However, this process proceeded without much long term consideration, and most early surveys were for short passenger routes that returned little or no profit. The importance of the surveys was that they obtained sanction and funds from the federal government for states and private business interests to use in mapping the best routes for railroad construction, an activity that had long-term positive results for railroad expansion. One example is an early map based on the survey of the route of the Western and Atlantic Rail Road of Georgia, 1837. The railroad constructed along this survey line stretched the 138-mile distance from Atlanta to Chattanooga. One could not have suspected the notoriety that this rail line would obtain in the Civil War when Union soldiers donned railroad employee clothing and seized a Confederate locomotive known as the *General*, thereby capturing a major Southern transportation route.[20]

Following the Civil War, U.S. railroad construction soared. In 1872 the nation built 7,340 miles of new track. At that moment, 60% of U.S. railroad track existed east of the Mississippi River and 40% west of the river. But the nation was undergoing a fundamental shift westward. In 1880 7,150 miles of fresh track ware laid, but the balance of overall track mileage had made a remarkable transformation: 20.4% east of the Mississippi River and 79.6% west. The building boom continued unabated: 9,800 miles in 1881, 11,500 miles in 1882, 9,000 miles in 1886, and 13,000 miles in 1887. By 1892 the United States had an estimated 174,600 miles of railroad track, or the equivalent of Europe, Asia, and Africa combined[21] (see Document 19). The railroad boom also stimulated locomotive construction. The Baldwin Locomotive Works in Philadelphia is a case in point. The industry employed 3,000 workers and turned out an average of ten locomotives a week. In 1861 it completed locomotive 1,000, and by 1880 had constructed some 5,000 locomotives for commercial use.[22]

Railroad safety was a constant concern. Accidents were frequent and gained widespread and detailed coverage in the press. One such incident was the 1888 collision of two trains on the Erie railway line near Avoca, New York. A mistake in track orders resulted in two trains being assigned to the same track approaching each other at a fast speed. A horrific crash occurred that caused injuries to several passengers and the death of one of the engineers whose head was completely severed from his body and found in the snow beside the track. His body was so wedged in that it took more than an hour to remove it from the wreckage. His left hand still gripped the lever that had applied the air brakes in an attempt to stop the train from the head on collision. Both locomotives were used for scrap metal, and the cost to repair the track and peripheral damage was estimated at $25,000.[23]

The Transcontinental Railroad

As the nation expanded westward at a rapid rate in the 1840s, many persons, gripped by the idea of Manifest Destiny or that the European Americans had been endowed by Providence to subdue and populate the continent, called for the linking of the nation east and west via the railroad. Congressional discussions concerning the feasibility of constructing a railroad to connect the Atlantic and Pacific Oceans occurred in the same decade and gained greater acceptance as the United States resolved the boundary dispute with Great Britain over the Oregon Territory, a war with Mexico brewed, and gold was discovered in California.

An odd coalition of individuals built the transcontinental railroad. The working men were Chinese and Irish. Presidents Lincoln and Grant and General Sherman provided leadership. The business, corporate, and engineer magnates formed at times a rogues' gallery of competing ambitions. In the end, these men accomplished what was considered nigh impossible. Historian Stephen E. Ambrose observed that "Next to winning the Civil War and abolishing slavery, building the first transcontinental railroad, from Omaha, Nebraska to Sacramento, California, was the greatest achievement of the American people in the nineteenth century."[24]

One of the early key promoters of such a venture was Asa Whitney, a distant relative of Eli Whitney, who became a prominent New York businessman and profited from overseas trade in China. Upon his return from the Orient in 1844, Whitney championed the cause of the intercontinental railroad. Whitney's idea was to use the intercontinental railroad to link China and Europe; the United States would serve as the middle man and was poised to profit handsomely from such a prospect. In addition, Whitney had as another goal the idea of human improvement. He believed that the intercontinental railroad would join the far flung regions of the nation into one entity, like a family, and would immeasurably strengthen the moral and social fabric of the nation. Finally, Whitney naively believed that the railroad connecting east and west would incorporate the Native Americans into the expanding American nation. Whitney urged congressional leaders to support his proposal and advocated an approach that would finance railroad construction through government grants of sixty-mile strips of land along an approved railroad route. In 1849 Whitney published a booklet that showed his proposed route for the railroad to the Pacific and additional subsidiary lines. Whitney became well-known for his skillful oratory on the matter and was frequently praised by the press. Even leading statesmen of the day such as John C. Calhoun, Stephen A. Douglas, and Jefferson Davis supported Whitney's proposal. However, the timing was ill-fated. After the nation obtained additional territory from war with Mexico and through negotiation with Great Britain over the Oregon Territory, the sectional crisis erupted in the early 1850s. In 1851 Congress rebuffed Whitney one last time, and he abandoned his effort for the railroad and retired to private life. Although Whitney lived to see the completion of the transcontinental railroad, it was an endeavor not done in accordance with his economic and philanthropic vision but rather through the auspices of federal government in collusion with profit-grabbing entrepreneurs.

During the 1850s the Army Topographic Corps made five surveys of potential routes for the transcontinental railroad. Each of the routes was deemed favorable, but no federal funding was forthcoming because of the heated Congressional debate over sectional issues. After the outbreak of the Civil War, business interests transformed the idea of the transcontinental railroad into a reality. Abraham Lincoln became convinced that such a railroad would have military purposes and also bind the west coast to the rest of the nation. He supported the Railroad Act of 1862, a measure that provided federal government financing for two railroad companies, the Central Pacific with its terminus at Sacramento and the Union Pacific with its terminus at Omaha. The two companies broke ground and began a seven-year race carving out railroad routes toward each other. The federal government provided land and sold bonds to help finance the venture. However, the Central Pacific spent $200,000 in bribes in Washington to obtain nine million acres of land and $24 million in bonds. The railroad owned its own construction company and made an overpayment of $36 million to that entity. The Union Pacific obtained twelve million acres of land and $27 million in bonds. It began the Credit Mobilier Company and overpaid it $50 million. The Union Pacific sold shares cheaply to members of Congress to ensure no investigation on construction practices would take place. Each railroad also charted a course in order to collect subsidies from towns through which they passed. Thus, in the initial phases of the construction, the companies set no eventual meeting place to join the lines.

By 1865 work on the transcontinental railroad began in earnest. The Central Pacific had created enough jobs for 4,000 men, although the back-breaking work and confusing management practices attracted less than 1,000 mostly Irish immigrant workers. At times these laborers grumbled about wages and carried the stereotype of spending their earnings on alcohol, thus reducing productivity. Reluctantly, the leadership of the Central Pacific Railroad employed Chinese workers who had to overcome a distinct anti-Asian bias prevalent in management and their fellow workers. Initially, the Chinese were assigned only the lowest tasks and paid wages lower than the Irish railroad men. The work ethic of the Chinese, however, soon impressed railroad officials and by 1868 12,000 Chinese workers were engaged on the project, more than 80% of the Central Pacific labor force. They were paid about $28 per month, a sum below that of their Irish counterparts. Eventually, some Chinese workers learned more skilled tasks such as masonry. Furthermore, the Chinese diet, frugal lifestyle, and penchant for cleanliness meant they avoided some of the diseases such as dysentery that ravaged the Irish from time to time and as a result had a better attendance record than their fellow laborers. The work of the Union Pacific Railroad began with much jubilation but also soon slowed due to a dearth of workers. Officials appealed to the War Department to employ freed slaves, but the government refused. A federal general also proposed using Native Americans captured during a campaign in 1864, but that idea faded as well. Two years after the groundbreaking, the Union Pacific had only forty miles of track in operation. Fortunately, thousands of discharged Civil War soldiers, joined also by Irishmen trekking west from eastern cities, gained employment on the railroad and the pace of laying down track increased. In early 1869 as the Union Pacific entered Utah it augmented its workforce with a large number of Mormons recruited after a plague of grasshoppers wiped out their crops.

The overall challenge in constructing the transcontinental railroad was daunting, as the companies not only had to subdue a formidable terrain comprising deserts and mountains but also had to contend with the Native Americans. The Indians resorted to violence on several occasions, killing U.S. soldiers and surveyors from the railroad lines who worked ahead of the construction. The Indians at times rustled livestock or sabotaged the rails by ripping them up or blocking the movement of goods. In one instance the Indians derailed a train and killed two crewmen. For the most part, the harassment by Native Americans was infrequent, although word of incidents or sightings of

Indians along the construction route generated fear and concern. Some tribes welcomed the railroad. The Union Pacific permitted Pawnee tribe members to ride its work trains for free. In return, members of the tribe conducted mock raids and battles to entertain dignitaries visiting the construction sites to check progress. In the end, however, the railroad proved to be a disaster for the Native Americans. They once again lost land as the tentacles of the railroad branched out in the later 19th century and squeezed them into federal reservations. The buffalo herds, that vital link in the survival of the Native Americans, nearly disappeared as thousands of sportsmen and hunters traveled west by rail to slaughter the animals. Ironically, it was the railroad that shipped the hides to markets in the east.

The process of putting down track was methodical and required the coordination of several tasks. One group of men directed horse-drawn carts over the newly placed track. Workers on each side of the cart unloaded rails and put them parallel to each other on the embedded ties. Men with gauges stooped down to verify that the rails were the correct distance apart. The next batch of men bolted contiguous rails on each side of the track and were followed by men who dropped spikes on the grade. Finally, workers with hammers placed the spikes and drove them into the ties with three solid taps. By June 1868 work had progressed to the point that the first locomotive arrived at Reno, Nevada on the Central Pacific Railroad. On April 8, 1869 the two railroad lines agreed to meet at Promontory Summit, Utah. They engaged in a contest to see which railroad could lay the most rail line in one day. On April 28, 1869 the workforce of the Central Pacific line surprised even its officials by placing 10 miles of track. After several delays, on May 10, 1869 Engine 119 of the Central Pacific and the *Jupiter* of the Union Pacific slowly approached each other and nearly touched, signifying the long awaited joining together of the disparate parts of the nation. The nation rejoiced almost instantaneously. Telegraph wires had been placed around the last spike and the sound of a sledgehammer driving it home was transmitted to cannon facing the oceans in San Francisco and New York causing them to fire and announce to the world the completion of the Transcontinental Railroad.

The impact of the Transcontinental Railroad was immediate. The next day a train departed from California carrying a cargo of Japanese teas in a testimony to the dream of Asa Whitney that the railroad would link Asia and Europe through the United States. Walt Whitman had published his "Passage to India" a year earlier in anticipation of the railroad's potential to join East and West. His vision soon faded with the opening of the Suez Canal six months later, joining Europe to India and the Far East without interaction with America. By 1891 only

5% of the transcontinental railroad's cargo had a destination for Asia, whereas 95% was local. Nonetheless, the railroad changed the United States forever. On May 15th passenger service commenced and carried travelers between San Francisco and New York in one week. Passengers traveling across country in the summer of 1869 paid $150 for a first class ticket. Within a year the cost had dropped to $136, and a third class ticket could be purchased for $65. The railroad lowered the cost of transporting goods, and within a decade the railroad transported more than $50 million in freight coast to coast. It brought the products manufactured in the east to the booming American population beyond the Mississippi River. Mail once transported across country at $2 per ounce cost only pennies within a year of the railroad's initial operation. The railroad also facilitated a production bonanza in the west as it ensured the mining, agriculture, and ranching industries particularly had a rapid and cost-effective means to ship their raw materials and goods to markets and industrial centers either in the east or west. In addition, the railroad provided a powerful stimulus to American culture. Passengers traveling across the country began to absorb the enormity, diversity, and beauty of the nation's landscape. Images of the frontier became the subject for writers, painters, and sculptors. Time and distance compressed but the exchange of ideas among citizens expanded. Within a few years a number of railroad lines snaked north and south from the transcontinental railroad and opened up millions of acres of land for settlement. By the end of the century additional lines had been laid parallel to the original railroad thereby weaving a tight transportation network throughout the nation.[25]

The U.S. Labor Force

The Dignity of Lowly Work
A lesson, Lord, those eighteen years to me;
Not elsewhere I could so divinely learn
That humble tasks are best, however I yearn
For higher sphere where I may work more free.
Blest were those patient toiling years to Thee,
If cross of death cast shadows on thy way,
What son was that so darkened in his light?
O Nazarene, out of their toils there came
That which we prize most dear – a brothers name.[26]

As the United States entered the Industrial Revolution, it faced the same labor shortage problem that Great Britain had encountered. What industrialization needed to take root was an adequate work force that could peddle its labor to factory owners in return for wages. However, in the early 19th century, nearly every adult white male still worked as a farmer or in other self-employed positions such as mechanics, artisans, or tradesmen, while women and children performed important tasks to supplement the family income. Only 10% of the population could claim to be employees or working for someone else. There were several reasons for this situation. First, the westward expansion of the nation continued to open up new land and kept many men "down on the farm" as land was cheap and plentiful. Indeed, the reverence for the agrarian worker lingered for a long time in America as the poem below emphasizes:

It was no curse that said to men,
"Labor thy lot shall be;
And with the seat upon thy brow
Thy hand shall nourish thee."
All who obey this high behest
Blessing in it have found;
And health and wealth are gathered best
By those who till the ground.[27]

Second, manufacturing was already being done on a small scale with the domestic or "putting out" system. Like his European counterpart, a merchant distributed materials such as yarn, straw, or leather, for example, to rural homes to be spun, plaited, or sewn, respectively. He returned on a designated date to pick up the finished articles for sale. Third, news of factory life emerging from Great Britain with its images of disease, monotony, squalor, family separation, and crime initially made American laborers more than wary of the experience.

For a few years, factory owners with facilities requiring only a small number of workers managed to survive, usually by recruiting widows and women with children and housing the family close to the mills while the men worked in the fields. Child labor was regulated by state laws in the 19th century. The first national child labor laws did not appear until the early 20th century, and these were declared unconstitutional by the Supreme Court.[28] The labor situation in the United States changed dramatically with the arrival new technology that caused the creation of larger factories and required not a dozen but perhaps hundreds of employees. An answer to this challenge appeared with the approach advanced by Francis C. Lowell (see Document 6) who in 1826 introduced one of the most innovative movements in American labor history.

Lowell had traveled abroad and while in Great Britain became fascinated with the textile industry. Because the British government forbade the export of any industrial technology, it is said that Lowell memorized what he observed. Upon his return to Massachusetts, he and his partner, Nathan Appleton, began their own manufacturing firm. Lowell's experience in Great Britain convinced him that he wanted a new type of labor force that did not resemble its impoverished laborers and their families. Thus, the saga of the Lowell mill girls was born. Lowell recruited young women of sound character to his factory system and provided work, supervised housing, and regular pay for a few years so they could return home with a dowry upon marriage. Lowell's project has received both praise and criticism from some historians. One school claims that his effort had commendable results while other scholars opine that his approach did not have all the altruism about which he boasted. While it is true that the hours were long and the pay low (there was a strike over wages), many of the girls looked back on the experience with gratitude for the opportunity to work and make new friendships. By the 1830s women made up approximately 80% of the textile mill work force in America. Sometimes factory owners recruited entire families, including the children, or widows who had a number of mouths to feed. Within a few decades, the toil of the factory worker began to be viewed as a positive and uplifting experience and one that generated additional loyalty to the nation as the following poem, "The Song of the Artizan [sic]," demonstrates:

Sing, comrades, sing!
Not alone in the workshop's clamor,
When wielding the saw and hammer,
In each of us, here, a king.
For as part of our noble nation,
We stand in a glorious station,
And learn to think, at every clink
Whatever the fools may say.[29]

Despite the success of the Lowell enterprise, some proprietors struggled with their workers. In 1846 one cotton mill owner, in an effort to reduce costs, lowered wages by 25%. His pool of workers dwindled, and he attempted to lure them back with a promise to restore wages to their previous level. Unfortunately, his business collapsed because his disgruntled employees had found other acceptable mill jobs.[30] Furthermore, in this early period of industrialization, the downside aspects of the new society surfaced. The number of urban poor began to be a visible problem and attracted the interest of reformers. The following poem, "Pity the Poor," illustrates this concern:

The winter-times are coming fast,
Pipes loud and shrill the autumn blast.
And leafless limbs are quivering;
And the houseless ones are shivering;
    With your eye
    You may spy
    Naked feet
    Mid the sleet
Then pity, oh! Pity the poor
Who stand in the cold at your door.
Who are the poor?
The poor! The poor are everywhere
They who life's labor never touch,
But at its table take too much,
Feel poverty's severest clutch,
As I opine,
The work-house were a bliss to such
Poor soul less swine.
There are so many in this city,
Few to aid and few to pity.[31]

The pool of available women to work in the factories dwindled by the 1840s, brought about in part by a decline in the birth rate in rural areas just as the new source of labor arrived: immigrants. The use of immigrant labor began in earnest in the 1820s during the canal age. By the 1840s a steady, growing stream of German, Irish, British, Scandinavian, and Polish workers escaping political upheaval, the collapse of the potato crop, or just seeking employment opportunities for even the most minimum of pay came to the United States. The labor force in one factory in Massachusetts changed from being just 4% immigrant labor in the mid-1820s to more than 50% two decades later. The immigrant tide swelled rapidly: 8400 in 1820, 23,000 in 1830, 84,000 in 1840, and 310,000 in 1850. The initial immigrants were mostly agrarian workers rather than industrial laborers. However, by 1850 just over 50% were farmers while the laborer pool had increased to 38%.[32] Indeed, almost one-half of the non-slave labor in the United States was performed by immigrants on the eve of the Civil War. The torrent of immigration continued in the last half of the century and is estimated to have been 14 million from 1860 to 1900. This new immigrant pool of workers stood in stark contrast to America's first immigrants in the 17th century. Whereas many of America's first immigrants were literate and skilled, their 19th-century counterparts were for the most part uneducated, unskilled, desperate for work, and easily exploited. These workers who were willing to toil long hours for minimum pay began to replace women and children in American factories and by the mid-19th century nudged industrial development forward in the United States.[33]

In many respects, the Civil War was a holding pattern in the nation's drive to industrialization. National productivity increased at the slow pace of only 7% over the period 1860 to 1865, primarily because all surplus labor had been siphoned off for the war effort. But during the five years following the war that percentage increased sixfold. Northern cotton textile production, which had actually declined during the conflict, doubled in the first year after the war and then was 50% higher again by 1869. During the war there was little iron to spare for capital or infrastructure uses because weapons created an insatiable demand for iron. The situation reversed itself immediately, and production increased from 1 million tons in 1865 to 3 million tons in 1873. Railroad construction actually declined during the conflict despite Congressional approval of the transcontinental railroad. In 1865 just over 800 miles of new construction took place. By 1871, however, nearly 50,000 new miles of track had been put into operation.

The war did encourage the growth of several industries. The Union army required the production of more than four million uniforms and three million pairs of socks. This substantial requirement led to the creation of ready-made sizes and the heavy reliance on the sewing machine to produce the garments. The idea of ready-made clothing was nearly foreign in 1860, but by the end of the century 90% of men's clothing fell into this category. Another industry that the war stimulated was that of milling machinery. Early in the war, this machinery drilled holes in the key components of guns. By the end of the war, this same procedure had been applied to the creation of cutlery, tools, locks, locomotives, etc. But perhaps no industry represented the new age dawning in the United States more than that of steel production. In 1865 the nation produced 16,000 tons of steel. Sixty years later the annual production was 56 million tons. The development of the Bessemer process (see Biographies) influenced Andrew Carnegie to establish a steel-making plant in 1875, even in the midst of the deepest economic downturn in the nation's history. Carnegie had a keen vision and became the epitome of the entrepreneurial spirit that dominated the last three decades of the 19th century. Carnegie, like other notables of big business such as Jay Gould, John D. Rockefeller, and Cornelius Vanderbilt, demonstrated that talent, ambition, personality, and at times the reliance ruthless tactics resulted in fabulous wealth and influence. Carnegie introduced the age of steel in America, as steel became the basic building material of manufacturing industries. His thrust dropped the price of steel from $50 a ton in 1875 to just $12 in the 1890s. Railway rails converted to steel in 1881, and by 1890 nearly 100,000 miles of new steel track had been laid in the country.[34] To state it most simply, between the years 1850 and 1870 the total dollar value of the nation's production more than quadrupled from $1 billion to $4.2 billion.[35]

After the Civil War the lot of most industrial workers had improved, although long hours and taxing work remained the norm. The increased speed and efficiency of industrial equipment also encouraged employers to demand more from workers. Efforts by the workers to organize were usually met with stiff resistance. Most early unions met in secret because identification with unionism would often result in the firing of a worker, and his public identification would make finding other employment difficult. Trade union membership in 1869 was estimated at 500,000. That number had declined by 1878, but a union voice remained active. In time two types of unions emerged. The first took an idealistic approach that advocated improved conditions not only for workers but also for society in general. Thus, the creation of the National Labor Union in 1866 and the Knights of Labor in 1869 stressed the eight-hour workday and educational opportunities, women's rights, and temperance. The second type of union worked for issues specific to members of its organizations and did not seek broad reform. The creation of the American Federation of Labor (AFL) in 1886, a loose federation of a conglomerate of different unions, is representative of this type.

The movement toward unionism was not entirely quiet. In an apparent anomaly the number of strikes increased three-fold at the same time that working conditions seemed to improve. For instance, in 1880 some 762 strikes and lockouts took place, costing an estimated $12 million in lost wages for laborers.[36] Some strikes gained widespread notoriety. Two examples are the Haymarket Affair of 1886 and the Homestead Strike of 1892. In the former a nationwide series of strikes by industrial workers had the goal of an eight-hour workday. On May 3, 1886 striking workers at the McCormick Reaper Works factory in Chicago clashed with police resulting in several deaths. The following evening a meeting was held near Haymarket Square under the auspices of several radical labor leaders. Just as the meeting adjourned a bomb was hurled into the group of police and gunfire erupted, killing a number of workers. Authorities rounded up labor activists and trials quickly ensued. After a series of appeals, three labor leaders were executed and several others went to jail. The Homestead Strike took place several years later in Pennsylvania at a Carnegie steel plant with a strong AFL union tradition. Discussions between management and labor representatives broke down over the issue of wage reductions. Plant leadership closed the facility and called in the Pinkerton Detective Agency to break the strike line. A confrontation turned violent and resulted in the death of 16 people. The National Guard arrived and restored order within a short period of time. The workers who returned to their jobs found themselves forced to endure twelve-hour days, wages reduced by 50%, and the loss of extra pay incentives.[37]

Despite these two extreme examples of labor unrest and the outbreak of other smaller confrontations, membership in union organizations on the eve of World War I only represented 15% of the non-agricultural workers in the United States. Although health and safety conditions did not improve substantially until the early 20th century, workers for the most part did enjoy higher wages and fewer working hours although on occasion they were tempered by extended periods of layoffs created by the unpredictable business cycle. The factories produced a seemingly endless variety of cheap goods. While the gap between rich and poor grew, in reality the lower classes did not get poorer because of their increasing purchasing power. Real wages—the actual purchasing power of earnings—rose in the last three decades of the 19th century, and the work week declined from 66 to 59 hours. The U.S worker became increasingly competitive with his British counterpart. The wages earned by U.S. workers in the late 19th century illustrate this point. In 1892 the average annual wage for workers in the U.S. cotton industry was $457.76, second only to Great Britain's $556.14. In the woolen industry the difference was $663.13 versus $915.64. And in the glass related industries the United States actually reversed the earlier situation and had wages measured at $859.64 compared to Great Britain's $501.69.[38]

The U.S. Centennial Exposition

Similar to the British Crystal Palace Exhibition of 1851, the United States hosted an exposition in Philadelphia to showcase the nation's cultural and industrial achievements during its first century. The U.S. Centennial Exposition marks the moment that the United States industrial prowess had reached a level of sophistication that would thrust it to world supremacy within half a century. President Ulysses S. Grant opened the exposition on May 10, 1876. The exposition hosted 37 nations and innumerable industrial exhibits housed in 250 pavilions stretched over 450 acres of land. In a fitting recognition of the shifting source of labor in America, the exposition was designed by a German immigrant, Herman J. Schwarzmann. The project cost $8 million and organizers calculated that nearly 10 million visitors would be needed to cover the expenses. On opening day only 76,000 persons attended, and officials expressed concern. However, by the summer of 1876 daily attendance had grown to between 150,000 to 200,000, and the worries subsided. Over the 159-day run of the exposition, daily admissions averaged 61,500 persons (the largest single day was 275,000 attendees) with a final tally of 9.8 million attendees. The exposition displayed the nation's growing industrial and economic might and introduced some of the latest American technology and know-how. A large 1,400 horsepower Corliss steam engine standing 70 feet in height and weighing 650 tons provided power for all the machinery in the exposition's Machinery Hall. After the exposition closed the engine went to Chicago and operated the Pullman train car factory for three decades before being sold for scrap at $8 a ton. In addition to the Corliss engine, exposition goers observed such new technical devices as the Remington typewriter, an early Alexander Graham Bell telephone, locomotives, printing presses, fire trucks, mining equipment, magic lanterns, a mechanical calculator, and an improved artificial leg, as well as new consumer products such as Heinz Ketchup and Hires Root Beer. America's centennial exposition outdrew the 1851 and 1862 London, 1855 Paris, and 1873 Vienna exhibitions and had virtually equal attendance with a second Paris exhibition in 1867. The remarkable aspect of this comparison is that the aggregate American population within seven days travel of Philadelphia numbered approximately forty-five million, whereas the European cities had more than 200 million people residing within seven days travel of all their exhibition cities. Furthermore, the nearly ten million attendees at the Philadelphia centennial site represented about 20% of the U.S. population in 1876. These statistics are testimony to the rapid maturity of the U.S. road and railroad network that had substantial infrastructure in place to bring large numbers of visitors to the exposition quickly, safely and cheaply.[39]

Technology

Although America's technological position was far behind that of Great Britain during the colonial era and the early years of the republic, the nation made great strides. Prior to the Revolution, the American Philosophical Society had been formed in Philadelphia for the purpose of encouraging useful knowledge. In 1824 the Franklin Institute attempted to mesh business and professional interests for the purpose of stimulating economic growth. Furthermore, the publication of the important technical journal *Scientific American* aided the spread of technical knowledge. The journal had 14,000 subscribers by the middle of the 19th century.[40] Indeed, in 1790 the United States established a patent office, modeled somewhat on the British example, to register inventions and protect the intellectual property of the inventors. The initial law was weak and had to be modified several times. However, its records indicate a steady stream of inventions: 3 patents in 1790, 158 patents in 1808, 544 patents in 1830, 1,050 patents in 1850, and 4,588 patents in 1860. Even women were able to obtain patents. The first U.S. patent to a woman was issued in 1809, and thereafter the issuance of patents to women averaged about one per year. By the late 19th century the situation had changed. In 1887 to 1888 the number had mushroomed to 250. Most patents by women had a connection to ladies apparel, but several achieved real technical sophistication such as patents for modified screw propellers, reaping machines, and furnaces for smelting ores.[41] Despite this activity, by 1850, for every two British workers toiling on the land three worked in manufacturing enterprises. At the same time the United States had only 15% of its workforce in industry. But the greater diversity of British manufacturing efforts, the specialization of labor, and the larger pool of business talent was on the brink of being outpaced by the United States. As previously stated, the United States had originally imported British technology by legal or illegal means. However, by the mid-19th century Great Britain was somewhat lethargic, as mill owners and workers tended to maintain equipment and procedures that had proven themselves rather than risking this security for new and possibly better techniques and inventions. The United States did have some advantages, including a growing ingenuity in a variety of technical fields and no fear of experimentation to seek newer and more efficient methods of production. The propensity for such unhampered approaches to technological development had its origins in colonial times. American farmers and craftsmen had to rely on trial and error and their own ingenuity to create new and improved tools and implements. No guilds or government regulation placed prohibitions on their efforts to save labor and improve efficiency. Productivity had increased by at least 50% as the nation shifted, albeit slowly, from agriculture to industry and began to rely more on machine power for production. Indeed, machines had become accepted aspects of the daily life of people.

This same attitude prevailed as more sophisticated machinery appeared in the nation's growing manufacturing sector. The variety of machine manufactured consumer goods seemed endless—cast iron stoves, window shades, flush toilets, gaslights, and standard furniture to mention a few—items that went in one generation from being unheard of or too costly to commonplace. As a further indication of the nation's appetite for new consumer goods, at least 1000 new patents had been approved by the government between the years 1840 and 1860. For example, in just over a decade after Elias Howe's 1846 patent for the sewing machine, the United States counted fifteen times as many of these devices as Great Britain. This single invention transformed the manufacture of clothing from a handicraft to machine production industry and thus drove the prices down substantially, so that even the lower classes could afford extra garments. A further stimulus to the growth of American technical ingenuity was the perfection of the concept of interchangeable parts. This development ensured the sustainability and profitability of mass production and virtually erased the pre-existing reliance on a large scale handicraft industry in America. The technology of interchangeable parts relied on the concept that components of a finished good are so uniform that they could be substituted for one another and still have a complete article produced. To be sure, the first idea in this vein was not American but rather British and French. Because neither country pursued the possibility in the late 18th century, the American inventor, Eli Whitney, was able to claim the process as his own. His financial frustrations over patent infringements with the cotton gin led him to pursue profit in arms-making and ultimately led to his successful demonstration of the disassembly and re-assembly of muskets for President Adams and Vice-President Jefferson in 1801 (see Biographies).

Even Whitney did not comprehend the ultimate impact of his procedure. Before this time machinists had to cut each nut individually, and the cylinders in the steam engine might have errors in uniformity up to 1/32 of an inch. In time the use of interchangeable parts not only made the process of creating like components for finished goods simple and rapid but it also led to the creation of uniform machine parts to produce the articles themselves, a transformation that was the real boon to industry. It ultimately revolutionized production costs, increased efficiency, and reduced the expense of finished goods to the consumer. The concept soon became referred to as the "American System" and spread to other industries such as clockmaking, sewing machines, farm items, watches, and even pistols. Even with the obvious benefits of interchangeable parts, fewer than two dozen industries employed the technique prior to the Civil War. Interestingly, the success of the American System did not immediately rebound on Great Britain and the continent. As U.S. manufacturers set up their operations in Great Britain following the Civil War, British observers expressed awe at the concept.[42]

In one respect, the nation's continued reliance on bringing new land under cultivation fostered the growth of inventions to make the harvesting of crops faster and more efficient. In fact the amount of land under cultivation doubled from 1850 to 1900 and increased three times by 1910. The farm population also increased by 50%, but its percentage of the overall labor force actually declined because of the growth of industry. In 1800 most farm work was done by hand, whereas by 1900 farm operations had become mechanized and power tools were the norm. Over the course of the 1830s and 1840s a series of devices appeared to make farm work more efficient and productive. The most significant invention was Cyrus H. McCormick's improved horse-drawn reaper in 1854. McCormick's reaper featured revolving blades that efficiently sliced the wheat and increased the harvesting capability from two acres a day to two acres an hour. As a further indication of the productivity increase, particularly after the application of steam and then diesel power to farm equipment, in 1800 it took approximately fifty-six man hours per acre to raise wheat, of which forty man hours were devoted to harvesting. By 1900 that total had been dramatically reduced to fifteen and nine man hours, respectively. Indeed, in 1800 the productivity of one farm could support just over four families. In 1900 the same farm could feed seven families.

Several other technical developments in the 19th century contributed to the acceleration of the United States to it eventual leadership in the industrial world after 1900. The appearance of the bicycle in 1878, for example, revolutionized transportation for individuals and families living in the crowded cities. By 1900 American factories produced one million bicycles a year. Two breakthroughs in communication technology, however, made a dramatic impact and deserve emphasis. The first was the perfection of the telegraph system by Samuel Finley Breese Morse (see Biographies) in 1844. Within his lifetime, telegraphic communication not only linked all of the nation's states but also wedded Europe and America by transatlantic cable. The second was the invention of the telephone by Alexander Graham Bell. Building on the work of other pioneer scientists in electricity and magnetic fields, Bell envisioned the transmission of speech electronically. In March 1876 he patented the first telephone in which sound wave vibration could be transformed into a fluctuating electric current and carried across wires and reconverted into identical sound waves at the other end of the circuit. The telephone's commercial and personal value became readily apparent. In 1883 there were 100,000 telephone subscribers, almost all in urban areas. In New York City there was one telephone for every 500 persons, as compared to one per 1,000 in Paris, one per 3,000 in London and Berlin, and one per 4,000 in St. Petersburg. By 1917 the

Unites States had twelve million telephones in operation.[43] In 1879 New Haven, Connecticut published the first commercial phone book listing 50 names and no numbers since all calls were operator assisted until a later date.[44] These two inventions—telegraph and telephone—revolutionized communications and sped up the sharing of important knowledge and influenced developments in Europe that resulted in the invention of the wireless radio in 1901. Another major technical advance was the incandescent light bulb developed by Thomas Alva Edison. Of humble origins, Edison was an inquisitive youth and established his first laboratory at the age of 12. In 1868 he became a telegraph operator for Western Union. By 1874 he had devised the quadruplex telegraph capable of sending two messages simultaneously in two directions. He established laboratories first in New York City and then his famous facility at Menlo Park, New Jersey. In the course of his life Edison obtained 1093 patents, including ones that resulted in the improved clarity and volume of the Bell telephone (1877), Wall Street stock ticker (1869), phonograph (1870), motion pictures (1888), and the device that won him international acclaim, the incandescent light bulb (1879). This latter invention resulted in the eventual creation of the General Electric Company in 1892 and the establishment of commercial electric lighting systems in the United States and abroad. By the late 19th century the force of electricity had found a variety of purposes. Industries supplied electricity and illuminated their formerly dimly lit assembly lines and powered motors and engines in the factories. The first electric trolley appeared in 1895, replacing the former horse-drawn trolleys, and within several years 10,000 miles of track were in place. Electric lighting appeared in homes as well as on city streets. By the early 20th century, electricity prepared the way for its eventual use as a power source for household appliances such as irons, washing machines, refrigerators, and vacuum cleaners, a development that eventually freed up more women to enter the U.S. workforce once again.[45]

One other technical innovation also contributed to the United States emergence as the industrial leader in the world by the early 20th century. Frank and Charles Duryea developed the gas powered engine in 1893, which resulted in the production of the earliest automobile. This development had grown from the discovery of petroleum and experiments with its potential earlier in the century. Interestingly, one of the first assessments was that fluid petroleum would have no functional purpose "except as a lotion for bruises and rheumatic afflictions."[46] Although it was acknowledged that petroleum could produce substantial light, its pungent odor was considered too offensive. In 1896 the Duryea brothers made and sold thirteen cars. In the same year a mechanic in his early thirties named Henry Ford created his first automobile, which resulted in the sale of more than 10,000 Model Ts in 1909. Two decades later he had established the largest industry in the nation with nearly 2,500 plants. These factories had an assembly line operation that married the product and process to mass produce cheap automobiles for consumption by a large segment of the American population. In 1929 more than 20 million automobiles traveled U.S. roadways, one for every five Americans, and nearly 17% of all U.S. patents had some connection to the automobile industry.

Urban Growth

During the first six decades of the 19th century, America experienced dramatic urban growth. In 1800 the United States had no cities with a population more than 70,000, and by 1860 there were two with half a million residents and fourteen with 100,000 in population. During George Washington's presidency, 95% of Americans lived in rural areas; in Abraham Lincoln's presidency this figure had declined to 80%. Following the Civil War the trend to urbanization accelerated. In 1865 no city in America had a population of 1 million persons, whereas by the late 1920s five cities had reached that population. This demographic shift moved the nation to the city. Agricultural labor made up half the workforce in 1865 but only one quarter in the 1920s. U.S. population growth advanced at a rate that far surpassed that of the world at large. From 1850 to 1920 world population increased at 55%, whereas the U.S. population grew from 23 million to 106 million, an increase of 461%. The trend to heavy mechanization on the farm had sliced cultivation time in half and displaced agrarian workers to seek employment in the industrialized cities. This development along with the large number of immigrants (see Document 17) entering the cities provided a wide variety of opportunities in an ever-expanding industrial base. In 1820, 350,000 Americans worked in manufacturing enterprises or handcraft trades. That number rose to 2 million in 1860. The total labor force increased nearly six times from 1.9 million to 11 million in these six decades. By the early 20th century approximately 300 American cities contained three-fourths of the U.S. population, and these cities were host to more than 80% of the nation's manufacturing enterprises.

The industrial city was the urban model from 1870 to 1920. The total worth of the nation's capital—buildings, factories, roads, machines, and livestock—is not entirely known, but its growth had been dramatic since the late 18th century and gained much momentum after the Civil

War. One example is the phenomenal construction that occurred in New York City. From 1868 to 1882, the city recorded the construction of nearly 30,000 new buildings with a total cost of $424 million. New York City illustrates the challenging living conditions that existed for the vast majority of the masses in industrial cities. The negative side of industrialization—garbage, grime, soot, overcrowded living conditions, low pay, slums, crime (see Document 18), and health concerns—appeared in American cities just as it had in Great Britain. The number of tenement houses in New York City attests to this new situation. In 1872, New York City had nearly 15,000 tenement houses with 500,000 residents (see Document 20); in 1890 the number was 37,000 with 1.25 million residents, and in 1900 42,700 tenement houses with 1.5 million inhabitants. The steady growth and the compact nature of the city is further illustrated by the block density, or number of persons living in one block, of New York City over time: 158 in 1820, 272 in 1850, and 5,000 to 6,000 in 1894. This crowding led to other problems not uncommon to urban areas: smoggy skies from the perpetual belching of coal produced smoke from the factories, a terrible din from the myriad of uncontrolled noises, piles of waste in the streets, congested thoroughfares, polluted rivers and waterways, and constant health concerns. Life expectancy was slow to improve under these conditions. In 1790 the life expectancy was 36 years of age and had crept only to 40 by the Civil War. In addition, the number of families needing assistance taxed the ability of churches and charities. It is estimated that in the years 1885 to 1890 some 136,000 families scattered throughout New York City in some 31,000 tenements required assistance. During these years, one in ten persons dying in New York was buried in Potter's Field.[47] Even by 1900 only 50% of children born in the United States could expect to reach 50 years of age, although life expectancy surged to an average of 60 years by 1929.

    Another blight that appeared was the number of abandoned and orphaned children. It is estimated that 100,000 children eked out a living in the streets of New York City by 1850. The number only grew over the next several decades as more immigrants poured into America. A unique effort to help this dispossessed group appeared under the auspices of Charles Loring Brace, a minister who became the pioneer in the idea of foster care. In conjunction with the Sisters of Charity, Brace sponsored Orphan Trains to transport some of these children west to place them in families seeking additional children. Few families actually adopted these children, but the "foster care" provided gave them hope and opportunity. The success of the project is found in the fact that less than 1% returned to New York, and the trains ran until 1930. Public services in urban areas in the form of fire, police, sanitation, etc. rarely existed in 1860, but following the Civil War the momentum for change was unstoppable.[48]

Conclusion

In many respects, the American experience in entering the industrial era reflected that of Great Britain. The long colonial linkage and the eventual warming of the relationship between the two countries in the 19th century led to the United States being the heir to British industrial developments. Yet, the United States also had distinctive trends that did not mirror those of Great Britain. Whereas Britain's agricultural production shrank during the industrial revolution and the nation had to import foodstuffs to support its manufacturing labor force, the United States saw the continued expansion of agriculture as the nation spread westward. This agricultural growth provided essential sustenance for the industrial workforce that expanded rapidly through the shift of population from farm to city and the arrival of millions of immigrants. Thus, the number and size of the nation's cities increased and changed the complexion of the United States from rural to urban. In addition, America's agricultural productivity ensured that the nation possessed sufficient exports to exchange for capital to support industrial expansion. Sustained agricultural development also stimulated the invention of more efficient and cost-effective farm equipment and meant that agricultural industries and the manufacturing sector existed side by side and mutually supported each other. The rapid expansion of U.S. industry after the Civil War resulted in the development of innovative business organizations with structures that became increasingly complex as the number and size of firms grew. For example, in 1870 the normal iron and steel firm had fewer than 100 employees. By 1900 that number had increased four-fold, a trend that found its mirror image in most other industrial enterprises. During the 19th century, the U.S. infrastructure in the form of roads and railroads expanded rapidly, a development that facilitated the mobility of the populace and the rapid transportation of goods and services and tied the nation together. New inventions and techniques emerged that changed the nature of workplace and the home. The United States experienced a prosperity that previous generations could not have envisioned. Indeed, the dramatic economic transformation of the late 19th century moved Henry Adams, the famous American historian and novelist, to lament that a boy born on the eve of the Civil War would have a life that more resembled the time of Christ than that of the U.S. in 1900. In 1908, just on the other side of that new century that Henry Adams had used as a benchmark, the United States had become a nation of modern industrial marvels. The year opened with the first electric ball ringing in the New Year in New York; Wilbur Wright made a manned flight of more than two hours, and the U.S. Navy sailed the Great White Fleet (sixteen battleships weighing 250 million tons and costing $100 million) on a 43,000 mile journey around the world. Mirroring the words of Queen Victoria more than a half century earlier, Thomas Edison perhaps said it best: "Anything, everything is possible."[49]

Notes

1. R. L. Heilbronner & A. Singer, *The Economic Transformation of America* (New York: Harcourt Brace Jovanovich, 1977), 9–13.

2. B. Hindle & S. Lubar, *Engines of Change: The American Industrial Revolution 1790–1860* (Washington, D.C.: Smithsonian Institution Press, 1986), 60–64.

3. Stalcup, *The Industrial Revolution*, 45–48.

4. R. Chernow, *Alexander Hamilton* (New York: Penguin Books, 2004), 32, 294–295, 371–372.

5. Stalcup, *The Industrial Revolution*, 52.

6. Chernow, *Alexander Hamilton*, 372–373.

7. D. C. North, *The Economic Growth of the United States 1790–1860* (New York: W.W. Norton Co. Inc., 1966), 17, 23.

8. Heilbronner, *Economic Transformation of America*, 34, 49.

9. Stalcup, *The Industrial Revolution*, 59–60; Heilbronner, *Economic Transformation of America*, 25.

10. Hindle and Lubar, *Engines of Change*, 112–114.

11. http://ww.swetland.net/cumberland.htm

12. Heilbronner, *Economic Transformation of America*, 30–31.

13. http://www.canals.org/erie.htm

14. Stalcup, *The Industrial Revolution*, 89–94; http:www.RobertFulton.org/htm

15. *Scientific American*, Vol. 14, No. 9 (June 15, 1859), 149.

16. Heilbronner, *The Economic Transformation of America*, 34–35.

17. *Scientific American*, Vol. 6, No. 33 (May 3, 1851), 257.

18. *Scientific American*, Vol. 10, No. 12 (December 2, 1854), 89.

19. *Scientific American*, Vol. 10, No. 36 (May 16, 1857), 299.

20. http://www.memory.loc.gov/ammem/index.html

21. *Manufacturer and Builder*, Vol. 13, No. 4 (April 1881), 87; *Manufacturer and Builder*, Vol. 21, No. 1 (January 1889), 1–2; *Manufacturer and Builder*, Vol. 25, No. 2 (February 1893), 32.

22. *Manufacturer and Builder*, Vol. 13, No. 7 (July 1881), 166.

23. http://www.nrhs.com/archives/trainwreck.htm

24. S. E. Ambrose, *Nothing Like It in the World: The Men Who Built the Transcontinental Railroad, 1863–1869* (New York: Simon and Schuster, 2000), 17–19.

25. http://www.pbs.org/wgbh/amex/tcrr; Ambrose, *Nothing Like It in the World*, 369–370.

26. *Harper's New Monthly Magazine*, Vol. 68, No. 408 (May 1884), 863.

27. *Scientific American*, Vol. 4, No. 11 (December 2, 1848), 81.

28. C. Nardinelli, *Child Labor in the Industrial Revolution* (Bloomington: Indiana University Press, 1990), 129.

29. *Scientific American*, Vol. 2, No. 13 (December 19, 1846), 97.

30. *Scientific American*, Vol. 2, No. 3 (October 10, 1846), 17.

31. *Scientific American*, Vol. 2, No. 14 (December 26, 1846), 405.

32. North, *The Economic Growth of the United States*, 24.

33. Heilbronner, *Economic Transformation of America*, 40; http://www.nps.gov/archive/lowe

34. Heilbronner, *Economic Transformation of America*, 67, 72, 90–91.

35. *Manufacturer and Builder*, Vol. 9, No. 2 (February 1877), 46.

36. *Manufacturer and Builder*, Vol. 12, No. 18 (December 1886), 267.

37. http://www.chicagohistory.org/hadc/chronology/html

38. *Manufacturer and Builder*, Vol. 24, No. 6 (June 1892), 133.

39. *Manufacturer and Builder*, Vol. 12, No. 8 (December 1876), 268; *Manufacturer and Builder*, Vol. 8, No. 10 (October 1876), 220.

40. Hindle & Lubar, *Engines of Change*, 77–79, 90–92.

41. *Manufacturer and Builder*, Vol. 21, No. 5 (May 1889), 48.

42. Heilbronner, *Economic Transformation of America*, 34.

43. *Manufacturer and Builder*, Vol. 15, No. 2 (February 1883), 27.

44. *Smithsonian*, Vol. 36, No. 11 (February 2008), 22.

45. http://www.nps.gov.edis

46. As quoted in *Smithsonian*, Vol. 36, No. 2 (May 2007), 10.

47. Manufacturer and Builder, Vol. 15, No. 1 (January 1883), 16; Heilbronner, *Economic Transformation of America*, 196.

48. *Florida Today*, January 20, 2008.

49. As quoted in *Smithsonian*, Vol. 36, No. 10 (January 2008), 42.

CHAPTER 6

THE INDUSTRIAL REVOLUTION ON THE CONTINENT IN THE LATE 19TH CENTURY

The rapid economic growth that Great Britain had achieved by the early 19th century far surpassed that of its continental neighbors. By mid-century Great Britain was the world's industrial giant and produced two thirds of the world's coal, one half of the world's iron and cotton textiles, and possessed a per capita income larger than countries on the continent. Britain's dominance of the global marketplace was unquestioned, and no nation could compete with its economic strength. Although some industrial developments had begun in Europe by the turn of the 19th century, in comparison to the British model, these activities were tepid at best. In 1851, as illustrated by the remarkable displays at the Crystal Palace Exhibition, Great Britain had achieved an advantage in almost every category of industrial achievement. Indeed, German representatives who saw the modern industrial wonders at the Crystal Palace Exhibition made a gloomy assessment that Great Britain would never lose its supremacy.[1] At that moment, the European nations held no illusion about challenging the British position in the near term. In reality, however, the situation had begun to change slowly in the years following the Napoleonic Wars, and industrialization gained additional momentum on the continent after 1850 as three centers—Belgium, France, and some German states— began to narrow the industrial gap.

Prior to the early 19th century a number of historical, political, geographical, economic, and social factors impeded potential industrial developments on the continent. The nations of Europe had a history of frequent warfare in the 17th and 18th centuries, and those conflicts did not run their course until the conclusion of the Seven Years War in 1763. Within one generation following that war, the French Revolution erupted in 1789 ushering in a long period of political and social disturbances that affected all the major nations of western and central Europe until 1848. Furthermore, in the midst of this era Napoleon's armies marched back and forth across Europe for nearly two decades disrupting opportunities for sustained economic and industrial development. Because many of the nations on the continent were larger than Great Britain in size and population, it was not easy to knit together their various regions. In addition, transportation costs remained high as it was difficult to move goods over long distances either by land or water networks. The vast majority of roads were poorly maintained and at times rivers became too shallow as a result of seasonal dryness, limiting the flow of traffic to link distant markets. In addition, few ports existed to join effectively the interior of these areas to the rest of the state. Further exacerbating this problem was the nagging retention of ancient high customs duties, tolls, and excise taxes that forced agents shipping goods to avoid these fees whenever possible. Also, local guild restrictions that had all but disappeared in Great Britain remained in effect in many places on the continent, and the strict rules and dictates of these old organizations long standing traditions impeded ingenuity and innovation.

Before 1789 most European states had not made any significant advances in agricultural practices that would increase food production while at the same time reducing agrarian labor requirements. Peasants who did work in the early mills or factories usually toiled in these enterprises only part of the year and returned to the farms during planting and harvest. This reluctance to break with old ways stifled the early development of a pool of full-time factory workers. The continent also had problems with the production of native supplies. Many resources needed for expansion such as wool for textile production or iron ore had to be imported from abroad. It was not until the discovery of rich coal deposits on the continent that western European nations changed from using their abundant timber for fuel. Even at that point, coal deposits were not located near ports or key population centers, and the high cost of its transportation to manufacturing centers added a burden to emerging industrial efforts. Thus, it would take the coming of the railroad in the mid-19th century before coal and other resources could be moved over long distances efficiently and cost-effectively for industrial purposes.

Other restrictions also hampered economic development. The patchwork political boundaries of the 300 German and numerous

The Industrial Revolution on the Continent in the Late 19th Century

Italian states, for example, resulted in a plethora of laws, court systems, currencies, weights, and measures that created additional barriers to trade. The formation of the *Zollverein* in the 1830s allowed the German states to take the first step on the path to overcoming these barriers but only the final unification of Germany and Italy by the 1870s finally dissolved them. In France the bureaucratic rigidity of the *Ancien Regime* restricted commerce and navigation and maintained a heavy tax burden that stifled change. France also maintained regional and local trade zones that intended to preserve these local economies and in essence discouraged the development of a cohesive national economy. France also continued to emphasize its luxury silk industry at the expense of diversifying production of other goods. The Low Countries also felt the lingering economic effects of earlier warfare. The Dutch had closed the Scheldt estuary in the 17th century thus blocking a key waterway to the North Sea for trade affecting the future Belgium, a situation not resolved until the French Revolution.

The distribution of wealth and income on the continent also was more unequal than in Great Britain. In some cases two separate economies operated. One produced fine articles for the more affluent members of society such as the aristocracy, church, and upper middle class; the other more poor, non-standard articles for the peasant and working classes. The lingering importance of regional dress and fashion styles lends further credence to the theory of two economies on the continent. Documents and diaries of travelers to Europe also speak to this economic cleavage. Arthur Young, the noted Englishman who journeyed to France in the late 18th century, refers to women, children, and farmers with bare feet, little meat consumption, dwellings without glass in the windows, and primitive wooden wagons that could haul only a single person or small load of goods.[2]

The upper classes on the continent also took longer to take advantage of the investment opportunities inherent in the new industries. The cost of commerce, banking, credit, and insurance exceeded that in Great Britain. Despite the fact that some aristocrats did recognize the potential of mining and manufacturing to accumulate more wealth, early continental industrial enterprises remained a class activity. Whereas British aristocrats formed investment alliances with entrepreneurs and inventors in the 18th century, it took Britain's continental counterparts much longer to engage in such partnerships. The bias against the middle class lingered—a group derided by the aristocrats and feared by the lower classes. Unlike Great Britain, in most cases continental men of extraordinary talent or technical skill in the 18th century had few places to seek capital to finance their enterprises or inventions. Until much later, those firms engaged in business on the continent remained mainly family affairs as an end in themselves in contrast to their British counterparts, who viewed industrial ventures as a means to make money. Thus, in France, the German states, and the Low Countries, such family-oriented firms looked for security, applied a conservative approach, and did not often take chances such as obtaining long-term loans or seeking alliances with other potential investors.

On the other hand, despite those obvious disadvantages and the gap between Great Britain and the continent, the situation was not as grim as it may first appear. Many countries on the continent had real potential for growth and shared some of the basic characteristics that had propelled Great Britain into the forefront. For example, great supplies of coal awaited discovery by the mid-19th century. A few technical developments were also at work alongside those in Great Britain. The French Jacquard Loom, which appeared in the early 19th century, is a prime example (see Biographies). In addition, 18th-century banks in a few areas such as the Low Countries and Switzerland offered loans to private enterprises similar to the experience in Great Britain. Even in pre-revolutionary France, the Bourbon regime supported a handful of national and private manufacturing enterprises and in 1786 completed a treaty with the British to allow certain British goods to penetrate the French market.[3] In addition, the short distance between Great Britain and its European neighbors meant that it was not entirely possible to shut off the flow of ideas and techniques from Great Britain to the continent. Indeed, before 1789, a small number of continental observers had traveled to the British Isles to learn about the latest industrial developments. The chaos and warfare of the French Revolution and Napoleonic eras did disrupt some of the early industrial developments on the continent but also helped to accelerate other political and economic changes. Napoleon abolished the Holy Roman Empire and France, Belgium, and the German states eliminated guilds and other commercial restrictions. It is also true that although Napoleon's Continental System closed off Europe from British competition and the acquisition of current technology, his anti-British program resulted in some independent developments and prepared the continent for more rapid advance and assimilation of technical innovation after 1815.

Despite these changes, the early industrial experience on the continent was different and more uneven than the British example. In the 18th century, governments on the continent had a more direct influence on the lives of their people. The evolution of industrial development followed this pattern. Whereas in Great Britain much of the early investment in industrialization came from the private sector, in Europe most governments provided grants for education and inventors, waived any import tax on purchased foreign equipment, and even financed infrastructure improvements such as roads, canals, and harbors and even early mill construction, particularly in the arms and luxury industries. In addition, governments established protective tariffs to protect their domestic goods from the cheaper British versions. These efforts proved costly and achieved only modest success. France had only a few cotton mills in operation by 1780 and a decade later could count relatively few working spinning jennies and water frames. The Arkwright water frame and Crompton mule did not appear in Saxony until the late 1790s and in the Low Countries at the turn of the century. Coke-blast furnaces were built during the same time in several German states but not in the Low Countries until the 1820s. The one major exception is that the continent did dabble in steam power at an early date. The first Newcomen engine arrived on the continent by 1721, and by 1750 it had been replicated and spread all over Europe. By 1790 thirty-nine improved atmospheric engines were located in the Mons area alone.[4] The dislocation and upheavals of the French Revolution and Napoleon occurred at this vital moment and severed the continent's link with Great Britain for nearly a generation. However, the embryonic stage of European industrial development left enough of an impression to prepare the continent for the real surge after 1815.

One important step was the acquisition of British techniques, a process that took several routes. The British government, most assuredly, feared the loss of its advantage and put strict laws in place against the exportation of the new industrial technology. At times the British levied stiff fines or prison sentences on persons violating the legal prohibitions. But penalties notwithstanding, it was virtually impossible to stem the exchange of ideas. British technical publications, engineering journals, and professional bulletins flowed to the continent, and their reprints provided details of inventions, machines, and factory enterprises to energetic individuals who thirsted for such information. Industrial spies also journeyed to Great Britain to seek information and return home with knowledge of machines and techniques. In addition, some legitimate agents who had approved commissions to purchase equipment for customers in Europe also received in-depth exposure to British technology. Furthermore, some Europeans gained employment in British factories and learned technical secrets. These workers drew sketches of equipment or built small models to take home and sell for a profit. Occasionally those persons smuggling secrets were apprehended, but it is certain that many individuals went undetected. Belgian agents, for example, stole equipment and whisked it home by rowboat or even resorted to kidnapping British workers.

Finally, the acquisition of detailed British scientific and industrial knowledge and its appearance in publications on the continent spurred the development of technical schools, particularly in France and the German states.[5]

The British could be their own worst enemy when it came to industrial information. Some industrialists were more open than others regarding the sharing of information, even to the point of providing foreigners with blueprints, models, and machine parts. British workers also received enticements to go abroad, although the British government considered this activity illegal until 1825. Records of continental enterprises in the early 19th century depict a number of British workers on the rolls, a fact that affirms that the British government failed to stop the loss of technical talent and information. These workers often found it profitable to go to the continent as employers offered high wages and bonuses to attract their skills. It is estimated that some 15,000 British workers were employed in French textile and metallurgy enterprises in 1830. A few industrialists on the continent groused at this windfall, complaining, for example, that their British workers were subpar and often drank excessively.[6]

After 1815 the British government debated the merits of maintaining such tough prohibitions against the exportation of technical information, machines, and labor. Beginning in the 1820s, several parliamentary commissions studied the issue. The grudging assessment was that it was exceedingly difficult to stop the losses. Even though some industrialists argued to maintain the strict laws in place, others believed that they hurt potential trade and exports to the continent and conceded that those nations would certainly turn elsewhere for technology and assistance if British sources were closed. Thus, the face of the entrepreneurs, factory managers, and workers on the continent increasingly took a decidedly British appearance after 1825.

The inability of Great Britain to stop the tide of industrial information to the continent and elsewhere and its ultimate capitulation had an impact that cannot be underestimated. Samuel Slater took the plan of the Arkwright textile factory to the United States in the late 18th century. Two British industrialists started the first Swiss textile mill. The William Cockerill family took textile machinery to France in the 1790s, and Napoleon granted its members French citizenship in 1810. The Cockerill plants employed 2,000 at Liege in 1812 and by the 1830s could boast the largest metallurgical and machine factory in the world. Belgium hired George Stephenson to establish its railroad. In 1838 Alfred Krupp studied the British railroad and mining industries. In many respects this seeding of continental industry by British entrepreneurs and workers did not reach its full potential as the cost of importing these persons was high. Many wanted to stay only short periods of time and then return home. Thus, they were paid by their time and not production results, and their real impact was what they taught European managers and workers rather than what they produced.[7] Nonetheless, despite the initial efforts to maintain its industrial seclusion and supremacy, by 1850 Great Britain had, perhaps reluctantly, accepted its role as the major contributor to the industrial development of the continent and the United States.

In 1815, however, the gap that existed between Great Britain and the continent was significant. Great Britain had expanded its overseas markets during the period from 1789 to 1815 and made substantial connections with Africa, South America, and East Asia. The size and sophistication of industrial machinery had leaped to new levels. The typical mule now had 1,000 spindles and was often powered by steam. Mills, blast furnaces, puddling furnaces, etc. had all increased in size. The steam engine's horsepower had increased from six to eight hp in the late 18th century and to fifty hp by the 1820s. In order to initiate industrial activity quickly, entrepreneurs in France, Belgium, and Germany did not attempt to purchase the latest equipment but rather sought smaller, used versions. The use of these obsolescent machines also meant that Great Britain would retain its competitive advantage for a few decades longer. After 1815 various European states took other direct actions to improve their industrial capabilities. Between the 1830s and 1850s, first Belgium and then France and the German states organized joint-stock investment banks that pooled the capital of thousands of investors and poured these assets into mining and heavy industry development. The Belgian joint-stock ventures were the most successful ones initially, whereas the French devoted a larger share of its capital into public works. By the time the continent entered fully into the industrial era, the larger pool of capital provided by governments and particularly the joint stock investment banks provided the financial basis for a rapid development of industry.[8]

The first continental industrial spurt occurred in Belgium. As was the case in Great Britain, a growing population contributed to this development. The Belgian population grew dramatically in the period from 1801 to 1850 from 3 million to 4.3 million inhabitants. By the mid-19th century, half of Belgians lived in urban areas, a situation that was decades ahead of the French and German experience. One major advantage that Belgium possessed was that the nation sat atop a large coal deposit and thus shifted at an early date to the use of mineral fuel. Indeed, during the 1830s and 1840s Belgium was the largest coal producer on the continent. By 1850 Belgium produced 3 million metric tons of coal per year, and that capacity jumped three-fold by 1873.

This seemingly endless supply of coal supported the iron industry. Belgium adopted coke blasting in the 1820s, and its major blast furnaces increased from 10 in 1826, to 23 in 1836, and 46 in 1847. The result was that the German states imported one sixth of their overall iron from Belgium in 1842, and that percentage had increased to two thirds by 1850.[9] During the same period the export of pig iron to the *Zollverein* rose from 9,500 tons to 76,000 tons. Belgian focus on heavy industry received financial banking from the joint-stock ventures and the establishment of the Bank of Belgium. The final key piece of development was Belgium's early decision to construct a rail network. By 1850 the nation had completed all of its major railway arteries to include key lines crossing north–south and east–west. Railroad mileage grew from 531 miles in 1850 to more than 2,300 miles in 1873.[10]

The trends did not occur in a similar fashion in all areas of the continent. The French experience speaks to this lack of uniformity in the industrialization process. France was the most populous country in Europe at the beginning of the 19th century. It continued to expand its population, but at a slower pace than the rest of Europe. While the overall population of Europe more than doubled in the 19th century, the French increase was merely 45%. This phenomenon was a result of lower birth rates rather than higher death rates. The most substantial urban growth was in the northern part of the country in cities such as Lille and Reims. While cities did increase in size, the average 19th century French worker still resided in an old city rather than a new factory town. Of the twenty-five largest cities in France in 1851, all but one had been chartered for more than 200 years. The slower population increase, however, meant that there were fewer workers to migrate to factories. By 1850 only 20% of all workers doing manufacturing work were employed in factories or mines. The nature of French industrialization resulted in a less revolutionary pattern of economic growth in comparison with Great Britain and its neighbors. Thus, many local and regional markets continued to exist and flourish. French industry joined with handicrafts and agriculture to ensure a slow but steady pace toward industrialization. Indeed, while the raw number of factory workers in the unskilled force increased in the 19th century, it has been estimated that the size of small scale artisans remained double that of factory workers until 1870. Yet, the more leisurely pace of the growth of factories ensured that skilled artisans survived as a group. Until the advent of interchangeable parts on a grand scale, French factory owners employed numerous machinists who were a separate class of artisans and were noted for their intelligence, skill, dexterity, and good judgment and stood out from the unskilled laborers in enterprises which they worked. While many artisans did labor for the

French national and international markets, the vast majority continued to make products and goods for local consumption—food, clothing, shoes, tools, utensils, etc.—until a substantially improved road network could be constructed later in the century (see Document 1). Many ancient French products such as silk, fine furniture, and porcelain also retained their local attraction and marketability. This combination of new industrial factories and the older craft industry with standard design techniques meant that France made a gradual and successful transition to the Industrial Revolution. Whereas the shift in Great Britain was the growing of unskilled labor in factories and mills, the French experience did not spell immediate doom for the artisan class.[11]

Therefore, French industrial growth initially lagged behind that of its contemporaries in Europe. However, there were success stories. By 1850 France had become the most important cotton textile manufacturer on the continent, although it remained no match for Great Britain. Unlike Great Britain, which concentrated its textile manufacturing in the two major centers of Lancashire and Glasgow, the majority of French textile firms were scattered north of the Loire River with the key centers in Normandy, Roubaix-Tourcoing, and in the Alsatian region and the remainder throughout the country. The pace of industrial development in the textile industry varied from region to region in the number of spindles in operation, the adaptation of steam power, and transition to more sophisticated power-driven machinery. For example, in 1847 Normandy had 83 mills that continued to operate with animal or hand power, and 22% of these mills had more than 10,000 spindles each. In 1832 Great Britain consumed 125,600 metric tons of raw cotton, while France's total was just 33,600 metric tons. By 1850 France's rate of consumption had doubled and kept pace with Great Britain's rate of increase, although its total consumption in actual tons still significantly trailed the British. French textile production in the period remained less than the British because its smaller factories, reliance on older machinery, and a less productive labor force resulted in a higher cost industry.[12]

In other industries progress was notable. Coal production increased thirteen times from 1820 to 1870, and iron production grew six times during the same period. In the area of technical development, the key invention of the Jacquard Loom used for fine cloth gave a real impetus to the textile industry and laid the foundation for future technological improvements. Finally, in the early 1840s the French government moved to establish a substantial railroad system. In contrast to the British private railroad enterprises, the French government initially financed construction and then leased the railway lines to private companies for niney-nine years. French railroad construction proceeded at a steady pace from roughly 300 miles in 1842 to more than 23,000 miles in 1900.[13]

The German states entered the Industrial Revolution later than France. The drawbacks were the lack of a strong national market because of the large number of individual states, a factor that changed rapidly with the creation of the *Zollverein* in 1834, the lack of tariff protection for native industries, a dearth of skilled workers, and the late appearance of an inventive spirit. The German industries also relied heavily on foreign, primarily British, technology until the 1870s. Even the German industrialists believed their situation was initially weak. In the 1830s a German manufacturer claimed that he could not locate one German laborer who had the knowledge and skill to make a machine screw.[14]

A review of several aspects of German industrial trends in the 19th century present a picture of a long but steady successful effort to compete with the British. Germany's population increase, although it trailed Great Britain's rate of growth, dramatically outpaced the French and rose from 23.5 million in 1810 to 33.5 million in 1850. Although it would not be until the turn of the 20th century that more Germans lived in urban areas than on farms, the rapid population increase did eventually provide more potential workers for factories. In the 1830s German coal mining leaped two-fold. With the introduction of new technology to dig deeper mine shafts, German coal production increased another seven times from the 1840s to 1870, particularly after the opening of the coal rich Ruhr valley brought new possibilities to German manufacturing. The German states experienced the slowest continental development in the iron industry. In the years from the 1830s to the 1850s, German pig iron and wrought iron production lagged far behind Great Britain and was only half that of France. In 1845, for example, the Dowlais ironworks in Wales produced 80,000 tons of pig iron whereas the largest Silesian ironworks managed to produce only 16,000 tons. Even the coke-smelting enterprises could not compete by mid-century. British smelting industries averaged 89 tons a week in the late 1840s, whereas the German states produced only about 14 tons. The introduction of the coke-smelting technique in the iron industry, however, resulted in a steady, annual 14% iron production increase in the 1850s.[15]

In the textile industry, the German states' total consumption of cotton rose seven times from 2,400 metric tons in 1832 to 17,000 metric tons in 1850. Although it surpassed Belgian production in 1834 and sliced the difference with France by mid-century, it still remained less than 10% of the British consumption at that time. The German textile industry mirrored that of the French in that it was scattered with specific concentrations in the Rhineland, Saxony, Silesia, and Bavaria. In addition, the enterprises were generally family run enterprises and remained small with few spindles in operation. These endeavors came and went as more profitable economic times waxed and waned. In most of the textile areas, entrepreneurs remained wedded to older practices and used equipment considered obsolete in Great Britain (some machinery dated back to the late 18th century). The first modern spinning mills did not appear in the Rhineland until the 1840s, and even then only a few of the textile processes used machine power rather than animal, water, and hand power. Only in the 1850s did conditions change. Additional capital from joint-stock ventures, including funds from Switzerland, began to appear in some of the German states. The number of steam engines and spindles in the *Zollverein* increased significantly, while the number of hand looms decreased. The weaving industry lagged behind that of spinning and did not get a boost until the introduction of the power loom in the mid-1820s and a surge in factory production in the 1830s.[16]

The continent remained a generation behind Great Britain in most categories of industrial development at the middle of the 19th century. Most industry in the key western European areas (France, Belgium, and the German states) remained scattered in a number of areas. Until the advance of the railroad that dispersion remained an impediment to more rapid economic advancement. This nature of continental enterprises meant that local domestic industry would remain important for a longer period than it had in Great Britain. There was nothing to compare to the British enclosure movement on the continent. Old patterns of land tenure persisted. Rural labor remained cheap and more agrarian workers tended to stay tied to the land. Other than in Belgium, there was a slower growth of cities and consequently the growth of the number of workers in mines and factories proceeded at a more moderate pace than in the British Isles. The cities on the continent, therefore, did not witness the ugly blight of slums, overcrowding, filth, and disease to the extent found in Britain. Great Britain reveled in the world of technology and most entrepreneurs, at least until the reform era of the 1840s, did not fret about the loss of employment of their workers if technology, efficiency, and production maintained profits. On the continent, an entirely different perception was at work. New factory owners, emerging in societies only recently removed from the older traditions that were tied to feudal and manorial rights, viewed themselves in a paternalistic manner. Workers were not mere factors of production that could be added or shed like the early British approach but rather agents of work that needed a strict guiding hand.

In many respects, the fear of proletarian unrest that reared its head in 1789 lingered in the minds of the new class of industrialists on the continent. Whereas in British political circles there grew to be a grudging realization in the 19th century that the workers' voice or the threat of a strike needed to be taken seriously, continental employers maintained the opinion that their workers should not disrupt the public order and that any efforts to organize were illegal and immoral.

1850–1870

Beginning in 1850 and for the next two decades, the landscape of the Industrial Revolution began to shift as the continental states experienced accelerated development in almost all measurable categories (coal consumption and output, cotton textile production, railroad mileage, the production of pig iron, and the increase in steam capacity). The race to catch the British proceeded at a fever pitch and points to an invigorated continent. With the lone exception of the cotton industry in the 1860s, the rate of industrial growth for Belgium, France, and the German states increased between 5% and 10% in this period. Great Britain's advantage remained in place, but its ability to increase capacity did not keep pace with its continental rivals.

By the early 1870s, the nations of Western Europe began to compete on more favorable terms with Great Britain. The statistics below (Table 1) reflect an accelerated growth that would challenge the British, although a quantitative and qualitative difference existed until the late 19th century.

During this two-decade period, the nations of Western Europe made this transition not only by expanding existing infrastructure, technology, and practices but also through the adoption of more

Table 1

	Railroad Miles	Coal*	Steam**	Pig Iron*	Raw Cotton*
Germany	14,800	36,400	12×	12×	2×
France	11,500	25,000	6×	3×	—
Great Britain	16,000	112,600	3×	3×	2×
Belgium	2,300	10,200	5×	5×	1.8×

* 1000 metric tons
** 1000 hp[17]

innovative and up-to-date approaches to industrial growth. The textile industry embraced the power loom and discarded the last vestiges of the hand loom. In the area of iron production, mineral rather than vegetable fuel became standard. The steam engine was the essential source of power technology and mechanization and had spread its tentacles to a growing number of industrial enterprises. In addition, these developments provided the foundation for increasing innovation and the appearance of new inventions that stimulated further expansion. The results were nothing less than spectacular. Railroad construction proceeded at a dizzying pace. More than 50,000 miles of new lines appeared from 1850 to 1870 in contrast to just 15,000 miles of construction in the 1840s. France constructed 9,300 miles in this era, while the German states added 7500 miles. Coal output from the Ruhr valley increased from 1.6 million tons in 1850 to 11.8 million tons in 1869 and overall German coal production increased from 4.2 million tons to 23.3 million tons in the same time period, while French output also rose dramatically from 4.4 million tons to 13.3 million tons.[18]

Only in the cotton textile industry did Great Britain fully ward off the growing capacity of the continent. The number of spindles in operation demonstrates that advantage. In 1834 the number in millions was as follows: Great Britain, 10; the United States, 1.4; France, 2.5; Germany, .6; Belgium, .2; in 1861, Great Britain, 31; the United States, 11.5; France, 5.5; Germany, 2.2; Belgium, .6; and in 1867 Great Britain, 55.5; the United States, 30.5; France, 7.4; Germany, 10.9; Belgium, 1.4. As late as 1913 Great Britain boasted three fifths of all cotton spindles in operation. Thus, not only did Great Britain maintain an edge in sheer quantity of spindles, but its power looms generally ran at a faster pace and had less waste than the counterparts on the continent.[19]

The obvious benefits arising from industrial expansion eventually broke down many of the social biases and traditional barriers that had been imposed by governments or lingered in the minds of the people. Changes in business, investment, and legal practices, as well as improving economies, also stimulated positive change. In response to a growing amount of bullion, the paper money supply increased three times in France and nine times in the German states and resulted in a fall in interest rates from 4% to 2%. Thus, additional capital and credit became more available for joint-stock ventures and other investment opportunities to funnel money into industrial enterprises. Correspondingly, new business enterprises arose as political authorities, albeit slowly at times, relaxed or modified controls on the formation of companies. Great Britain took the first steps in the 1850s, and France and the German states followed in the 1860s and 1870s. Prussia was a prime example of how loosening restrictions led to the formation of new companies. Prior to 1850, 123 firms had been registered; from 1850 to 1870 that number was 295; from 1870 to 1874 the number soared to 833. Other legal changes facilitated growth. Great Britain discarded its statutes on usury in 1854, and the Netherlands, Belgium, France, and the German states accomplished the same over the next decade or so. Furthermore, laws prohibiting foreign companies from crossing into other nations began to be repealed in the 1850s and 1860s. A rash of additional commercial and financial reforms took place in the same period. A revision of laws occurred regarding debt payment, patents, and levies on rivers and major water arteries such as the Scheldt estuary and the North and Baltic Seas further led to important commercial treaties and furthered broad economic change and cooperation.[20]

By 1870 Europe's industrial map had essentially been drawn. There were relatively few major sources of key raw materials such as coal fields and iron deposits left to discover. The infrastructure of transportation and communication had made great strides and would be enhanced throughout the rest of the century. Advanced techniques had been introduced into a variety of industrial enterprises, and new innovations continued to be adopted and employed. Modern business, banking, and investment procedures had proven to be exceedingly profitable. By 1870 Great Britain's role as the industrial leader of the world remained secure. Britain led in all major areas of industrial capacity. However, over the next three decades the margin of difference dwindled as the nations of Europe entered into a mature stage of development and coped with the new challenges facing their respective societies.

The Late 19th Century

By 1900 the industrial landscape of the Western world had undergone additional transformation. In the last decades of the century, Europe experienced what some historians have labeled the Second Industrial Revolution. The continent had become a behemoth-like engine of manufacturing, and the variety and quality of goods produced was beyond the comprehension of persons born just a generation earlier. New scientific and technological achievements occurred at a rapid pace, and the growth of prosperity was characterized by an urban society with rising standards of living, improved methods of transportation, and a growing life expectancy based on better health and sanitary conditions. In reality, two distinct economic regions had emerged in Europe. The first was the industrialized area that included

Great Britain, Belgium, France, Germany, the Netherlands, northern Italy, and certain portions of the Austro-Hungarian Empire. In stark contrast was the mostly rural and agrarian region of southern Italy, the remainder of the Austro-Hungarian Empire, Spain, Portugal, the Balkan areas, and Eastern Europe, a zone that supplied important foodstuffs and raw materials to the industrialized nations.

New Approaches, Technologies, and Their Applications

Following 1870 Great Britain faced growing challenges to its position as the industrial leader of the world. In some cases, the problem was self-made. Britain's long-dominant productive industrial plant operated by proven machines and techniques and financed by large investments over time was securely in place. However, the leaders of many of Great Britain's industries, somewhat suspicious of innovation and change, found it difficult to shift to new and more up-to-date technologies and organizations. On the other hand, the later entrants into the Industrial Revolution such as Belgium, France, and the German states had fewer ties to the past and were more than eager to embrace change by creating more modern facilities and quickly adopting new inventions and techniques in manufacturing.

Other developments were beyond Great Britain's ability to control. For example, the late 19th century witnessed an even closer merger between science and technology in order to make new applications in industry. New disciplines such as organic chemistry and electrical engineering emerged and provided knowledge and challenges that were beyond the abilities of the original inventors and tinkerers earlier in the Industrial Revolution. More European companies began to place additional capital investment into research and development activities to prepare for the next generation of technology. In Germany, a proliferation of technical schools occurred in the latter part of the 19th century. These technical schools awarded advanced degrees and graduated thousands of students annually, many of whom found positions in a variety of German industries. Furthermore, the advancing technology in communications and marine transport and the addition of thousands of miles of railroads stimulated the growth of national and world economies, one that the nations of Europe, as well as the United States, eagerly participated in for markets for their products, securing raw materials, or seeking new profitable investment ventures.

New products and innovations helped to reshape the industrial map of Europe. After 1870 steel rather than iron became an essential material for the construction of machines, buildings, rails, ships, engines, and weapons. From the mid-19th century until World War I the amount of steel production in Europe rose nearly 128 times and Germany's production was double that of Great Britain, although by that time the United States had taken the lead. France and Germany also made great strides in the chemical industry, which had an increased demand for alkalis to use in the paper and soap industries as the standard of living improved and sanitation and health became primary concerns for consumers. The production of sulfuric acid provides ample evidence of the German capacity to outstrip the British. In 1900 Great Britain produced almost twice as much sulfuric acid as Germany (one million to 550,000 tons). On the eve of World War I, the situation had undergone a dramatic reversal. Germany produced 1.7 million tons, whereas Great Britain produced 1.1 million tons. Improved artificial dyes also gained popularity for use in cotton and silk fabrics. By 1900 Germany controlled 90% of the dyestuff market.

The development of electricity also changed the nature of European industry. Electricity possessed the unique characteristics of transmissibility or moving energy easily and quickly over short or long distances by wires without any real loss of energy, and the ability to convert to alternative forms of energy such as light, heat, and motion. Electricity also had two other important consequences. First, it meant that machinery was not fixed near the power supply. Second, electricity became an important alternative energy source to those countries that did not possess adequate supplies of coal and brought them into the industrial era sooner rather than later. The first power stations appeared in Great Britain in the early 1880s, but very soon they spread across the world and spurred the growth of other industries such as the telephone, electric lighting, and devices for homes and city streets, electric railway cars for transportation, and factory machines. The arrival of the internal combustion engine also had a similar impact. The first crude internal combustion engine powered by gas and air appeared in 1878, but it did not prove suitable for universal use as it required the machine to be tied to the source of supply. The discovery and application of liquid fuels such as petroleum and its distilled derivatives solved the problem. These agents had a combustion rate and efficiency equal to gas but had the advantages of a power output twice that of coal. The initial drawback was the cost of 4–12 times that of coal in 1900. However, large oil deposits were discovered after 1900 and the perfection of refinement techniques soon drove the cost downward. By the early 20th century oil gradually began to replace coal as the power source for ocean vessels and the improved internal combustion engine found application in the new automobile and aviation industries. Yet, despite the advantages that electricity and petroleum provided for powering industry, on the eve of World War I coal remained the primary source of energy, measuring nearly 90% of the world's energy output, with Great Britain's energy output from coal being 92%, Germany's 82%, and France's 73%.

Mass Society

The increase in industrial production with its emphasis on new patterns of consumption, urban growth, and social class changes virtually obliterated the last vestiges of the old world order and resulted in an emerging mass society after 1870. This new environment incorporated tens of millions of people into the economic changes that Industrial Revolution had wrought. The scope and scale of society expanded to include new perceptions about class distinctions, redefined concepts about work and leisure time, increased political participation by the lower classes, and new expectations about standards of living.

The rising population fueled much of the change. In 1850 Europe's population stood at 270 million. In 1910 that number had swelled to 410 million. From 1800 to 1914, a dramatic shift from farm to city had occurred and the vast majority of Europeans now dwelled in cities: in Great Britain 80% of the population lived in the cities; in Germany, 60%; and in France, 45%. Even Eastern Europe was not immune to urbanization as its city population stood at 30% by World War I. In 1800 only 21 European cities had a population of more than 100,000 inhabitants, whereas in 1914 that number had risen to 147 and continued to grow. London's population had soared by more than six times to 6.5 million and Berlin's from 172,000 to 2.7 million. The advanced industrial capacity provided new opportunities for work and attracted hordes of people to migrate from the rural areas to the city. The cities also gained population from improved health, sanitation, and living conditions as a result of the pressure of reformers and the decision of political authorities to embrace changes such as increasing fresh water supplies through the creation of elaborate dams and reservoirs and the construction of sewage systems. These changes gained the notice of American engineers and attest to the progress that had been made in the late 19th century. In July 1881, Ralph Hering of the Engineers Club of Philadelphia reported on his trip that examined the sewerage works of principal European cities. He stated that compared to American cities, the European cities took better care in the construction, inspection, and maintenance of their sewers. Hering related that he and the Crown Prince of Germany took an hour's walk through the sewers of Hamburg and as far as odor was concerned there was little or no difference from going into a common cellar.[21]

The cities emerging in the last decades of the 19th century developed a distinctly modern appearance. The older boundaries of European cities gave way under the pressure of an increasing population. The redesign of Paris under Emperor Napoleon III with the creation of wide boulevards, parks, public buildings, university buildings, an opera house, and museums occurred in areas formerly the residence of the working classes. In Paris and other expanding cities, these persons became displaced and moved to the adjacent countryside and towns that soon thereafter became incorporated back into the metropolitan areas. One of the most visual and controversial events in late 19th century France was the construction of the Eiffel Tower. Despised by some and praised by others, it was a grand testimony to the industrial age. Opened to the public in May 1889, it became the tallest structure in the world at 984 feet or twice the height of the Washington Monument. Its skeletal structure comprised 6,875 tons of iron.[22]

European class structure also took on a new look as a result of this changing nature of society. The traditional upper classes remained very small, perhaps numbering only about 5% of society, although this group controlled nearly half the wealth in 1870. That percentage had declined precipitously by World War I. Throughout the course of the 19th century, aristocratic classes increasingly invested in the enterprises of the leading industrialists and businessmen and in some cases the mergers were sealed by the intermarriage of these groups. In addition, growing numbers of the industrialists purchased land to enhance their social respectability, and landed aristocrats bought homes in the city to enjoy the new urban living styles. Even older established educational patterns broke down as members of the new industrialist classes sent their sons to elite schools formerly reserved for the landed aristocracy.

The middle class also experienced change in the latter part of the 19th century. This class had a broad array of professions and occupations within its ranks, ranging from professionals such as well-to-do industrialists, business managers, large merchants, lawyers, doctors, engineers, architects, accountants, and chemists to white collar workers such as salesmen, bookkeepers, bank tellers, and secretaries, and finally small shopkeepers and traders. The lower classes, including peasants, encompassed about 80% of the European population overall, with a larger urban working class population in Western Europe consisting of a large breadth of groups including skilled artisans, semi-skilled workers, and unskilled laborers.

Families and gender roles also experienced significant changes. Birth rates dropped substantially throughout the course of the 19th century as most women did choose to wed. Birth control and new attitudes and perceptions about family life contributed to this decline. The restriction of employment opportunities for middle class women limited them to either accept marriage or seek the limited positions open to their sex—ecretarial, teaching, nursing, retail clerks, etc. The family became the central institution in the middle class. The traditional view that men dominated the workforce and women should remain at home to care for the family took deep root and dominated social mores and is often referred to as the cult of domesticity. This emphasis on the woman's role as wife and mother created a different sense of family compared to the older rural and agrarian world. The wife's idealized role took on that of character builder and nurturer for the children, protecting them from the taint of the outside world. Most middle-class families also hired domestic servants to free the wife from household duties and allow her more time to spend on establishing the proper home environment, emphasize the education of children, and encourage their future pursuits. The idea of a woman's right to work generated tremendous attention not only in middle-class circles but also in the lower classes. Over time even the idea of lower-class women working in factories came under assault by working men or working class organizations as they supported the moral argument embraced by the middle class related to the cult of domesticity and the role of the wife and mother. But the fact remains that by 1900 women still constituted 23% of the French and 15% of the British work force.[23] Prior to the movement for compulsory education, sons in lower-class families might perform odd jobs or seek apprenticeships while daughters would work at some job until marriage. Many lower class women found that their only outlets outside of the home were to become domestic servants in the domiciles of the upper or middle class families, work part-time in seedy, low-paying sweatshop industries, or resort to prostitution in order to survive. Women in this latter category usually broke out of the cycle by returning to work or eventually marrying.[24]

The improved standard of living after 1871, which included better wages and a decline in the cost of goods, meant that the working classes had the means to purchase more items than just the essentials of food and housing. With additional cash in their pockets and a reduction in the work day and week, the lower classes began to enjoy the results of this new mass society such as the revolutionary emphasis on education, the rise of literacy, and the growth of leisure time pursuits. Education took on more significance in the 19th century. Beginning in the latter half of the 19th century, the states of Europe increasingly viewed elementary education as a necessity. Having the ability to read, write, and perform simple calculations was merely the beginning. The industrial age required more persons to have highly advanced technical skills and theoretical scientific knowledge and the ability to combine these two for practical applications.

Great Britain and Germany took the lead in education but had different approaches and results. Initially, Great Britain had a more relaxed idea and relied heavily on private initiatives to develop its educational institutions. Reports by several government commissions revealed that by 1860 nearly half of Great Britain's school-aged children received some form of elementary education. In the end, a key purpose of educating the lower classes was to tame this large horde of the proletariat and have them join the mainstream of British society. In Germany the idea of compulsory education dated back to the era of Frederick the Great. Although the quality of education was haphazard, by the 19th century the situation had been reversed and German schools were the envy of the rest of Europe. By the 1860s, 97.5% of Prussian children attended school. The Saxon level was 100%. The German model required more years of schooling than in Great Britain and in addition established a foundation for civic-mindedness. As the 19th century progressed, the convergence of technical, scientific, and vocational education helped to ensure that workers were better prepared and needed less expensive and time-consuming on-the-job training. By 1900 state sponsored education systems had gradually appeared across Europe, and boys and girls usually between the ages of 6 and 12 attended some form of compulsory public school. In addition to providing moral instruction, civic education, and training for the increasingly complex skilled labor required in the factories, a literate electorate came to be viewed as essential as the suffrage was extended to most adult males. By 1900 illiteracy had virtually ceased to exist in the industrialized states of Western Europe, while it remained slightly more than 20% in the rural Eastern and Southeastern areas on the continent. The rise of literacy can be readily seen with the increase of newspapers (circulation of millions of copies a day), magazines, periodicals, and novels that had as their target a public with an insatiable appetite for reading not only for news and information but also for pleasure.

Leisure time was not new in the modern industrial world. In agrarian society it was directly tied to the tempo of farm life and the daily and seasonal work patterns of peasants and artisans. Urban life had a different rhythm. Workers in the factories toiled to a set clock, and their home and work life were generally separated by activity and distance. Thus, evening time, weekends, and holidays presented new opportunities for leisure activities. Transportation by rail or streetcar meant that one could engage in a growing number of pursuits not tied to the local neighborhood. Vacations and trips to beaches, formerly the purview of the well-to-do, became more common place for the public at large. Amusement parks, dance halls (London reportedly had 500 in the 1880s), and organized, professional sporting activities such as European football (soccer) gained wild popularity with the masses. Although these activities were often touted as a means to enhance people's lives, in reality they certainly stimulated new business opportunities and provided distractions from the ordered and monotonous pace of everyday life of the working classes.

By 1900 the growth of industrialization and its attendant economic developments had created a true world economy. The working classes had for the most part begun to share in the benefits of the new modern society that had been created. That result had not been assured if one looked at the situation at mid-century. The legacy of the French Revolution and the spread of the Industrial Revolution led to increasing tensions between the factory owners and their laborers. Workers on occasion attempted to organize trade unions to advocate improved conditions and wages but in reality this activity had limited goals, such as to assist unemployed workers, and thus gained only minimal support. Effective change awaited the growth of socialist trade unions and the socialist parties after 1870. These trends received their impetus from the theories developed by Karl Marx around 1850. Karl Marx was from a middle class German family with Jewish roots. After earning a university degree, Marx's atheist and radical political views led him to move to Paris where he met Friedrich Engels, the son of a German cotton manufacturer. Engels had worked in his father's textile mills in Great Britain and had become convinced that factory workers were slaves to wages, a view he advanced in his 1844 work, *The Conditions of the Working Class in England*. The Marx–Engels collaboration got support from a group of mostly German socialist revolutionaries who had formed the Communist League. Marx and Engels published the *Communist Manifesto* in 1848. This work was the clarion call to action to those who advocated creating a radical working-class movement. Based upon earlier French socialist thought and German idealistic philosophy, the *Communist Manifesto* argued for the historical determination of economic forces. According to Marx and Engels, history had been replete with the struggle between the haves and the have-nots: the ancient clash between aristocrats and slaves had been replaced by one between the medieval landowners and the serfs, and that conflict had evolved into the 19th-century version with the bourgeoisie and its government support having the goal to suppress the industrial working classes or proletariat. Marx and Engels predicted that a bitter fight would ensue and result in the ultimate victory of the proletariat over its middle-class masters. Government would wither away and a classless society would emerge, and progress in all scientific and technical areas would ensure greater prosperity for all persons in society.

The failure of the revolutions in 1848 led Marx to London where he continued to express his ideas regarding economics. His major work, *Capital*, was unfinished at his death but was eventually completed by Engels. He and Engels harangued against a number of common industrial practices of his day including child labor. They argued that this common practice not only exploited the children involved but also the worker class at large by lowering the wages for adult laborers.[25] Marx turned increasingly to efforts at organizing the working classes. He joined the International Working Men's Association, a body that had as its stated goal improving the lot of the working classes. Its thrust was unsuccessful and eventually fell to the work of the trade union movement after 1870. In Great Britain, France, and Germany, trade unions won the right to organize and strike. By 1900 British trade unions had 2 million members, and that number doubled by World War I. The French and German experience was different. The trade union movement had a more direct link to the political process, as unions became affiliated with socialist parties. In France there were a number of socialist parties and the various trade unions split amongst them, leading to a weaker unified effort. The German approach was the most successful. Beginning in the 1860s, the trade unions forged a stronger alliance with the political structures in Prussia and other German states. As goals were achieved, the workers opted to seek incremental improvement within the political system rather than advocate revolution. By 1914 Germany had a trade union movement with 3 million members, second only to Great Britain, and 85% of these members belonged to socialist unions.

The real impetus for stability after 1870 was the trend toward full political democracy and reform in Western Europe. Great Britain built upon the Reform Bill of 1832 and the reform of factory conditions in the 1840s by passing two additional important measures in the 19th century: the Reform Act of 1867, which doubled the number of males eligible to vote from one million to two million, and the Reform Act of 1884, which virtually enfranchised all adult males in Great Britain. After the Franco-Prussian War, the Third Republic in France guaranteed universal male suffrage and established a political order that lasted more than six decades. The French government also addressed issues such as child labor. The first child labor law for the French had appeared in 1841, but real change did not get codified until 1871. The law required that no French child under the age of 12 could work in mines or industry. It also stipulated that children between 12 and 16 years of age could work no more than 12 hours a day. It also provided for sanitation and educational standards for working children. By the 1880s all child laborers had legal protection. The new German state also instituted voting rights for all adult males. In addition to the extension of suffrage, these states also enacted laws that provided for sickness, accident, and disability benefits as well as some form of pension plans. Germany also addressed child labor. Building upon earlier Prussian law, Germany banned children under the age of 12 from industrial employment. It further required that all children 12 to 14 years of age work only 6 hours a day, with 3 additional hours designated for schooling purposes. These measures, while introducing some reform, were in fact limited in their scope and generally in response to the perceived threat and strength of the growing socialist parties and the trade unions in the 1880s.[26] However, along with improved working conditions and a better health and sanitation environment in the urban areas, the increase in voting rights and social welfare legislation as well as other incremental reform measures did much to gain a broad base of citizen loyalty to the modern nation state.

Conclusion

By the turn of the 20th century, the Industrial Revolution, particularly that phase that had begun after 1850, had forever changed the map of Europe. Belgium, France, and several German states marshaled their resources and eventually obtained the techniques that had thrust Great Britain into the leadership role in the Industrial Revolution. By the end of the 19th century they began to compete with Great Britain in a number of areas. Like Great Britain, the Industrial Revolution produced a transformation of the societies on the continent. The booming population and the dynamic urban society that it spawned had provided Europeans a new sense of national identity. The creation of a mass society ensured that even the working classes played an important role. The increase in the standard of living, the appearance of new forms of transportation that bound all regions of nations together, the growth of educational opportunities and literacy, the sense that work was not an end to itself with the participation of more people in leisure time activities, and the increased role of citizens in the political process forged a Europe that would have been unrecognizable in 1800. This phenomenal material prosperity convinced the vast majority of Europeans that they were truly living in an age of progress, one that offered unlimited potential for the future.

Notes

1. Landes, *The Unbound Prometheus*, 178.
2. A. Young, *Travels in France during the Years 1787, 1788, 1789*, as quoted in J. H. Robinson & C. A. Beard, *Readings in Modern European History*, Vol. 1 (New York: Ginn and Company), 232.
3. Stalcup, *The Industrial Revolution*, 37–39.
4. Landes, *The Unbound Prometheus*, 139–141.
5. Stalcup, *The Industrial Revolution*, 39–43.
6. Stearns, *The Industrial Revolution in World History*, 43.
7. Ibid.
8. Landes, *The Unbound Prometheus*, 145–146.
9. Ibid., 196–197.
10. Stearns, *The Industrial Revolution in World History*, 44–46.
11. Beaudoin, *The Industrial Revolution*, 19–25.
12. Landes, *The Unbound Prometheus*, 162–165.
13. Stearns, *The Industrial Revolution in World History*, 44–46.
14. Ibid., 47.
15. Landes, *The Unbound Prometheus*, 152, 180; Stearns, *The Industrial Revolution in World History*, 47–48.
16. Landes, *The Unbound Prometheus*, 167.
17. Excerpted from table in Landes, *The Unbound Prometheus*, 194
18. Ibid., 201.
19. Ibid., 215.
20. Ibid., 198.
21. *Manufacturer and Builder*, Vol. 13, No. 8 (July 1881) 166.
22. *Manufacturer and Builder*, Vol. 21, No. 1 (January 1889), 1–2.
23. Stearns, *The Industrial Revolution in World History*, 55.
24. Ibid., 59–62.
25. See K. Marx, *Capital*, Vol. 1, translated by S. Moore & E. Aveling (New York: International Publishing, 1967), and Freidrich Engels, *The Conditions of the Working Class in England*, translated by W. O. Henderson & W. H. Chalons (Stanford: Stanford University Press, 1968); Nardinelli, *Child Labor in the Industrial Revolution*, 67.
26. Nadinelli, *Child Labor in the Industrial Revolution*, 128, 138, 145–147.

CHAPTER 7

THE INDUSTRIAL REVOLUTION BEYOND THE WEST

By 1870, major portions of the Western world had achieved or were on the road to a sophisticated level of industrialization, although areas such as southern Italy, Spain, Portugal, and a few isolated other isolated spots within the Western orbit such as Ireland and the American South, had made only minimal progress by comparison. In other parts of the globe, no set of favorable conditions similar to that of the Western nations, such as the availability of abundant resources, enterprising entrepreneurs, technological advances, the growth of capital for investment, rapid urbanization, etc., existed to facilitate industrial growth. That is not to say that industrialization had no impact on the non-Western regions. On the contrary, the rapid trends in industrialization in Western nations in the 19th century led to their intrusion into other parts of the world for both economic and strategic reasons. Western entrepreneurs built factory enterprises and introduced technology into these areas and sought resources and markets, while some Western workers sought opportunity in the newly emerging enterprises. As a result, significant interaction with Western nations occurred and in many instances left these regions with no easy path to industrialization and an increased dependence on the West for economic viability. Until the 1860s, East Asia (except for China and Japan) and sub-Saharan Africa remained virtually free from Western industrial intrusion, while the Middle East, Latin America, and India experienced some degree of influence. However, only Russia and Japan, for very different and unique reasons, began a significant economic transformation within their societies, based upon national decisions to industrialize.

India, the Middle East, and Latin America

India and the Middle East each had the opportunity to industrialize relatively early. However, despite attempts to replicate the success of the West, each of these areas failed to generate widespread industrial development. In India, the efforts were feeble at best. The East India Company had operated in Calcutta since the late 17th century, and British colonial rule had established close ties with its elite classes. In the 18th and early 19th centuries, a few colleges and scientific research facilities and a banking operation had appeared, and some of the existing commercial enterprises and the more primitive manufacturing activities came under the sway of the British. In the 1830s, British capitalists and entrepreneurs controlled portions of the Indian coal mines, sugar refineries, and a few textile mills. The British introduced their equipment and machinery into these ventures in an effort to establish a modern industrial base. However, these efforts proved futile. The cheap British textiles that flowed into India erased the jobs of millions of rural villagers who relied on traditional domestic manufacturing practices for their livelihood. The next stage of development occurred with the introduction of the railroad in the 1850s. Passenger travel commenced in 1853. Some initial fear existed that the Hindu population might reject railroad transportation as being too dangerous. Instead, the populace relied on railroads for transportation, but it did not stimulate noticeable economic change. Railroad construction merely connected the interior agricultural regions with Indian ports. This linkage meant that the traditional cash crops flowed more freely to the coastal areas for export, and British imports had easier access to penetrate the interior.[1]

The Middle East confronted industrialization from a position of a long-standing bias against Western culture. Aside from the acquisition of some Western armaments, the Ottoman Empire had remained virtually free of any Western intrusion and appeared oblivious to the speed and depth of Western industrialization occurring on its periphery. By the late 18th century the situation had reversed itself as the Ottoman Empire sought additional Western military technology. The reaction of the British to Napoleon's military escapade in Egypt in 1798 did not go unnoticed. Shortly thereafter, Muhammed Ali seized control of Egypt and began to modernize its society. He established textile mills, sugar refineries, paper mills, and armories to strengthen Egypt's economy. In the end, this effort failed. Like the experience in India, Egyptian factories could not compete with European enterprises, and the heavy reliance on cash crops to generate income ensured they would be used to purchase European goods and commodities rather than promote industrial development. The Ottoman Empire also attempted to imitate developments in Europe. The first factories appeared in the 1840s, albeit with European machinery and personnel expertise. The government pushed coal and iron production and instituted a postal service in the 1830s, a telegraph service in the 1850s, and the railroad in the middle of the 1860s. However, despite these small efforts, the Ottoman Empire's industrial growth also was a victim of the overwhelming influence of European entrepreneurs and investors and the exchange of cash crops for cheaper European manufactured products.[2]

By 1820 Latin American nations had won independence from their European masters. The long tradition of Spanish and Portuguese influence hampered industrial development of its former colonies, as these nations fell outside of the orbit of industrialization occurring in the rest of Western Europe. In addition, the creation of a semblance of political stability took several decades in Latin America and further impeded industrial growth. The real impetus for embracing change came from the economic and commercial connections that Latin American areas had previously established with other Western nations undergoing industrialization. Brazil introduced steam power into a sugar mill in 1815. Coffee producers saw the advantage of steam power, and by mid-century the country had nearly 150 steam engines in operation. Again, however, the pattern followed that of other non-Western areas in the 19th century. The use of new technology, such as the steam engine, merely reinforced Latin American reliance on its cash crops for export in order to obtain sufficient funds to purchase Western technology. In the 1830s railroad development began in Cuba and appeared in Brazil and other regions of Latin America two decades later. Brazil offered financial incentives for assistance in railroad construction and extended its railroad mileage from a paltry ten miles in 1852 to 800 miles by the early 1870s. Mexico only built 369 miles of railroads in 1880, at a time when worldwide construction was booming. Several other Latin American countries such as Mexico, Chile, and Paraguay also attempted to modernize their economies by emphasizing ship building, iron production, and railroad construction, but these efforts achieved only meager results in the face of the more dominant influence of Western powers. But Latin American countries also suffered from resisting the investment interests of its neighbor the United States. Brazil and other countries remained tied to the heavy, bulky, and more expensive European industrial machinery rather than adopting the emerging more light and delicate and less expensive machinery from the United States.[3]

In truth, the splash of these early efforts fell far short of what was required to establish a modern industrial society in India, the Middle

East, and Latin America. A number of factors precluded the creation of the Western model of industrialization in these areas throughout most of the 19th century. Several conflicts between countries, political instability, the failure of the populaces to abandon their reliance on traditional cash crops for export in exchange for European goods and commodities, primitive education systems, cultural differences, the lack of internal infrastructure development as represented by the relatively modest amount of factories built, and the dearth of railroad mileage and the continued heavy dependence on European entrepreneurs, investment, and technology prevented these portions of the globe from making any serious transformation to industrialized societies.

Russia

Russia more quickly understood the advantages of gaining Western technology for economic, political, and military purposes. In many respects, Russia was in the best position of any other non-Western power in the 19th century. Russia had already obtained and mimicked Western shipbuilding and metallurgy technology since the reign of Peter the Great in the 17th century. By the early 19th century, Russia had been incorporated into the continent's diplomatic scene, particularly after its efforts in the last phase of the Napoleonic Wars and the peace settlement at Vienna. Afterwards, Russians were not uncommon sights in Western capitals and the cultural ties between Russia and the rest of Europe became more solidified, although the long-standing suspicion of Russia's strategic ambitions remained foremost in the minds of many Europeans.

Russia had some exposure to industrialization in the first half of the 19th century. Western agents assisted in the construction of steamboats and then railroads. The first steamboat appeared on the Volga River in 1815, and regular passenger and commercial service began five years later. The first railroad connecting St. Petersburg and its suburbs appeared in 1837, and in 1851 a line opened between St. Petersburg and Moscow. American engineers who gained the sponsorship of the Russian government gave the main impetus to the effort. George Whistler, father of the famous American painter James Whistler, was the key person in the railroad ventures. Although he noted the eagerness of the Russian workers he trained, Whistler was also disturbed by their slovenly behavior. Great Britain exported textile machinery to Russia in 1843, and a German in Manchester shipped materials to Russia and even encouraged a number of British workers to take employment in Russian textile mills. Russian entrepreneurs began a frantic importation of British machinery. The number of imported machines rose 30 times in the period from 1825 to 1860. Furthermore, these machines provided models for native machine manufacturing and by 1860 Russia manufactured more machines than it imported. The number of factories engaged in machine building jumped more than fourfold from nineteen in 1851 to ninety-nine less than a decade later. The majority of the revenues for these endeavors came from the Tsar's taxation of his people to obtain money to lure entrepreneurs from Great Britain and the German states to Russia for their expertise.[4]

Despite these initial efforts, Russia did not industrialize prior to 1860 and remained first and foremost an agricultural nation. The ancient ties of serfs to the land prevented any significant move of peasants from rural to urban areas. Western powers also took great advantage of the Russians. As more Western investors poured into Russia, they secured the export of important products such as timber, hemp, grain, etc. for European markets, a fact that kept many peasants tied to the farm to whet this voracious appetite. Also, few Russian cities had developed even a primitive manufacturing tradition, making the transition that much more difficult. The artisan class was small and did not increase substantially even when Russian urban areas experienced some modest growth beginning in the 1860s. For decades Russia had to encourage the immigration of foreign artisans, particularly from Great Britain and Germany. To be sure, Russian exports rose dramatically for the first six decades of the 19th century, but that increase is misleading and resembled more the cases of India, the Middle East, and Latin America because they were primarily based on raw materials and resources aimed for Western use.

Russia renewed its efforts to industrialize in the 1860s. The disastrous results of the Crimean War (1854–1856) forced the Russian leadership to concede that it lagged behind the West in technological affairs. That conflict proved first-hand to Russia that the industrializing states of Great Britain and France had far surpassed it in the capability of rapidly transporting large numbers of men and high quality war material to the front lines with steamship power. Russia, on the other hand, possessed few railroads and had only several thousand miles of usable roads. Russia moved quickly in the 1860s. The emancipation of the serfs in 1861 led to a host of other reforms, such as the creation of a state bank to centralize finances and credit and the enactment of new commercial laws to facilitate the growth of business. Railroad construction also proceeded at a healthy pace from 700 miles in 1860 to 21,000 miles in 1894 to 36,000 miles in 1900. By the 1870s, French, Belgian, German, and American firms and subsidiaries had established healthy operations in Russia. In addition, by that decade a large number of foreign engineers had arrived in Russia to direct the efforts of Russian workers. A number of nagging issues had to be addressed such as worker resentment of foreign managers, property disputes, and at times inadequate equipment. In spite of these difficulties, slow but steady progress was made.

After a period of retrenchment brought about by conservative tsarist regimes in the 1880s, a new industrial push occurred in the 1890s. The leading figure in this surge was Sergei Witte, the Russian Minister of Finance, who had the formidable task of instituting policy changes to strengthen the Russian state in the face of an evolving strategic challenges arising in Europe. Witte had earlier experience in the buildup of the Russian railroad network and stressed a further extension of the system, a program that doubled mileage in the decade from 1895 to 1905 and resulted in the important trans-Siberian railroad that connected the heartland of Russia to Vladivostok on the Pacific Ocean and made more readily available vast resources of coal and iron to support development of heavy industry. Witte also attempted to strengthen the Russian currency and monetary system by accumulating a substantial gold reserve.

These trends encouraged the growth of foreign capital in Russia, which in the 1890s represented roughly 20% of the investment in Russian industry. By World War I that amount had doubled. The number of industrial companies also had a healthy increase in the period from the emancipation of the serfs to the end of the century. Before 1860 only eighty companies existed in Russia. By 1873 the number had jumped to more than 3,500. In the 1890s, the number increased by more than 200%. The discovery of huge deposits of oil in the Caucuses in 1870 made Russia the world's second leading producer by 1900. Other areas had similar growth: coal, 131%; pig iron, 190%; manufactured iron, 116%; and cotton manufactures, 76%. Overall industrial growth posted healthy gains from 6% in the 1880s to 8% in the 1890s, although after 1900 the growth slowed. Russia's growth rate when compared to Western nations from 1860 to 1913 also attests to its potential and ability to compete. During that period Russia's growth rate was roughly equal to the United States, twice that of Germany, three times that of France, and four times that of Great Britain, although it should be noted that Russia started from a lower position of comparison.[5]

Nonetheless, by the early 20th century, despite retaining a heavy reliance on an agrarian economy and the existence of a very conservative political regime opposed to significant change, Russia had climbed its way to the position as the fourth largest industrial nation in most identifiable categories. Success, at least on the surface, had been

The Industrial Revolution beyond the West

achieved. However, this rapid change and the momentum for further development clashed with other opposing forces at this propitious moment. Most Russian workers toiled in huge industrial enterprises. In 1900 about one-third of the Russian factory labor force worked in factories with a minimum of 500 persons, a figure more than two times that of Germany, and an additional one-quarter of Russian workers toiled in factories that employed 1,000 or more persons. The conditions facing these workers resembled those that Great Britain's industrial laborers had experienced a half century earlier. Women and child labor was widespread and abuse was commonplace. Workers at times toiled fourteen hours day for low wages and faced fines or reduced pay for tardiness, low quality work, or resistance to authority. Many men left their families in the rural areas and moved to factory towns seeking work. This family separation created additional tensions and often resulted in a decline in morality, heavy drinking, and frequent job changes. Living conditions were often extremely depressing as exhibited by the makeshift construction of housing, overcrowding, poor or almost nonexistent sanitation, and the exorbitant prices in the factory owner stores. Other negative factors were also at work. Some foreign workers recruited for Russian factories had negotiated special privileges related to pay and other benefits, thus drawing additional resentment from Russian workers. The few feeble efforts to enact factory reform lacked adequate enforcement provisions.[6]

Worker's efforts to organize and appeal for improvement began as early as the 1870s. The Russian workers movement had a distinctly different complexion than that of Western nations. The peasants who had labored under such strict conditions for so long carried their frustrations to the factory environment. Socialist ideas arrived in Russia at the same moment they circulated amongst intellectuals and worker organizers in Western Europe. The significant difference was that by the late 19th century, government action and political and social reform had begun to incorporate the workers into the overall fabric of Western society. Russian workers, on the other hand, faced the prospects of the conservative government's policy of inaction in the area of reform and a prohibition of worker organizations and strikes. In addition, aristocratic and urban elites frequently looked upon the working classes with disdain, adding to their discontent and fueling more reasons for friction and some protest actions in the 1870s and 1880s. It was in the environment of the factory cities that Lenin and other Marxists found welcome support for their ideology in Russia and formed the Socialist Workers Party in 1898. As the 20th century dawned, economic hard times and a devastating loss in the Russo-Japanese War of 1904 to 1905 led to the great strike in 1905. The ensuing political revolution that year merely patched together a false sense of normalcy that would be disrupted in a dramatic fashion by World War I and the Russian Revolution of 1917. Thereafter, the early promise of industrialization and modernization in Russia charted a divergent course from that of the West.

Japan

Japan's transition to an industrialized society took another route. In the middle of the 19th century Japan did not appear poised to embrace industrialization. Under the Tokugawa Shogunate, Japan had been virtually isolated from most foreign influence since the early 17th century and did not fully comprehend the significant changes that were sweeping across the Western states. In 1720 a long prohibition against Western knowledge was partially lifted. Dutch merchants entering Japan found a small group of Japanese interested in gaining more information about Western science and technology. This so-called Dutch School of Learning was an important vehicle for keeping channels of knowledge alive for future use. Japan also did not possess abundant resources. Coal and copper were in short supply, and textiles had to be imported. Finally, the traditionalists in Japan clung tightly to their belief that maintenance of the status quo was the only option for retaining the purity of Japanese society and culture.

Japan, like Russia in the Crimean War, had to experience the brunt of Western military power before making the decision to change. In 1852 Commodore Matthew Perry, commanding the U.S. East India squadron, had instructions from President Milliard Fillmore and the Secretary of the Navy "to open commercial intercourse with the Japanese government" for the purpose of engaging in trade and having Japanese ports available for obtaining coal and other supplies for its whaling fleet. On July 8, 1853 four black ships under his command sailed into Tokyo (Edo) Bay and amazed Japanese onlookers who had never before seen steamboats or such a sizeable number of guns. He demanded to see high ranking members of the Japanese government. Although he was unsuccessful in 1853, he returned in 1854 and the Japanese realized their weak position. After weeks of negotiations, the Treaty of Kanagawa was signed on March 31, 1854. The provisions declared friendship between the two nations, opened several ports for American vessels, obtained the promise of Japanese aid to shipwrecked sailors, guaranteed U.S. purchase of supplies in Japanese ports, and got approval for a permanent U.S. consul. Commodore Perry presented a large number of gifts to the emperor (see Documents 10 and 11).

Other Western powers soon entered Japan and forced the nation to sign treaties that gave them great advantages.[7]

The Perry mission and the subsequent arrival of a number of European powers created a crisis in the government that rapidly caused the ultimate collapse of the Tokugawa Shogunate. The result was the restoration of the traditional power of the imperial dignity in 1868, a historical event known as the Meiji Restoration. In reality a small number of nobles controlled the machinery of government in the name of the emperor and made the decision to imitate Western ways but to do so within Japanese societal norms in order to maintain independence from Western influence. According to an ancient Japanese saying, "What the upper likes, the lower learns to like still more."[8] In the 1870s the imperial government soon took a direct hand in promoting change. (see Document 8). The marriage of politics and capital was the key component to instituting the growth of mass production. Thus, Japan initially emphasized the development of technology over scientific research and development, as had the United States in the early stages.[9] A prime example of this thrust can be found in the growth of the Japanese cotton textile industry. In 1880 Japan had only two mills with 20,000 spindles each. In 1900 the number of spindles had grown to 1.3 million, and by 1913 that number of spindles was 2.2 million.[10] In time foreign capital and later Japanese private investors played the major role in the nation's efforts to industrialize and modernize. The first major initiative was the creation of a national railroad system to unify the country and provide a conduit for rapid economic growth. It was a difficult prospect at first, as it cost virtually the same to ship an item 50 miles by rail as it did to transport it to Europe. However, the situation soon changed dramatically. In two decades the Japanese had constructed nearly 2,000 miles of track with only 550 miles funded by the government. Soon the government and private capital poured their energies into coal, lead, copper, gold, and silver mining enterprises supported by procuring modern technical machinery from the West. Shipbuilding and shipping companies also garnered assistance in order to break the Western grip on trade and commerce. In this industry initiative and dedication led to the creation of such colossus enterprises as the Mitsubishi Company, which had as its initial enterprise the ferrying of passengers and freight items along the Japanese coast. Eventually, this company diversified and entered insurance, banking, and mining businesses. This approach set the standard for later industrial and business ventures known as the *zabaitsu* or large industrial companies that secured foreign banking loans and established important political ties within the government in order to gain and maintain advantage. The Japanese government also fostered the growth of textiles but preferred an emphasis on heavy versus light industry. The push for heavy industry had distinct military overtones and proved its success with victories in conflicts with Taiwan in the 1880s and China in the 1890s.

These great strides in creating an industrial base took place despite the inability of Japan to impose any tariffs on Western goods until the early 20th century. The continued pressure of Western nations forced Japan to cope with this inequitable situation. Government policies and support, the cultural unity of the Japanese people, and the industrious nature of the Japanese workers all contributed to a successful transition. One example was the productivity of the Japanese farmer. Once feudalism was abolished in the 19th century more free trade opportunities emerged. Many farmers obtained titles to their land, and even if they worked for landlords they often got access to modern farm equipment and a new batch of fertilizers to increase crop yields. Output for agricultural products, particularly rice, soared. Japan's population growth also accelerated from thirty million in 1868 to forty-five million in 1900. Like the British and later continental experience, the increased productivity of a smaller number of farmers allowed for a portion of the agrarian labor force to move to urban areas and factories.

The Japanese natural penchant for adoption and adaptation had other characteristics. Beginning with the Iwakura mission in 1871, the government sponsored agents to travel to the West and see firsthand how their societies were organized to support industrialization. Currency reform and the establishment of the Bank of Japan also occurred during this period. An important area of emphasis was universal education, one that did not have a gender bias. By 1890, 64% of boys and 31% of girls attended primary schools. By the early 20th century, 98% of all children between the ages of 6 and 13 received a primary education, and a healthy percentage of older children pursued additional formal learning opportunities. The reverence for education played an important role in maintaining a highly skilled workforce and a cohesive society. Japan also sent students abroad to study modern ideas in Western colleges and universities and specifically to learn languages, science, and technology. In addition, Japan created the Imperial University and Schools of Mechanical Engineering and Agriculture. Military officers studied the German and French armies and British navy, and the government adopted the Western model of universal conscription. In 1889, Japan introduced its version of a constitutional monarchy with the creation of a parliament or diet, although the ruling clique behind the scenes maintained the responsibility for the actual day-to-day exercise of power.[11]

Japanese industry also initially depended heavily on raw materials, technology, and machine parts from the West in order to produce goods for sale abroad. The shift from rural to urban took place at a moderate pace. Factories changed these work approaches for good, even though the vast majority of them were small enterprises. This situation seemed to mirror the same dilemma that faced other areas of the world that attempted to industrialize. To offset a trade imbalance, one answer was silk exports, which increased from 2.3 million pounds in 1870 to ten million pounds by 1900. Furthermore, Japan took a different approach by moving quickly to develop its own industrial infrastructure and break the hold of Western powers. This transition to an industrialized society occurred gradually and ultimately redefined work roles in Japan. Agrarian workers, which made up 80% of the Japanese workforce in 1870, still constituted a healthy 67% of the total at the turn of the 20th century. But the skill of the Japanese also impressed the West. According to one account, at the 1876 U.S. Centennial Exposition in Philadelphia, "It is especially the tools of the Japanese workmen which attracts the most attention," as their implements are "handled with much ease and produce the most admirable results."[12] At a later worldwide technical exhibition, Japanese construction workers were praised for their "nimbleness and neatness" and the quality of their labor.[13]

The lot of the Japanese workers, like their European and Russian counterparts, was initially difficult. In the pre-industrial world, agrarian workers had a tempo of work and leisure, and artisans in urban areas belonged to regulatory guilds and had sufficient time for worldly pursuits. Conditions were generally poor, especially in the mining industry, as workers often toiled under extreme temperatures and the fear of corporal punishment. Workdays averaged twelve hours or longer. The low level of wages exacerbated this situation and also led to worker migration from job to job. Long hours and low pay also cut into leisure time, and workers had a monotonous cycle of working, eating, and sleeping. The Japanese workforce also had a larger percentage of women than that of Western nations, although the majority was found in smaller enterprises. By comparison, in 1900 women comprised just over 10% of the workforce in Great Britain, about 30% in France, and 62% in Japan. Women workers in Japan also faced more hardships than their Western counterparts. Often their wages were lower than men, and at times they were not paid on a timely basis by their employers to ensure their appearance on the job. Health conditions were frequently horrid and many women got sick because of the poor conditions.[14]

Child labor was another matter. The Japanese government drafted a factory law in 1887 that resembled Germany's legislation. This act would have placed constraints on the ages and hours that children could work in industrial enterprises. High ranking political and business leaders, however, resisted its implementation, arguing that it would slow industrial growth. The legislation languished for several decades until Japan's first factory law was passed in 1911. This act also had limitations but did provide for inspectors to ensure that children under the age of sixteen did not work more than twelve hours a day and that their employment could not occur between the hours of 10 P.M. and 4 A.M. The call for such reform came primarily from liberal politicians and humanitarians in higher education, who pushed for changes in an effort to blunt the power of highly influential industrialists. In reality, after 1900 the Japanese government had become convinced that a reduction in child labor would lead to higher employment of adult males and thus reduce potential labor unrest.[15]

Although industrialization created some initial stress as men left home to find employment and a large number of women entered the labor force, Japan had a remarkably rapid and successful transition from an isolated, agrarian society to a modern industrial state. After the arrival of Commodore Perry, the nation made a decision to embrace Western political and economic techniques. But the Japanese approach to industrialization did not undermine its ancient values and customs and fit nicely with its long-held belief in paternalism. The fabric of Japanese society remained tightly woven and characterized by strict obedience and respect given to government officials and employers. It should be emphasized that Japan at the turn of the 20th century was only one-twentieth the size of the United States but possessed a robust population of forty-five million people. Japan was an ancient country with long-held traditions, whereas the United States was new and growing. Yet Japan made the most of its resources and potential, a fact that can be measured by its expanding influence in the Pacific by 1900 and the admiration and awe of its accomplishments expressed by the Western powers.[16]

Conclusion

During the second half of the 19th century, the Industrial Revolution had a variety of effects on the non-Western world. The power of the industrialized nations of the West overwhelmed the efforts of areas such as India, the Middle East, and Latin America to become equal partners. Political difficulties, cultural differences, lack of education, little home-grown entrepreneurship, few means to attract capital resources, and the creation of virtually no industrial proletariat spelled doom for their transformation to industrialized societies. For the most part, these areas continued to provide cash crops and raw materials to Western nations in return for purchasing finished products and commodities and only limited amounts of machinery and technology that might have assisted their entry into the Industrial Revolution. In contrast, two distinct areas, Russia and Japan, were the exception to the norm and did make significant progress toward industrialization in the last half of the 19th century. Their success was remarkable when compared to other areas of the world and came about in spite of significantly different starting positions and conditions. Neither country possessed the advantages that Western nations had parlayed into the creation of industrialized societies. Both nations retained a larger agrarian class and did not experience dramatic urbanization. In addition, they operated within the constraints of government structures that looked at industrialization with different perspectives. Russia and Japan had to obtain sufficient capital for investment and also Western technology in order to compete, and did so without having to develop their own large class of inventors or pool of new inventions. Finally, a dearth of native resources and the inability to secure them from external sources for a time seemed questionable at best. By 1900 both Russia and Japan solved these problems and proceeded to develop a level of industrialization that astounded contemporary observers. In so doing, these nations took on many of the characteristics of the nations that had previously industrialized. Each experienced significant technological and organizational changes related to the new economic realities that altered the nature of work and society in their respective countries. But Russia and Japan did so in an environment in which they had to react to the pressure of the previously industrialized nations while at the same moment transforming their traditional societies. However, in the end Russia and Japan took different paths to industrialization and had different results. Japan succeeded without social unrest that might have disrupted the economic growth of the nation. Russia, on the other hand, found the experience more painful in the long term and as a result faced the consequences of the social and political upheavals in the Revolutions of 1905 and 1917. Thus, by the 20th century the Industrial Revolution had extended its impact beyond Western societies. Its scope and influence was somewhat muted in areas such as India, the Middle East, and Latin America but became a transforming force in others such as Japan and Russia. As a result the nature of the world's economies and the course of world history had been changed forever.

Notes

1. Stearns, *The Industrial Revolution in World History*, 74–76.
2. Ibid., 75–76.
3. Ibid., 77; *Manufacturer and Builder*, Vol. 22, No. 1 (January 1880), 13; *Manufacturer and Builder*, Vol. 11, No. 1 (January 1879), 4.
4. Stearns, *The Industrial Revolution in World History*, 72–73.
5. Ibid., 99–103.
6. Ibid., 100–103.
7. *Commodore Matthew C. Perry's Expedition to Japan and Related Activities as Described in the Annual Reports of the Secretary of the Navy, 1852–1854* (Navy Department Library, Department of the Navy, Naval Historical Center, Washington, D.C.), http://history.navy.mil/bios/perry_mc_secnav.html
8. C. Okuma, "The Industrial Revolution in Japan," *The North American Review*, Vol. 171, No. 538 (November 1900), 678.
9. Hindle & Lubar, *Engines of Change*, 273.
10. Landes, *The Unbound Prometheus*, 241; Okuma, "The Industrial Revolution in Japan," *The North American Review*, 684.
11. Nardinelli, *Child Labor and the Industrial Revolution*, 147; Okuma, "The Industrial Revolution in Japan," *The North American Review*, 681–682.
12. *Manufacturer and Builder*, Vol. 8, No. 4 (April 1876), 73–74.
13. *Manufacturer and Builder*, Vol. 25, No. 4 (April 1893), 94.
14. Stearns, *The Industrial Revolution in World History*, 124–129.
15. Nardinelli, *Child Labor and the Industrial Revolution*, 138–139.
16. Okuma, "The Industrial Revolution in Japan," *The North American Review*, 688.

Women at work on looms. Courtesy of Library of Congress.

A skirt in the process of manufacture. Courtesy of Library of Congress.

New York Foundling Asylum. Sister Irene and her flock, New York City, ca. 1890. Courtesy of Library of Congress.

Garbage in the streets, tenement area, New York City. Courtesy of Library of Congress.

New York City—Among the Poor—A Summer Evening at Five Points. Courtesy of Library of Congress.

How street-cleaning authorities in New York City guard against summer epidemics. Courtesy of Library of Congress.

First trip of Fulton's steamboat to Albany, 1807. Courtesy of Library of Congress.

Our Bicentennial—President Grant and Dom Pedro starting the Corliss Engine at the Philadelphia Exposition. Courtesy of Library of Congress.

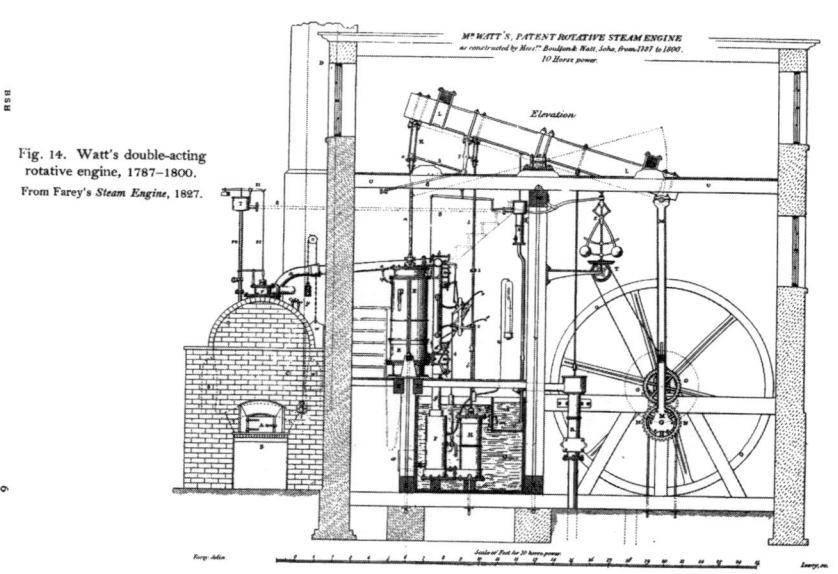

Watt's double-acting rotative steam engine, 1787–1800. Courtesy of Library of Congress.

Cotton Gin, 1854. Courtesy of Library of Congress.

First locomotive to cross the Allegheny Mountains, ca. 1840—people seated on cow catcher. Courtesy of Library of Congress.

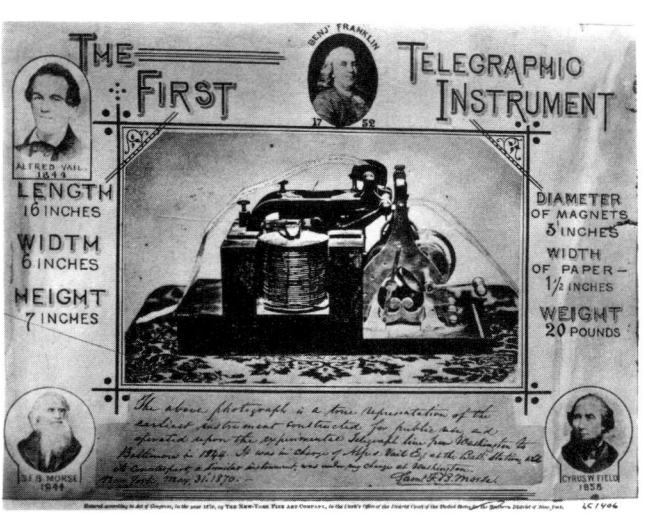

The first telegraphic instrument. Courtesy of Library of Congress.

"Substance and Shadow." *Punch Magazine* cartoon, July 15, 1843. The lower classes observing the upper class depicted on canvas. Courtesy of Library of Congress.

"The Meeting of the Ways": The old world giving way to the new industrial age. Reproduction of color drawing by S. M. Arthurs, ca. 1830s. Courtesy of Library of Congress.

The experimental railway of John Stevens at Hoboken, 1825. Courtesy of Library of Congress.

A Polish miner's life. Courtesy of Library of Congress.

The great railroad strike of 1877. Courtesy of Library of Congress.

Spinning, reeling, warping, and weaving woolen cloth, ca. 1749. Courtesy of Library of Congress.

New York City—"Doing the Slums." Courtesy of Library of Congress.

BIOGRAPHIES

Sir Richard Arkwright (1732–1792)

Richard Arkwright is often referred to as the "father of the modern factory system." Was he a genius at organization or merely a "tough and unpleasing" taskmaster who duped others? The truth lies likely somewhere between these extreme viewpoints. The youngest of more than a dozen siblings in a poor Lancashire laborer's family, he did not have a formal education but was taught to read and write by his cousin. He worked as an apprentice to a barber and became an entrepreneur upon the death of his first wife. He subsequently remarried, and his second wife provided a small sum for Richard to expand his barbering business. Arkwright purchased a tavern and began a wig-making enterprise. He learned about dyeing hair and traveled extensively across north western England collecting human hair for making perukes or wigs.

His journeys brought Arkwright into contact with weavers and spinners who worked in the expanding British textile industry. As the fashion and demand for wigs declined, Arkwright turned to the idea of spinning cloth. Living nearby was Thomas Highs, who had developed the prototype spinning jenny perfected later by James Hargreaves, and John Kay, a noted clockmaker. These two enterprising men had collaborated on building a mechanical spinning machine. Kay is a significant figure because as a clockmaker he understood the intricate working of gears, an important talent that would pay dividends for the scheming Arkwright. At this point the ambitious and perhaps diabolical side of Arkwright emerged. He apparently got Kay drunk and convinced him to construct two models of High's machine. He then used the models to secure investment in his own venture. Arkwright whisked Kay away with him to Manchester, Liverpool, and subsequently Preston to prevent Highs from discovering the deception.

In 1768, after several years of hard work and a number of fits and starts, Arkwright, in his supervisory capacity, along with Kay and two other craftsmen working in virtual seclusion, constructed a full-scale version of High's machine, a contraption that initially became known as the spinning frame. Arkwright had chosen a quiet spot to pursue his enterprise because already bands of hand-spinner workers, fearful of losing their livelihoods, were attacking machines in Lancashire. The device the team developed had three sets of wooden draw roller devices (in existence since 1738) which spun 128 threads at a time at different and increasing rates of speed to make a stronger yarn with less physical exertion. For the first time a weaver could use domestically produced yarns to thread looms. The carding, drawing, and roving now could be combined into a systematic process. Furthermore, this device did not require skilled labor to operate it. Arkwright secured a patent for his machine in 1775.

However, there were some initial drawbacks. The size of the spinning frame made hand operation virtually impossible. At first Arkwright used a team of horses to provide the power for his device. Because this approach became too expensive, with the help of investors he built a larger facility in Derbyshire and used a waterwheel to power the machines (now referred to as water frames) by connecting a paddlewheel to a crank attached to the machines inside his facility. Because Derbyshire had a dearth of male laborers, Arkwright recruited women and children from other localities to work in his mill while their men worked at home turning the yarn into cloth. It is at this point that Arkwright's claim as the "father of the factory system" comes into play. Although Great Britain's earliest factory facility dates to 1742, Arkwright was the first person to envision expanding the scope and size of such enterprises with the establishment of two factory mills by 1774. In 1790 his growing factories boasted an employment of 5,000 workers, perhaps two-thirds of them poor children and orphans who worked thirteen hours a day from sunrise until after dark. It should be emphasized that the use of children as workers was a standard and legal practice in Arkwright's time. However, he would not employ children younger than six or seven years of age. Thus, some contemporary observers labeled his child labor policy as more benevolent and humane than other employers. His detractors claim that he developed harsh psychological techniques and ruled through fear because he hired children and orphans at the lowest possible wages. Indeed, Adam Smith in his *Wealth of Nations* justifies the use of children in the factory environment as part of the capitalistic principle of employing what the "market will bear." The criticism of Arkwright is not only based on the use of children but also on the fact that Arkwright's mill was constructed like a fortress to keep the workers from straying. In addition he had a window, known as the Cromford Window, built on a wall of his house that overlooked his Cromford Mill. This opening provided an unimpeded view of the activities of the mill. Thus, the workers had a sense of being watched even when Arkwright was not on the premises.

Whatever the truth, Arkwright gained enough influence to become a local magistrate despite maintaining his work schedule of sixteen-hour days, often driving a carriage between his various mill sites. His factory village, therefore, was not the product of any governmental action but rather the maturation of Arkwright's own vision, investment, persuasion, and hard work. Arkwright's innovation ensured that Great Britain sat poised to produce enough cloth to handily outsell by under-pricing other nations.

Trouble soon reared its head. One of Arkwright's investors died, and the second dissolved the partnership, leery of Arkwright's plan to expand his business into Manchester and even Scotland. In addition, fire-bombers were still busy at work destroying automated activities as they sprang up in Great Britain. Arkwright's workers, however, were fiercely loyal, likely because of their assurance of steady employment, and literally hundreds of armed men were ready at a moment's notice to defend the mills against attack. Indeed, Arkwright kept a cannon loaded with grapeshot just inside his Cromford Mill to deter "the rabble." Unfortunately, his facility at Chorley, an early steam-powered mill, let down its guard and was destroyed by an irate band of hand-spinners. According to legend, Arkwright began its reconstruction even before the embers had cooled.

Even more worrisome were the patent battles that began to occupy Arkwright's time and energies. He fought off a growing number of "competitors" who had pirated his inventions and established their own factory communities in an effort to duplicate his financial success. In 1785 the swirling confusion of patent infringement claims led the Court of the King's Bench to rescind his patents. The court heard testimony from Thomas Highs, Kay, Kay's wife, and James Hargreaves's widow. These witnesses claimed that Arkwright had indeed based his fortune on the inventions he had pilfered from their family members, an accusation that bought them some compensation. Despite his battles with the hand-spinners and the claims challenging his originality, it is nonetheless true that Arkwright was the chief architect behind the birth of the factory system with its regimented and specialized labor in one location. The dramatic shift in production process gave the employer virtually total control over the product and its means and cost of production.

After a series of appeals, Arkwright's contributions and services were eventually recognized by the crown and led to George III granting him knighthood for "services to His Majesty's subjects in general." He also became High Sheriff of Derbyshire and his son and namesake attended Oxford and socialized with the British aristocracy, a far cry from Awkwright's humble origins. He bought land and was assimilated into the old social system of England. Arkwright amassed a sizeable estate and left his heirs 500,000 pounds, a substantial fortune in his day.

Arkwright's ultimate contribution was providing an organizational framework and new production techniques for the booming cotton industry of the 18th and 19th centuries. The market for cheap cotton was almost infinite. His efforts to stimulate mass production through the factory system, despite often nagging legal challenges and the resistance of those persons wedded to old production techniques, triggered a geometric leap in national productivity, first in Derbyshire, then in Lancashire and Scotland, and eventually across the nation and the growing industrialized Western world. His methods and factory organization and operations were copied around the globe. Once steam power became standard, the growth of the factory system roared at an exponential pace and the former flourishing local cottage industry model faded into memory as new factory towns with continually active mills belching black smoke dominated the once tranquil rural landscape.

Henry Bessemer (1813–1898)

Henry Bessemer was born in Charlton, Hertfordshire, England. His father was a French émigré who had escaped the Revolution to become an engineer and type founder in England. The young Henry demonstrated the same prowess as his father in mechanical ability and interest in engineering and invention. Indeed, his father was so elated that he often permitted Henry to skip school and perform experiments in his workshop at home.

At the age of 17, Bessemer journeyed to London to peddle his various ideas. He dabbled with the concept of wax casts for sculptors but found no takers. He also invented a die cast to impress ornamental scrollwork on Bibles, but this endeavor also failed to attract any investors. Finally, in 1832 he achieved success when he invented a device—a "gold dust" machine—that ground up the pigment for the gold paint used in decorating china. He made a fortune as his secret formula was adopted to adorn a sizeable portion of the gilded decorations of his era.

Bessemer married and purchased a home in London. At this point he sat poised for his greatest contribution: cheaper steel production. His steel process is the perfect example of how military considerations can influence technological development. During the Crimean War he experimented with new types of artillery projectiles. He first developed the idea of a spinning projectile whose motion provided a better trajectory to the intended target. Because the British military was not receptive, he approached the French. The French government expressed interest but one serious problem needed resolution. At times the projectile exploded prior to exiting the cannon tube. Bessemer saw the necessity of creating a stronger artillery piece. This realization set him off on a new course. Steel was a natural material and had long been produced. To be sure, the Chinese had manufactured steel for nearly a millennium, although their process, known as the "hundred refinings," was extremely slow as the name itself suggests. In the early 19th century steel was scarce and expensive to produce because of the existing inefficient method to remove carbon from the iron ore. Thus, steel was not available for larger construction projects such as railroad rails, bridges, ships, etc. These structures were made of wrought iron created from a process known a puddling, a procedure that not only was expensive but also demanded workers who possessed strength, endurance, and skill. The belief in Bessemer's day was that cast iron had to be converted to wrought iron by removing as much carbon as possible and then be converted to steel by the reintroduction of carbon. The steel produced in this manner retained a higher percentage of carbon than Bessemer deemed acceptable. Furthermore, previous methods of making steel took up to ten days by heating powdered charcoal to a red-hot capacity. This method produced only minimal batches of expensive steel and was used to make merely small implements such as tools, cutlery, and machine parts.

After much study Bessemer concluded that cast iron could be transformed to steel in one step by applying a dedicated blast of cool air to the molten iron. His contention was not widely accepted initially, as most persons associated with steel-making thought that cool air would likely cause the iron to gel before it could be manipulated. Bessemer set out to prove them wrong. He constructed a large, fully equipped workshop with a large egg-shaped furnace to aid in his experiments. Bessemer further modified his furnace with a perforated bottom to allow for the blown air to be introduced through the vents. This furnace became known as the Bessemer converter and is the real key to his contribution. The converter itself was constructed of steel and lined with silica and clay and mounted on supports or trunnions that enabled the converter to tilt forward or backward. In the initial step, a blast of cool air was applied and one-half ton of molten pig iron was poured into the converter. The oxygen from the air kept the mass ignited, thus negating the need for additional fuel. After the mass quit burning the converter was tilted to pour out and remove the impurities such as silicon, manganese, and carbon in the form of a slag. The remaining pure mass was poured into ladles from which the now malleable steel was emptied into molds. The whole process lasted no longer than fifteen to twenty minutes, and the larger converters could handle from eight to thirty tons. The typical output was twenty tons in twenty minutes. Bessemer's approach, also referred to as the pneumatic conversion process, not only promised to hasten the production of steel but also greatly reduce the associated financial costs.

In 1856 Bessemer received a patent for his process to manufacture steel without additional fuel. His patent claimed that he had developed "the fusion of steel in a bath of melted pig or cast iron in a reverberating furnace, as herein described." He then set out to construct the Sheffield Iron Works. Interestingly, an American, William Kelly, was simultaneously working on the same process as Bessemer. To his ultimate chagrin, Kelly had kept his experimentations private and did not initially seek a patent. And, no evidence exists to suggest that Bessemer had any inkling of this independent effort. About a year after the Bessemer patent, Kelly obtained an American one, although by that time Bessemer's steel process and quality had secured a positive reputation that led to a rapidly expanding business. Thus, Kelly's operations never achieved anything approaching the level of success of Bessemer's process.

Bessemer enjoyed tremendous financial success, and his process had far-reaching ramifications. His patents resulted in a five-million-pound profit. And, by the late 1860s, Great Britain was producing 110,000 tons of steel annually. Steel was first used in the construction of railroad rails in 1857. His steel beams were employed in the construction of the earliest skyscraper, the Chicago Home Insurance Building in 1884. In 1878 Sidney Gilchrist Thomas used the Bessemer process to remove phosphorus from steel (Bessemer had used phosphorus-free ores thus restricting his selection). Ten years after Bessemer's patent, Charles and Ernest Siemens and their partner, Pierre-Emile Martin, introduced the open-hearth system. Bessemer himself liked to cite the British Prime Minister, William Gladstone, who remarked that the Bessemer patent was a near approximation of the later Siemens-Martin patent. Nonetheless, the upshot of the efforts begun by Bessemer and followed by Kelly and the Siemens-Martin team resulted in a dramatic increase in the world's production of steel from 0.5 million tons in 1870 to twenty-eight million tons in 1900. However, Bessemer converters remained in limited use until finally discontinued in the 1970s.

Henry Bessemer was a tireless inventor. Among his subsequent inventions were the steamship cabin, which remained stable while the ship rolled in order to preclude seasickness, a solar furnace, an astronomical telescope, and a diamond-polishing machine. In the end Bessemer held 120 patents, although none would have the significance of his Bessemer converter and steel-making process. Unlike the experience of many inventors of the Industrial Revolution, Bessemer's achievements were recognized during his lifetime and he achieved substantial financial reward. He became a member of the Royal Society in 1877, and Queen Victoria knighted him in 1879. Although his steel production process did not reach its fruition until he was in his seventies, it was without a doubt the most important development in the steel industry. Indeed, in the opinion of many observers, the Age of Steel that Bessemer helped to usher in ranks in importance with the Bronze and Iron Ages of the past. Thus, steel, along with iron, became the underpinning of modern industry and transportation as lighter and stronger steamships became the norm for passenger travel and hauling cargo in a burgeoning worldwide marketplace. Upon his death in 1898, his admirers could attest that the industrialized world would have taken a different course without Henry Bessemer.

Isambard Kingdom Brunel (1806–1859)

Isambard Kingdom Brunel was one of the most important engineers of the 19th century. Although his life was cut short by a stroke at age 53, his impressive body of work included numerous innovative design projects for bridges, tunnels, viaducts, docks, and super ships that greatly facilitated the rapid growth of Great Britain's ground and sea transportation system at the height of the Industrial Revolution.

Brunel's French father was a distinguished engineer in his own right who had fled to England to escape the horrors of the French Revolution. He married an English woman, and in 1820 the couple sent their son Isambard to France to study mathematics and science. Two years later the younger Brunel returned to England to join his father who was supervising the construction of a tunnel under the Thames River from Rotherhithe to Wapping, a project not completed until 1843. Isambard was injured in a cave-in during the construction and went to Bristol to recuperate. While in Bristol, he entered into a design competition for the construction of a suspension bridge over the gorge through which the Avon River flowed. His several submissions won over the judges because they not only addressed the essential practicality and stability in their design of the bridge but, as he observed afterwards, also demonstrated vision, grace, and taste. These traits made his work noteworthy and set him apart from most contemporary engineers.

The Avon gorge project resulted in the erection of the Clifton Suspension Bridge. Brunel's span measured 700 feet, a distance never before attempted. The bridge's height was a breathtaking 245 feet above the river level. Work on the span began in 1831 and reached fruition in 1864. Unfortunately, only the end piers of the bridge had been completed before Brunel's death in 1859. His engineering associates took it upon themselves to see the project to its completion in his honor. As a testimony to his achievement, the Clifton Suspension Bridge remains in use to this day.

Brunel's Avon project progressed slowly and gave him the opportunity to become involved in another venture. Civic officials desired to establish a railway connection between Bristol and London, a distance of just over 100 miles. This project initially raised concern amongst the local landed gentry and landlords who were fearful of the impact of this new technology with respect to noise and the disruption of the countryside. Indeed, even the famous Duke of Wellington expressed his trepidation claiming that expansion of the railway system would result in an indiscriminate migration of the lower classes. In 1835 Parliament settled the matter by passing an act creating the Great Western Railway.

Brunel became the main engineer for the project. This endeavor required substantial planning and skill to overcome a number of engineering obstacles presented by the terrain between Bristol and London. In 1836 construction began simultaneously at two sites at each end of the railway's course. Brunel's effort resulted in the construction of a number of innovative and impressive tubular, suspension, and truss bridges as well as tunnels and viaducts along the route in order to ensure the railway had the most direct route possible. The first section of the railway opened for business in May 1838. Once completed in 1841 the entire line had been labeled, "Brunel's Billiard Table," and had cost 6.5 million pounds, more than twice the original estimate. It even featured the first public refreshment rooms, facilities that allowed passengers to debark for ten minutes to attend to personal affairs. Interestingly, the Great Western Railway officials soon came to frown upon these conveniences as they slowed the pace of the trains. To compensate, in 1845 the company instituted express service along the line.

Despite Brunel's remarkable success, the project also had several glitches. First, he advocated the adoption of an atmospheric railway rather than a locomotive, arguing that it provided more reliability on steep gradients. However, the technology to use the atmospheric railway was very sophisticated and the materials available were not substantial enough to offset the costs. Brunel abandoned this proposal after a year's effort, assumed full responsibility for its failure, and took no funds for his effort to employ the atmospheric railway. Second, Brunel advocated a railway with a broad gauge of just over seven feet. The standard gauge on existing lines was four feet, eight and one half inches. His broad gauge did offer the advantage of a more smooth and stable ride. However, he faced stiff opposition from his good friend and rival, Robert Stephenson, son of the famous George Stephenson, whose substantial railroad network employed the standard gauge. In 1846 Parliament resolved the controversy by denying the use of the broad gauge on any new lines. However, the politicians did compromise and allowed any broad gauge lines already in existence to add a third rail, a modification that permitted rail transportation to pass unimpeded across the railway. However, the ultimate adoption of the standard gauge resulted in the removal of the last Brunel broad gauges in 1892.

In addition to his contribution on the Great Western Railway, Brunel designed several important sea-going vessels. Brunel convinced his investors that a transatlantic shipping network would work well in conjunction with railway services at the ports. He organized the Great Western Steamship Company in Bristol. In the late 1830s he had designed and supervised construction of the *Great Western*, the first steamship to make transatlantic service. The *Great Western* was constructed of wood, measured 236 feet in length, and was powered by sail and paddlewheels. Its first voyage to New York took fifteen days and the return two weeks. Formerly, a one-way journey by sail alone took a month. The *Great Western* ultimately made 74 trips to New York. In the early 1840s he designed the *Great Britain*, a 3,270 ton iron-clad vessel powered by steam and a screw propeller. It consisted of state rooms and cabins for 360 passengers and boasted an exquisite dining room. It was later modernized to transport 630 passengers and traveled between London and Australia for nearly two decades. The *Great Britain* ended up as a relic in the Falkland Islands until it was rescued in the 1970s and returned to Bristol for restoration.

In the 1850s Brunel, assisted by John Scott Russell, a noted engineer and naval architect of the day, designed and constructed the *Great Eastern*, the largest ship ever built at that time. It was 693 feet in length, 120 feet wide, and weighed 18,900 tons. The vessel housed 4,000 passengers, although on its maiden voyage only 38 ticket bearing passengers made the journey. The ship also had enough fuel storage capacity to make the entire trip from London to Australia without a refueling stop. Unfortunately, the *Great Eastern* seemed to be jinxed. Scott Russell had underestimated the cost to build the ship, and its construction came to a halt in 1856. Brunel, true to his nature, persevered and won new financing. In spite of construction delays, technical problems, and his own illness, which prevented his participation in the initial launch, the *Great Eastern* sailed. However, within a few hours the ship experienced an explosion that might have destroyed a lesser vessel. Furthermore, Brunel himself died within a week of the accident. The combination of the explosion and Brunel's death was too much to overcome. The *Great Eastern's* passenger business did not fare well, even though the ship represented a scale and technical capability never before seen in passenger vessels. Smaller and swifter ships run by competing companies retained the major share of the transocean passenger service. The *Great Eastern* never made a profit and was finally broken up in 1888. It retained the title as the world's largest passenger ship until the launch of the super ships in the early 20th century: the *Lusitania* in 1907, the *Titanic* in 1912, and the *Imperator* in 1913. However, prior to its demise, the *Great Eastern* found an even more significant purpose for its mammoth size and powerful engines. In 1866 Cyrus Field, the American entrepreneur who had teamed up with Samuel Morse on the initial concept of a transatlantic cable, employed the ship to lay 5,000 tons of telegraphic cable under water between Newfoundland and Ireland. The ship continued in its new role for a number of years and laid telegraphic cable on the ocean floor across the globe.

Isambard Kingdom Brunel is one of the heroes of the Industrial Revolution in the 19th century. He was an heir to the many developments in invention, technology, business organization, and political support that had evolved since the 18th century. Brunel's genius is that he brought together the complex aspects of technical skill, engineering principles, and entrepreneurship in new and effective ways. In so doing he created sophisticated infrastructure and vessels that propelled persons and goods across imposing landscapes and the vast oceans and became a model for enterprising individuals that followed him. He had a distinct and creative approach, becoming personally and professionally involved in every aspect of his projects. Brunel had the ability to attract financial support, maintain the loyalty and productivity of his work force, and sustain high standards in a very competitive environment. It is true that he took many risks, but in no case did he endanger the persons for whom his projects were intended—the railway and ship passengers of the general public and the labor whose sweat and toil constructed his sophisticated projects. Rather, Brunel and his shareholders assumed the risks themselves. Despite periodic disappointments and failures, Isambard Kingdom Brunel's achievements reflected the best spirit of technical innovation and vision for the future in the rapidly changing 19th century.

Edmund Cartwright (1743–1823)

Edmund Cartwright was an English clergyman exemplifying the 18th-century "universal man," or a person who simultaneously excelled in diverse fields. He was one of three successful brothers of a prominent Nottinghamshire family. His brother John was elected to Parliament while George was an army officer and explorer who first brought Eskimos to England. Edmund was educated at University College, Oxford, became a fellow at Magdalen College, and later obtained a Lincoln Cathedral prebend or church position. He also received critical acclaim (including from Sir Walter Scott) for his poem *Armine and Elvira* and successfully cured several parishioners of typhus by dousing them in yeast, a procedure adopted by many 18th-century physicians.

An unintended encounter led the curate Edmund Cartwright to become an important figure in the production of cloth. During the summer of 1784, Cartwright met in Manchester several men who were engaged in a discussion of Richard Arkwright's spinning machines. The conversation emphasized that once Arkwright's patent had elapsed, so many new mills would appear that there would not be enough people available to weave the cotton that would certainly be produced. Cartwright suggested that Arkwright might be wise to devise a weaving mill, a comment that his companions apparently scoffed at as being impractical to automate.

Cartwright took the challenge to heart. Although he had never set eyes upon a handloom or even thought about such a mechanical apparatus, upon his return home he set about constructing a powered model of the handloom. Perhaps he relied on knowledge given to him about the Indian method of slinging warp threads over the branch of a tree or he recalled a drawing of a Greek machine in an early 18th-century text at Oxford. Nonetheless, he secured his first patent in April 1785. Cartwright's original loom was primitive and required two men to power the device. In the next three years he worked tirelessly to improve his invention and secured additional patents. By 1788 his power loom also rolled the cloth off the loom and could detect a broken thread.

Despite his inventive spirit, Cartwright was neither a savvy industrialist nor a shrewd businessman. He was also the victim of those persons who feared the changing times. In 1785 he established a factory at Doncaster to house his looms. However, this facility never became more than a testing site for his inventive efforts. By 1790 he had sold a license to Robert Grimshaw to construct up to 500 new looms. Soon public distrust arose, especially about his efforts to apply steam power to the looms. A factory intended to house the looms burnt down after the installation of the first twenty-four, most certainly the work of handloom weavers who feared for their livelihood if this new contraption took root. Threatening letters appeared frequently, and he abandoned his project as he faced bankruptcy. Indeed, other manufacturers, also afraid of the backlash, failed to purchase Cartwright's machinery. By 1793 his family came to his aid and sold their estate at Marnham to settle his debts.

Faced with this opposition and disappointment, Cartwright dabbled in a few other inventions. He designed a wool-combing device that would do the work of twenty men. Cartwright developed interlocking construction bricks and floorboards of incombustible materials. Each of his effort resulted in financial disappointment and practical opposition. He attempted to interest Robert Fulton in a modified Watt steam engine that increased power by one-third, but the latter had settled on the Watt–Boulton engine at the urging of his business partner Robert R. Livingston, the U.S. Ambassador to France. In subsequent years Fulton denied accusations that he had pirated Cartwright's plans and claimed them as his own.

Cartwright's disillusionment led him to accept the Duke of Bedford's offer to manage a farm at Woburn. As well as serving as the Duke's chaplain, he worked for seven years on experimental farming techniques, winning a medal from the Board of Agriculture in 1805 for an essay on artificial manures. Cartwright thought that his attempts at inventing mechanical devices had totaled 30,000 pounds and included his family estate at Marnham. However, in recognition of his ingenuity and lifetime achievements, a group of well-to-do cotton manufacturers, including Sir Robert Peel, persuaded the English government to award him a stipend of 10,000 pounds. This sum allowed him to leave his Woburn position and retire to a small farm in Kent.

Edmund Cartwright obtained the sobriquet "The British Archimedes" in song. He was in many respects a man ahead of his times. His efforts to construct and market the power loom anticipated the developments following the end of Richard Arkwright's patents—a power loom operated by horses, water wheel, or steam engine. However, breaking the bottleneck of power sources and bias proved too much for him. In the quarter century following his invention, only 2,400 power looms were in operation in the entire country. No shortage of handlooms or their operators existed, and coal remained expensive. Another sixty years passed before the pendulum would swing in the direction that Cartwright had envisioned in the 1780s. Cartwright spent his last years comfortably but never lost his desire to construct machines. His last project was a device that would be powered by explosives, perhaps the first hint of the internal combustion engine.

Sir Edwin Chadwick (1800–1890)

Edwin Chadwick was the leading voice calling for vast improvement in sanitation and public health in 19th-century Great Britain. Born in Manchester, Chadwick most assuredly was influenced by his politically progressive father who admired the ideas of radicals such as Joseph Priestly and Thomas Paine. The family moved to London in 1810, and Chadwick received his education from private tutors and studied for the law. While undergoing his legal studies he worked part-time as a journalist for several newspapers and honed his skills of inquiry and clarity of writing, two traits that would serve him well in later years.

Chadwick developed an important circle of acquaintances in London. His articles for several professional journals attracted the friendship and encouragement of John Stuart Mill and Jeremy Bentham, the leading British Utilitarian thinkers of the age. In fact, Chadwick and Bentham lived together for a short period of time. Chadwick joined the London Debating Society, a club for Utilitarians and assisted Bentham in the completion of several of his works. During this period, Chadwick developed and refined his concept of the "sanitary idea," a notion that drove his professional career and led to the health and sanitation reform movement in Great Britain.

Chadwick's true influence began when he entered the civil service. In 1832 Prime Minister Earl Grey appointed him as the Assistant Commissioner of the Poor Law Commission and a year later elevated him to the Chief Commissioner's post. In 1833 he was part of a Royal Commission that investigated the condition of children working in factories. His research was so thorough that he was chosen to write the majority of the report published in 1834. That paper urged Parliament to limit the child workday to six hours. Although this recommendation did not win approval, it did eventually influence Parliament to pass the Ten Hours Act in 1847. Chadwick also made several other proposals not acted upon, such as holding employers responsible for accidents on the job, restricting liquor sales, urging healthy recreational opportunities for the masses, providing pensions to discharged soldiers and sailors, and teaching them a trade during their military service.

Chadwick's work gained him some notoriety and in 1834 he was appointed as secretary to a new Poor Law Commission that monitored compliance with the Poor Law Amendment Act from 1836 to 1848. This body prodded Parliament to take action to improve the lot of the urban poor and destitute. Chadwick's intense belief in the righteousness of his cause at times created problems as his opponents viewed him as arrogant, obstinate, single-minded, and intolerant and placed him in the utilitarian movement camp. A depression in 1837 led to thousands of laborers entering Victorian workhouses. During the general elections of 1837, Chadwick was the target of demonstrations by the lower classes, who protested his efforts to limit such public relief. These groups wanted funding where he believed that financial support for improving public health and factory conditions would accomplish the desired end to relieve suffering.

One significant area of concern was epidemic disease, a curse that ran rampant in Great Britain between 1830 and the early 1840s. In 1831 Asiatic cholera first appeared in the nation and claimed more than 50,000 lives. Influenza followed, and in parts of 1833 the number of burials doubled and then quadrupled in London. From 1838 to 1842, the number of typhus cases averaged 16,000 a year. Scarlet Fever killed 20,000 in 1840 alone, and Whooping Cough snuffed out 50,000 lives in the years 1838 to 1840. Timing was crucial. In 1837 and 1838 cholera and typhoid epidemics decimated London's poor population. In response Chadwick successfully lobbied for the creation of a sanitary commission in 1839 to address the health crisis created by the outbreak of these diseases.

Chadwick had been intrigued by reading a report on the conditions of industrial towns and decided to conduct his own research. Between 1838 and 1842 he interviewed and gathered reports from more than 2,000 local officials, factory owners, and physicians. In 1842 at his own expense he privately published his most significant work, *The Sanitary Conditions of the Labouring Population*. The report stated that disease was directly related to living conditions and that public health reform was sorely needed. As part of the report, Chadwick provided statistics comparing the life expectancy of professional classes, tradesmen, and the laboring classes in a number of cities. For example, the age of death for these three groups was as follows for the indicated British cities: Bolton: 34, 23, 18; Manchester: 38, 20, 17; Leeds: 44, 27, 19; Derby: 49, 38, 21; and Liverpool: 35, 22, 15. In addition to these alarming statistics, Chadwick discovered that on the average for every one person who died of old age or violence in 1839 eight perished due to disease. Finally, he calculated that one child in three born in England in the 1820s and 1830s did not live to reach the age of five.

In many respects, the report confirmed the suspicions of many politicians, medical officials, and even the public at large regarding the relationship between conditions in which people lived and the outbreak of disease. It was apparent that working class neighborhoods had stagnant piles of filth and garbage and overflowing drains in the streets, polluted water, cellars filled with human and animal excrement, overcrowded dwellings with little or no ventilation, and noxious odors fouling the air. Indeed, Chadwick's emphasis on the conditions of residences was so pointed that he generally downplayed any role that factories and mills contributed to the problem. Thus, his report stands in stark contrast to other contemporary critics of British industrial society such as the socialist Friedrich Engels and William P. Alison, Professor of Medicine at Edinburgh University, who argued that higher wages and less poverty, rather than improved living conditions, would help alleviate the bleak situation of the working classes. These critics raised Chadwick's ire. He went so far as to state that the mortality rate of children under five years of age was higher than that of children aged five to ten years who worked in the factories, proving that the workplace was safer than the residence for the lower classes. He even argued that some factory owners allowed employees to use the hot water discarded from their steam engines for baths. Eventually some 7,000 copies of the report became public as Chadwick sold or gave copies to newspapers and other publications. Its impact led to parliamentary investigations, additional newspaper reports, and the growth of lobby groups such as the Health of Towns Association. Even Charles Dickens, who initially had opposed Chadwick over the latter's efforts to eliminate public poor relief and workhouses, changed his opinion of the reformer after reading the report.

Chadwick's intended his efforts to pressure political authorities to recognize their special role in improving working peoples' lives in order to develop a healthier population that could be more productive and less costly to support. The initial government response was negative. Prime Minister Robert Peel and his Conservative Party did not embrace Chadwick's report. The status quo remained unchanged until the elections of 1847, which swept the Liberal Party and Prime Minister Lord John Russell into power. Growing public sentiment and the memory of the epidemics of the previous decade led to the passage of the Public Health Act in 1848. This measure instituted a Central Board of Health at the national and local levels, albeit with limited powers. The boards had oversight responsibility for street cleaning, trash collection, sewage systems, water supplies, and the construction of burial grounds. Chadwick's report had noted that some graveyards had fifteen times the number of bodies that could be neutralized per acre of ground. However, the boards lacked any enforcement powers and had minimal impact. Chadwick was appointed as Sanitation Commissioner and lobbied Parliament for policies to bring fresh water supplies to cities and towns, install water closets in all dwellings, and develop a method to carry urban sewage to outlying areas as a means of producing cheap fertilizer.

The momentum for reform halted temporarily in 1854. Lord Palmerston became the Home Secretary and, although he saw the apparent need for health reform, he faced several obstacles. First, individuals and groups with vested interests such as landlords and water companies had used their political influence to erode the impact of the already weak 1848 legislation. Chadwick's service as Sanitation Commissioner also became a liability because of his difficult personality and unpopularity. Therefore, Chadwick agreed with Palmerston that he should resign, and he accepted an annual pension of 1,000 pounds. Chadwick's official public career thus came to an inglorious end. Even so, the House of Commons failed to renew the Public Health Act, leaving final reform still years in the future.

Despite the loss of his official platform, Chadwick remained a powerful private voice advocating reform. Between the mid-1850s and the 1870s, he championed a variety of causes such as the adoption of civil service examinations, improved military sanitation because of the high rate of disease amongst the British troops in the Crimean War, a far-ranging agricultural drainage policy to improve soil fertility, and the introduction of sanitation techniques in the tropical territories of the British Empire. Indeed, at Prime Minister Gladstone's request, Chadwick studied the possibility of a postal telegraph and the problem of storm and sewage drainage for which he proposed separate systems for storm drains and the carrying of sewage from individual residences. Chadwick's final bid to regain a public posture for his reform ideas failed as he ran unsuccessfully for Parliament in 1867.

Chadwick eventually received the acclaim that he had certainly earned. Societies of Medicine and Hygiene in France, Belgium, and Italy recognized his contributions in the areas of public health and sanitation. Great Britain also honored him with a knighthood in 1889 during the last months of his life, a late recognition that some observers attribute to his difficult nature in dealing with parliamentary and government officials over the years. His obituary in the *Sanitary Record* of July 15, 1890 perhaps best sums up the man: "He was a large-minded man, who saw things in their just proportions, and realized how many methods contribute to the same end."[1]

John Fitch (1743–1798)

The application of steam power to water travel is often associated with Robert Fulton and his launch of the *Clermont* on the Hudson River in the early 19th century. In reality, his achievement was the culmination of efforts that began in Europe in the early 18th century and found one of its earliest successful applications by the unheralded American inventor John Fitch in the late 1780s.

John Fitch was born the fifth of sixth children in 1743 in Hartford, Connecticut. He began his education at age four and developed an insatiable appetite for reading books on mathematics, geography, and astronomy. His father was a harsh disciplinarian and forced him to do farm labor, an activity for which he developed a deep aversion, and he ran away to sea at age seventeen. He hated the life of a sailor and subsequently became an apprentice to a clockmaker, although he ended the agreement with his master when he was required to do farm work as part of his responsibilities.

Fitch returned to Connecticut and began his own clock repair business. He married Lucy Roberts in 1766 and took up making buttons from discarded brass kettles. Lucy's temper tantrums led to quarreling, and Fitch abandoned his family, work, and his home state and resettled in New Jersey. He opened up a clock repair, brass, and silversmith business. Unfortunately, British troops destroyed his shop during the American Revolution. He then helped to provision the colonial army at Valley Forge with beer and tobacco. He also repaired arms for American troops but failed in his bid to gain a permanent commission in the American army. After several failures in business enterprises, Fitch left New Jersey and purchased land in Virginia, becoming a tobacco merchant. Fitch also obtained land warrants and a surveyor's commission and made two trips to Kentucky to survey land. His second venture occurred in the spring of 1782 during the last sputtering of the American Revolution in the backcountry. Delaware Indians loyal to the British captured Fitch and his survey team. Several members of his party were scalped and killed, but he and the others were moved north and turned over to the British army in Detroit. They remained prisoners until exchanged at Christmas of that year. His survey work eventually paid off and resulted in his creation of "A Map of the Northwest Parts of the United States of America," the first cartographic representation of the new nation drawn, engraved, and printed by the same person. The map returned a significant profit and earned Fitch some notoriety.

Fitch's surveying travels piqued his interest in developing ways to traverse the rugged American frontier. He was denied petitions to become an official surveyor in Pennsylvania and gain a position in the U.S. Mint, two additional events in a long series of disappointments that would color his life. However, if one takes Fitch at his word, he had a moment of inspiration on Sunday walk in April 1785, similar to James Watt's "eureka moment" regarding the steam engine. What captured Fitch's fancy was the movement of a horse-drawn carriage. He pondered what it might entail to remove the horse and propel the carriage by some other means. It is unclear whether or not Fitch had seen the operation of a Watt steam engine but he immediately envisioned such a possibility for transportation, not along inland roads but rather on water using the principle and power of condensed vapor unleashed in the device.

Fitch traveled to Philadelphia, the technical capital of America, in order to gain financial backing. However, his harsh life and earlier disappointments had molded him into a brusque, gruff person who turned off many potential investors, including individual members of the Congress, a Spanish ambassador, and even the American Philosophical Society, which boasted Benjamin Franklin as a member. Fitch remained persistent, and his efforts eventually convinced a handful of investors to put up a modest amount of money for his project. This sum provided Fitch with enough cash to construct his first boat. With the assistance of Henry Voight, a German-born machinist, the initial vessel measured forty-five feet in length and weighed seven tons. The craft moved forward by the motion of six paddles on each side, one set dipping into the water while the other set finished that motion and prepared to dip into the water once again, replicating the efforts of human paddlers. Fitch fashioned his craft after recalling his earlier survey and mapping expeditions when he observed Indians paddling their war canoes in such a manner. Of course, Fitch's creation employed the power of an eighteen-inch cylinder steam engine and moved at the rate of four miles per hour, a speed that was only one mile an hour slower than Fulton's more famous New York to Albany sail nearly two decades later. Fitch demonstrated his boat's capability in Philadelphia on August 22, 1787 in front of a public gathering that included members of the Constitutional Convention. His efforts so impressed the Governor of Pennsylvania that he presented Fitch with a silk flag in honor of the achievement. As was the case with other inventors, Fitch had to fight for his patent rights. He successfully blunted a stiff challenge from James Rumsey of Maryland who had experimented with steam power for river transportation and operated a craft on the Potomac at four miles per hour.

Fitch followed this first successful venture with a larger boat destined for a Delaware River run. He named this vessel the *Thornton* after his major investor William Thornton. His boat raced upstream against the wind and handily outpaced all competing sailboats and human powered oar craft. By 1790 he operated the *Thornton* on the Delaware River carrying passengers and freight between Burlington, New Jersey and Philadelphia, Pennsylvania, a distance of twenty miles. Schedules for the *Thornton*'s trips soon appeared in the local newspapers such as the *Pennsylvania Packet*, advertising fees and stops in between at Bristol, Bordentown, and Trenton. The craft carried up to thirty passengers at a speed of nearly eight miles per hour. During its six months of operation, the *Thornton* traveled some 2,000 miles, transported more than 1,000 persons, and experienced few and minor mechanical or operational problems. *New York Magazine* raved about the performance of

Fitch's craft, stating that it outshone sailing vessels in remaining on a direct course even against a "contrary wind."

Fitch, however, was under agreement to produce a second boat. The *Perseverance* was scheduled to be ready in November 1790. However, a storm blew it away from its dock and it became grounded on an island. Fitch's efforts to repair the craft did not happen quickly enough, and his investors lost their sole rights to operate steamboats on the river. Although he did construct four boats in the period from 1785 to 1796, the number of passengers did not increase substantially and the public remained skeptical about the prospects of steam powered river transportation. Stagecoaches remained faster and less expensive means for long distance travel, even though such rides were noticeably more uncomfortable. In the end, poor ridership, lack of entrepreneurial skills, and the delay of his repairs to the *Perseverance* drove Fitch out of business.

Fitch even journeyed to France in 1793 to seek that nation's support for his proposed projects. That country was in the throes of revolution, and interest in investment in such a questionable project was nonexistent. This venture cost Fitch so much money that he had to journey to Britain and hire himself out as a sailor to work his way back to America. In 1796 he briefly dabbled with new designs such as the screw propeller and took Robert Fulton on rides on a New York lake. In the end, it was just too soon for investors, the general public, or a foreign country to embrace such forward-thinking innovation. Furthermore, his difficult personality also discouraged people from serious consideration of his ideas.

After this series of disappointments, Fitch retired and moved to Bardstown, Kentucky where he owned property from his surveying days. Squatters had seized much of his 1,600 acres of land, and he took steps to reclaim his property. This effort apparently took the last measure of Fitch's energy. He spiraled into a deep state of despair. He lived with a tavern owner and began to consume alcohol heavily, apparently with the intention of drinking himself to death. His landlord received acres of land in return for pints of whiskey. Under a doctor's care for what would now be a diagnosis of depression, Fitch took a large number of opium pills and passed away in his sleep in July 1798.

John Fitch was a visionary who had laid the groundwork for future steamboat development that Oliver Evans and Robert Fulton perfected in the early 19th century. In 1792 Fitch predicted to one of his shareholders that, whether or not he personally achieved success, steam powered vessels would in the not too distant future cross the Atlantic Ocean and become the standard means of river transportation. While John Fitch's name today is not widely associated with the steamboat, it is apparent that his technical insight, grit, and determination were the foundation upon which later developments rested. Despite building four working steamboats, he never received his due recognition and certainly not the financial reward of his successors. A generation later, the January 1836 issue of *Mechanics Magazine* lauded Fitch's accomplishments and lamented his lack of recognition, stating that misfortune had robbed John Fitch of his claim to the "most noble and useful invention."[2]

James Hargreaves (1720–1778)

James Hargreaves was a Lancashire weaver who traditionally has been credited with the invention of the "spinning jenny," a device that facilitated the processing of an increasing quantity of harvested cotton. Some historians have reassessed Hargreaves's role as an inventor, claiming that Thomas Highs, a poor artisan from Leigh, had actually designed and built the spinning machine in 1763 or 1764 several years before Hargreaves's model burst on the scene. Highs, however, had no money to secure a patent and merely rented several models before eventually abandoning his invention. Others claim that Hargreaves received credit for the spinning jenny simply because the unscrupulous early industrialist Richard Arkwright found it beneficial to recognize his machine. Whether Hargreaves was indeed either the inventor or improver of the spinning jenny or merely lucky through his association with Arkwright is of little consequence. His persistence in perfecting and initially marketing the spinning jenny are proof enough of his significant contribution to the Industrial Revolution, and it is likely his name will forever be wedded to the invention.

Hargreaves had no formal education and never learned to read or write. He eventually became a carpenter and weaver, as in his era the agricultural lifestyle meant that he derived his income from farming and weaving cloth. In 1740 he married a local woman and the couple had thirteen children, with his girls likely helping him to spin thread for his loom. Hargreaves most assuredly experienced the same frustration as others who had placed John Kay's flying shuttle on their looms. The family could not keep pace and supply him with sufficient thread. Legend has it that Jenny, one of Hargreaves daughters, inadvertently knocked over a spinning wheel and as the spindle tumbled and rolled across the floor, Hargreaves had the inspiration for the spinning jenny. However, local records do not confirm that Hargreaves had a daughter by that name. More likely, the word is simply one that evolved from "gin," a shortened version of the word engine.

Hargreaves first machine appeared in 1767; his main tool for its construction being a simple hand knife. He turned the traditional spinning wheel 90 degrees to a horizontal position so that it could operate multiple spindles at once. His first jenny had eight spindles, an improvement over Highs's six, and other versions soon followed. A moving carriage bearing the spindles stretched the thread as it pulled away from the body of the machine, simultaneously creating a twist to the cotton. The spindles wound up the thread as the carriage returned and then the process repeated itself. The thread produced by his jenny was coarse and broke easily, but the machine dramatically increased the amount of thread that a single person could spin. The single wheel on the spinning jenny controlled the spindles—initially eight and later up to eighty. Family and friends quickly began using his models. Unfortunately, financial success did not follow. The courts rejected his first patent because he had made and sold several machines outside the patent application window.

Hargreaves's jenny performed the work of eight people and thus decreased the need for labor. As a result, the early reaction to his invention was negative. In 1768 neighbors who were spinners and had witnessed the early success of the machine felt fear and jealousy. An angry mob gathered and marched to a barn and destroyed twenty of Hargreaves's machines under construction and then continued on to his residence. If legend is correct, the rioters forced Hargreaves to use a hammer and personally destroy one of his spinning jennies. Afterwards, Hargreaves fled to Nottingham where there was a warmer reception for new technology. He built a small spinning mill and refined the jenny but became increasingly frustrated at his inability to obtain a patent. By this time, carpenters in Lancashire had built scores of replicas of his machine and increased the number of threads to eighty or more. His patent rejected and dreams in shambles, Hargreaves died in relative obscurity in 1778. By the time of his death it is estimated that 20,000 jennies were operating in England.

The impact of Hargreaves's invention was dramatic. The spinning jenny fit perfectly into the framework of the existing domestic textile industry. The machine was cheap to construct, small enough to fit into a cottage, easy to operate (even for a child), and the spinners could now keep pace with the weavers. It became the foundation upon which later textile technology developed. In the early 1790s Richard Arkwright had put the water frame into mass operation, and soon Samuel Crompton married the best parts of the two machines to produce his "mule" and the textile industry soared. Cotton yarn exports increased more than three-fold from the 1760s to 1780 and by the early 19th century was ten times that produced in the 1780s. Thus, James

Hargreaves's jenny ended the reliance on the ancient spinning wheel and opened the door for the major developments in the English textile industry in the early phase of the Industrial Revolution.

Joseph-Marie Jacquard (1752–1834)

Joseph-Marie Jacquard's inventive spirit led to the development of an improved loom that not only revolutionized the weaving process in the 19th century, but its technical implications had a major impact on technology in the 20th century. Jacquard was the son of a weaver in Lyon, France. Because his family had little means and he received only a meager education, his father found him employment as a bookbinder. His employer, who gave the boy some very elementary lessons in mathematics, noticed that Jacquard had a real flair for computations and mechanics.

Upon learning that his father was dying, Jacquard returned to the family and took possession of his father's two looms and became a weaver himself. He became obsessed with improvement of the looms and soon had to sell the family cottage and the looms to get out of debt. In the midst of this turmoil Jacquard married, but his financial situation forced him to leave his wife in Lyons to work making straw bonnets while he moved to Bresse for employment and continued to work on improving his loom concept. The French Revolution interrupted his pursuits, and he joined the Lyonese volunteers against the French army. During the course of the next several years he experienced the death of his son fighting at his side and fled back to Lyon to remain in hiding while his wife continued her hat making. After emerging from his concealment he obtained employment with a manufacturer and at night continued to improve his loom. His employer, upon learning of his interests, advanced him money to modify the loom. Within several months, Jacquard had invented a loom that substituted mechanical power for the hand-labor of the weaver.

In 1801 the loom was displayed at the Exposition of National Industry in Paris and received a bronze medal. His facile mind continued to seek improvements and projects, and his employer provided him with additional funds to pursue them. Soon his work became known to officials of his *Department* and he received an invitation to the see the Emperor in Paris. After a lengthy interview, an impressed Napoleon provided Jacquard with comfortable lodging in Paris and a workshop to continue his projects. One of the advantages of this arrangement was that Jacquard was able to obtain other machines and inventions to study. One such device was a loom for weaving flowered silk invented by Vaucanson, a noted French inventor who had died in 1782. Jacquard diligently studied the operation of Vaucanson's loom that had as its essential feature a pierced cylinder whose holes when they revolved regulated the movement of needles that deviated the warp threads to produce a specific design. Jacquard worked to improve the device. He added a series of punch cards to control the sequence of movements and the weaving of patterns and reduce the heavy manual labor component in the process. The result was a machine that permitted weavers to focus on the quality of designs and standardize production. He presented his rich fabric to the Empress Josephine. The result pleased Napoleon, who ordered a number of the looms to be built according to Jacquard's specifications. In 1806 the French government specified that the Jacquard loom was public property and awarded him an annual pension and a royalty on each machine that was constructed.

Jacquard returned to Lyon and experienced a rude reception. Similar to early British inventors, the weavers of Lyon viewed Jacquard's loom as a threat to their jobs. It took troops to hold back the angry mob and prevent the confiscation and destruction of his inventory of looms. He was publicly denounced, hanged in effigy, and had one of his looms smashed to bits. At one point, riots broke out and Jacquard himself was dragged through the streets briefly before being rescued. Some British silk makers tried to persuade Jacquard to journey to their homeland for refuge, but he opted to stay in France. They did adopt his loom, an action that forced the Lyon weavers to do the same. To their delight, the Jacquard loom actually increased employment opportunities tenfold. In 1812 it is estimated that France had 11,000 Jacquard looms in operation employing some 60,000 persons, a figure that continued to rise in subsequent years. Jacquard went from being the most scorned man in Lyon to a hero. He continued to perfect his loom. In 1820 he received the French Legion of Honor, and he died at Oullins in 1834. In 1840, the city of Lyon erected a statue in his honor, although his family members drifted into poverty and even had to resort to selling the gold medal bestowed on him by King Louis XVIII.

The Jacquard loom was not only a revolution in the 19th century weaving process, but it also had far-reaching implications. The idea of punch cards that made repetitive tasks easier was a forerunner of the early modern computer technology. Of course, the Jacquard loom did not make computations, but the punch cards that are controlled by humans in reality stored information that was used to create a specific tapestry. It also permitted the same loom and weaver to make a variety of designs. Thus, weaving moved from the domain of the individual to the realm of mass production, at least according to 19th-century standards.

Samuel Finley Breese Morse (1791–1872)

Samuel F. B. Morse was born in Charleston, Massachusetts, the son of a Congregational minister. Morse was an intellectually gifted youth who entered Yale at the age of fourteen. He majored in art, his first passion, but also attended other lectures, including ones on electricity. He earned money in college painting small portraits of his friends. Following graduation, Morse briefly served as a bookseller's apprentice but received his parents' blessing to attend the Royal Academy of Arts in England. He met the poet Samuel Taylor Coleridge and several future American and British painters and actors, acquaintances that began for Morse a life-long series of friendships with famous persons in the world of politics, education, invention, and the arts.

Morse returned to the United States in 1815 and divided his time between New England, Washington, D.C., and the South. He was a talented artist and fulfilled a number of painting commissions for portraits of such notables as President James Monroe, Eli Whitney, and Noah Webster. After his marriage in 1818, Morse spent more than a year painting a large scene of the House of Representatives in the Capitol Rotunda.

Morse eventually moved to New York City to seek additional opportunities. The City of New York commissioned him for $1,000 to paint a portrait of the Marquis de Lafayette during the French patriot's final visit to America. Morse poured himself into a number of activities. He served as President of the New York Drawing Association and the National Academy of Design. Morse also helped create the publications *Journal of Commerce* and *Academics of Art*. He also remained attracted by developments in electricity, particularly the invention of the electromagnet, and attended a number of lectures on the field at the New York Athenaeum.

In the late 1820s, after a series of personal tragedies that included the deaths of his first wife, son, and both parents, Morse sailed to Europe to ease his grief and pursue other painting ventures and study in England, France, Switzerland, and Italy. However, Morse's career soon took another course. In the early 1830s the American scientist Joseph Henry had discovered the powerful property of electromagnetism created through many layers of insulated wires. He demonstrated how magnetic signals could be sent over long distances, the first suggestion of the telegraph. On his voyage home from Europe, Morse had lengthy conversations with Charles T. Jackson, a Boston physician, who informed him of Henry's and simultaneous European experiments regarding electromagnetism. An intrigued Morse began sketching his idea of how to use electromagnetism to transmit messages with a dot and dash system.

After returning to the United States, he immediately began work on what would become his claim to fame—the telegraph. In 1836 Morse constructed a recording telegraph and demonstrated it for Dr. Leonard Gale, Professor of Science at New York University. He used a series of relays to open and close the switches further away through the use of magnets—a fundamental principle in the telegraph system. Gale became his partner, and by 1837 a message could be sent through ten miles of wire reels in the professor's university lecture room. After witnessing a demonstration, Morse's friend, Alfred Vail, joined the team. Vail possessed substantial financial resources through his family's iron works. These three men formed an important collaboration that led to Morse's perfection of the telegraph. Morse spent seven years toying with different approaches to his design. He demonstrated his telegraph to friends and colleagues, spending nearly his entire savings on his project. At one time his net worth dropped to $0.37! He eventually obtained financial support from several investors, partnerships, and the sale of a few paintings.

Morse ran into other trouble. Charles T. Jackson, the man with whom Morse had conversed on his sail home from Europe, made claims that he, not Morse, was the inventor of the telegraph. Morse obtained statements from passengers of the ship who supported his bid, and he filed for his patent in the fall of 1837. Unfortunately, this incident began a long series of court battles that would drain time, monetary resources, and energy from Morse's efforts to perfect his system.

As the tempo of developments related to the telegraph increased, Morse decided to abandon his painting work and concentrate solely on the device. He modified his approach. His telegraphic dictionary initially had words represented by number codes. He switched to using a code for each letter, a technique that made it unnecessary to encode and decode every word. In early 1838 he demonstrated his telegraph for several groups including scientists at the Franklin Institute in Philadelphia, members of the U.S. House of Representatives Commerce Committee whose chairman was F. O. J. Smith of Maine, and President Martin Van Buren and his cabinet. Smith was so impressed that he sponsored a bill to fund $30,000 to construct a fifty-mile telegraph line. Smith did not reveal to his colleagues that he had purchased part interest in Morse's telegraph, but the bill failed.

This legislative failure left his American effort flagging, thus Morse journeyed once again to Europe to secure additional patents. He visited England, Russia, and France and succeeded only in the latter country. While in Paris he met Louis Daguerre, the inventor of the Daguerreotype, and published the first U.S. description of this style of photography. Morse returned to America, finally secured a U.S. patent for the telegraph, opened up a daguerreotype studio, and taught the process to a small number of individuals, including Matthew Brady, the famous Civil War photographer.

In the early 1840s, an undeterred Morse conducted further experiments with the telegraph. His original instrument worked by printing the message on a piece of ribbon paper through the use of a pendulum and electromagnet that produced a series of ridged slugs in the form of dots and dashes in a distinctive pattern for each letter of the alphabet according to a code Morse had devised. The message produced then was given to a decoding official who translated the message. By 1845 Morse had modified his receiver so that trained telegraphers listening to the noise pattern in a sounding box could record the message quickly. Morse also thought into the future and realized that some signals would be required to be sent to points separated by bodies of water. He experimented with laying several miles of cable underwater between Battery Park and Governor's Island in New York and successfully transmitted a signal between the two sites.

Morse gave additional demonstrations to officials in Newark, Philadelphia, New York, and Washington, D.C. Congress expressed renewed interest in his invention. In 1843 after an extremely close vote, eighty-nine to eighty-three with seventy Congressmen not voting, the House of Representatives appropriated $30,000 for an experimental 41 mile telegraph line between Washington, D.C. and Baltimore. The construction initially employed underground lines in lead pipes, but that approach proved unworkable so Morse shifted to the use of a single wire strung on glass insulators that were mounted on trees or poles placed above ground. The mastermind behind the installation was Ezra Cornell, whose fortune led him later to found Cornell University. Morse was now ready for the most important moment in the telegraph's development. On May 24, 1844 he sent a message from the Supreme Court chamber in the U.S. Capitol in Washington, D.C. to his assistant Alfred Vail waiting at the B&O Railroad Depot in Baltimore, Maryland. The message when decoded stated, "What hath God Wrought?"[3]

Morse gave credit for the message to Annie Elsworth, the daughter of a friend, who took the quote from the Old Testament passage: Numbers 23:23. The initial test left Morse humbled. A week later he wrote his brother in a very pensive tone obviously feeling great pride but also a sense of major responsibility from what he described as "an astonishing invention."[4] Furthermore, in the fall of 1844, Morse cautioned Alfred Vail against use of the device to promote partisanship.

Following Morse's demonstration, telegraph developments moved rapidly. An event in Britain proved the benefit of the new technology. In 1845 John Tawell murdered his mistress and attempted to escape by train to London. However, telegraph operators wired ahead his description to London police officials who apprehended Tawell as he stepped off the train. In the same year, Morse picked Amos Kendall, the U.S. Postmaster-General, to join his investment team as his agent. By 1846 this collaboration resulted in the creation of the Magnetic Telegraph Company and the extension of telegraph technology to connect Washington, Baltimore, Philadelphia, New York, and Buffalo. However, Morse had to fight patent infringement in the United States as a flurry of telegraph companies appeared in the late 1840s, some constructing their lines parallel to his earlier ones. In 1848 six New York City daily newspapers formed the Associated Press to share the cost of telegraphing news. By 1850 nearly two dozen telegraph companies and 12,000 miles of wire had been laid in the United States. The Supreme Court, however, upheld Morse's patent in 1854 and extended his sole possession of telegraphy for seven years, and the challenges to his system waned.

During the 1850s and 1860s Morse's invention experienced remarkable growth. In 1852 the telegraph linked London and Paris. By 1853 Florida was the only state east of the Mississippi River that did not have the telegraph. In the mid 1850s the British and French governments used the telegraph to communicate with commanders in the field during the Crimean War. Furthermore, serious efforts began to connect the United States and Europe. Morse and Cyrus W. Fields became partners to lay a transatlantic cable. On its fourth attempt, Queen Victoria transmitted a message to President James Buchanan but the cable broke several weeks later. However, ten European countries paid Morse 400,000 French francs to use his invention. In 1859 the Magnetic Telegraph Company merged with Field's American Telegraph Company. In 1861 Union and Confederate forces adopted the telegraph to communicate while conducting military operations. In the same year a transcontinental telegraph extended to California. By 1865 the International Telegraph Union had formed to establish rules, regulations, and standards for the telegraph industry. In 1866 the transatlantic cable was successfully laid, and a second one was soon added. By 1880 more than 100,000 miles of undersea cable had been laid across the globe. Also in 1866 the rival Western Union Telegraph Company merged with the American Telegraph Company to create the largest U.S. telegraph company.

Samuel Morse was a remarkable individual whose early career as an artist provided no hint of his future development of the telegraph system, one of the most important inventions in an era dominated by men of remarkable technical ingenuity. Morse was a highly complex person. Besides his artistic and technical pursuits, he had a great interest in politics, twice running unsuccessfully for mayor of New York on an anti-immigrant platform and once losing a Congressional bid from the Poughkeepsie district in New York. However, Morse, unlike many other inventors, achieved wide acclaim in his lifetime. He received accolades and awards from the governments of France, Spain, Portugal, Denmark, Prussia, Austria, and Italy, as well as from the Sultan of Turkey. In addition, important scientific societies and associations in France, Belgium, and the United States granted him special recognition, and Yale University awarded him the degree of Doctor of Laws. In 1871, a year before his death, New York City unveiled a statue of Morse. The inventor fittingly sent a farewell message around the globe—a world his telegraph had connected. The man who had spent nearly every penny on his ingenious idea lived the last decades of his life comfortably on a 200-acre estate along the upper Hudson River. What had God Wrought? Indeed!

Thomas Newcomen (1663–1729)

Thomas Newcomen, a Dartmouth iron monger (hardware salesman) and a sometimes lay-preacher, had passed from the scene before the full eruption of the Industrial Revolution. However, Newcomen's contribution cannot be overemphasized, because his atmospheric steam engine became the prototype device that with later modifications powered rapid industrial growth initially in England and then later throughout the Western world.

Newcomen's engine was arguably the most important development in a long line of devices designed to overcome the problem of water seepage into coal, tin, and copper mines. As miners dug deeper to reap greater profits, the mines quickly filled with water. Indeed, Newcomen was not the first person to dabble with steam power to expel water from mines. In fact, one of his contemporaries, Thomas Savery (1650–1715), had obtained a patent in 1698 for his so-called "fire engine," a device to extract water from mines by using the heat force generated by fire. In truth, Savery's machine was not an engine at all, as it contained no moving parts and merely applied high-pressured steam directly on the water it sought to raise. Because Newcomen feared a patent dispute, he became Savery's partner, despite the fact that his invention was far superior to the fire engine of his colleague. The real significance of the Newcomen engine is that it first brought together the essential hardware—cylinder, piston, and a separate boiler—and processes to tap the potential of steam power, the key elements that would be utilized by the improved steam engines for the next century.

He commenced his experiments with the same device—a cylinder and piston—that the ancient Romans had employed to bring water from the mines. However, he soon decided to add a brewer's copper kettle to house water and a furnace to heat the water. He then installed a water jet inside the piston cylinder to condense steam. When the water boiled and the steam condensed it, the piston was forced to move within the cylinder creating a vacuum. The weight of the atmosphere above forced the piston down, this motion creating the real power stroke of the engine. Thus, his device actually is often more correctly described as an atmospheric engine. The up-and-down movement was harnessed to a "walking beam"—a huge horizontal beam of wood that balanced like a seesaw and was connected at one end to the piston of a pump. The Romans had used endless shifts of sweating men and panting horses to work such a pump. Newcomen's result was dramatic—an engine that produced in just two days what fifty men and twenty horses previously could replicate only by working twenty-four hours a day for a week.

Despite its improvements on earlier devices, Newcomen's engine had several key drawbacks. The most significant one was its crude inefficiency, especially when compared to the later 18th century modifications and improvements. Furthermore, the constant heating and cooling required the boiler to obtain more fuel, a problem somewhat masked initially because the device was primarily used in coalmines where there was a ready source of fuel. This insatiable demand for coal, however, became a nagging problem at other mines and led his successors to seek more efficient solutions.

The first Newcomen engine operated at a coalmine at Dudley Castle in Straffordshire in 1712. It was an instant success, raising 120 gallons of water 153 feet in one minute. Soon a number of flooded mines reopened and miners once again found employment. By 1769 at least 120 English coal mines sported Newcomen engines. A French observer once marveled at the Newcomen engine and compared its operation to that of the human body: heat spawned all the engine's motions; the circulation that took place in the engine's tubes was like blood in a person's veins; valves opened and closed at the proper moments like in the human heart; the machine fed itself; the engine rejected what it used regularly; and it drew from its own work everything required for support.

There can be little doubt that Thomas Newcomen is a pivotal figure in the Industrial Revolution. His crowning achievement is that he constructed the initial efficient steam-powered device, a prototype steam engine. This important initial link soon led James Watt and others to thrust Great Britain and other countries headlong into the Age of Steam and the industrial era.

George Stephenson (1781–1848)

George Stephenson was a major contributor to the early development of the modern railway system. He was born the son of a colliery fireman in Wylam near Newcastle Upon Tyne. As a young boy he herded cows but also developed a keen fascination with machines associated with the mines, and spent much of his free time learning about their components and operations.

At the age of 14 he joined his father in the mines and several years later began attending night classes to learn how to read and write. In 1802 he became a colliery engineman and in this role operated a stationary steam engine to haul coal up from the mines or to transport heavy loads of ore, rock, or coal along wooden or iron rails. He married a local servant farm girl and had a watch and clock repair business in the evening hours. His wife died unexpectedly in 1806 and left him to care for their young son Robert. Indeed, Robert obtained a formal education and ultimately brought scientific knowledge into a partnership with his father. George tinkered and Robert understood scientific principles and became an excellent manager. In 1808 George moved to the Killingworth mine as an engineman and spent his Saturdays studying engines, particularly several Newcomen and Watt models, by disassembling them to learn the intricacies of their operation. His skill was recognized, and by 1812 he had been promoted to the position of colliery enginewright. In this role he delved into the problem of the large number of explosion accidents caused by the gases that filled the mines. By 1815 he and Sir Humphrey Davy independently had developed a safety lamp that could be used without the fear of igniting the inflammable gases. The claims and counter claims between the two men resulted in Stephenson's reluctance to trust contemporary scientists, a trait that led him to follow his own inclinations rather than rely on those of others.

During this same period, Stephenson learned of the work by William Hedley and Timothy Hackworth to develop a primitive locomotive. After he convinced his superior to let him construct a similar engine, Stephenson's genius became apparent. He conducted an exhaustive study on the phenomena of friction and heat. In 1814 he built a locomotive called the *Blutcher* that could haul eight wagons containing thirty tons of cargo uphill at the speed of four miles per hour. His creation was certainly not the first locomotive, as Richard Trevithick's steam coach had appeared in 1798. However, Stephenson's model modified the existing locomotive designs by using flanged wheels for adhesion to the track, developing a means to transfer movement from pistons to wheels by using a drive-rod and crank mechanism, eliminating the intermediate gearing technique employed by his predecessors and employing a pipe exhaust system to increase the fire's draft and thus produce more power. By 1820 he had constructed sixteen engines for the Killingworth mine and a few other enterprises. His work so impressed the mine owners that they assigned him to construct an eight mile railroad. At this point, Stephenson became convinced that steam railroads would be most efficient if their track was as level as possible. Thus, he anticipated the marriage of railroad construction and civil engineering. Stephenson's handiwork resulted in a number of railway lines and machines. The track was placed down in sections. The initial portion of the line was worked by moving locomotives and subsequent portions by fixed engines and cables. Once the railway obtained a height of 250 feet above sea level, the coal wagons traveled down over 2 miles of incline. Stephenson used fixed engines and locomotives and thus created the first railway totally independent of animal power.

By the early 1820s developments were in place for a dramatic event to spur on railway development. On April 19, 1821 Parliament passed a law that permitted a company owned by Edward Pease to construct a horse railway to link the mines in West Durham, Darlington and the Tees River at Stockton. Stephenson intervened and convinced Pease that a horse-drawn load on an iron rail could weigh no more than ten tons but that his existing *Blutcher* locomotive at the Killingworth colliery could haul 500 tons. The discussion intrigued Pease, who then visited Killingworth to observe Stephenson's locomotive. He was immediately impressed and hired Stephenson as the chief engineer of the Stockton and Darlington Company. In order to use Stephenson's *Blutcher*, Pease successfully obtained a Parliamentary modification to the original act that permitted the use of a locomotive or moveable engine as well as the horse railway.

Stephenson soon collaborated with William Losh, who owned the Newcastle ironworks. The pair patented their own iron rails but discovered that another engineer, John Birkinshaw, had created malleable fifteen-foot-long iron rails. Stephenson decided that, despite the added expense, the Birkinshaw rails were the best option for the Stockton and Darlington line. Work on the railway line began in 1822. During the construction phase, Stephenson observed that even a slight change in gradient could reduce the hauling capacity of the locomotive by up to 50%. Thus, he spent considerable time and energy in supervising the construction of cuttings, tunnels, and embankments in order to reduce the gradient along the route as much as possible.

The Stockton and Darlington line opened in September 1825. The event drew a large audience to observe Stephenson at the control of his locomotive. His vehicle named *Locomotion* hauled more than three dozen wagons filled with passengers and sacks of coal and flour. The maiden journey took two hours to travel nine miles. However, the impressive portion of the trip was the final descent into the Stockton terminus as the *Locomotion* obtained a top speed of fifteen miles per hour. This successful event won Stephenson wide acclaim and resulted in his appointment as the chief engineer for several other railway lines including the important Liverpool and Manchester Railway. Liverpool was a key port for the importation of cotton, and Manchester boasted a number of booming textile factories. He encountered significant engineering challenges, including crossing a soft and unstable peat bog, constructing a large viaduct across a valley, and building sixty-three bridges, two tunnels, and a two-mile-long rock cutting to straighten the route as much as possible. In addition to the obstacles presented by terrain, Stephenson faced additional struggles. Competitors wooed their friends in Parliament in order to gain an advantage, and angry armed farmers threatened to use force to stop construction across the rural landscape. In addition, wild misperceptions about his locomotive circulated amongst the public: birds would be killed in midair, women on trains would miscarry, passengers would be killed by sparks, cows would halt milk production, crops would be polluted, and people could be torn apart traveling at ten miles per hour. Perhaps to dispel these erroneous notions, Stephenson provided a famous British actress a ride on his locomotive. She was mesmerized by the experience and described her steady, unwavering journey on a machine belching white breath as magical as a fairy tale.

In response to the growing interest and potential associated with railway transportation, the Liverpool and Manchester Railway decided to host an 1829 competition. The winner would receive a 500-pound award, but the greater purpose was to determine which railway mode of transportation—stationary engines with horses and cables or steam-powered locomotives—would rule the future of the railway system. Each participating locomotive had to weigh less than six tons (in order not to break the rails), haul three times its own weight, and maintain a minimum speed of ten miles per hour. The locomotives had to run up and down a portion of the railway twenty times in order to approximate the distance between Liverpool and Manchester. Although ten locomotives originally promised to compete, only five showed up on the assigned date. One locomotive was eliminated when a horse was discovered inside. Two additional locomotives experienced early mechanical problems. The George and Robert Stephenson entry named the *Rocket* easily bested the remaining competition.

The Liverpool and Manchester Railway began operating in September 1830. For the official opening, the British Prime Minister, the Duke of Wellington, and many high ranking officials attended. With wide-eyed spectators gawking at the scene and cannon booming, the event consisted of eight locomotives which took thirty dignitaries for a demonstration ride. Ironically, the dangers and possibilities of the new technology became immediately apparent when one of the attendees, William Huskisson, a government minister, was struck and killed by a passing locomotive as he stepped from a train. Thinking quickly, George Stephenson whisked the injured minister by train to the nearest doctor. Unfortunately, this rescue effort was in vain and William Huskisson became the first fatality of the railroad era (see Document 2).

Stephenson's influence grew rapidly. His success stimulated the great age of railway construction in Great Britain, and his vision for a national rail network soon became a reality. He became the chief engineer for four additional prominent railways and continued to develop more efficient locomotives. Within a short period of time nearly 200 separate rail networks existed. However, competition, mergers, and bankruptcies very quickly reduced that number to about two dozen. By 1838 five hundred miles of track had been laid. Five years later, 2,000 miles of track snaked across Great Britain and by 1852 the country boasted nearly 8,000 miles of track.

The impact of railway development was dramatic and far reaching. Transportation expenses fell significantly as the railway either complemented or competed more efficiently with the former monopoly of the canal system. Railway transportation also resulted in a decline in food prices, as outlying districts could rapidly ship agricultural products over large distances and in many instances undercut the prices of existing farmlands around the towns. By the mid-19th century commerce was the acknowledged lifeblood of the nation, and the railway system was its artery and vein network. The railway also transformed the social life of Great Britain and ultimately the Western world. In 1828 the first lines opened in France and the United States, in 1835 in Belgium and in several German states, and in 1839 in the Netherlands and in the northern Italian states. Great Britain and these other states soon had paying customers who sped across the landscape at thirty miles an hour or more according to set timetables. Time and distance compressed so significantly that the railway became the visible symbol of progress. Numerous pictures and prints soon depicted the energy associated with the railways, and even poems and narrative verse praised the speed and rhythm one experienced on journey by rail. By the time of his death, George Stephenson's influence on the development and growth of the British railway system signaled that a dramatic upheaval had occurred in the former rural, agrarian, and slow-paced Western society and that a new, modern, and bustling era had dawned.

Thomas Telford (1757–1834)

Born into an impoverished family in an isolated valley in Scotland, Thomas Telford's innate intellect, drive, and energy led him to become one of Great Britain's greatest civil engineers. His prolific lifework consisted of the construction of a treasure trove of roads, bridges, tunnels, canals, harbors, and churches in the British Isles. His handiwork is still indelibly etched into the landscape of Great Britain today.

After moving to Edinburgh, Telford became a stonemason's apprentice at the age of fourteen. In 1782 he went to London and attached himself to an architect charged with the construction of Somerset House. His work in London likely attracted the attention of Sir William Pulteney, a Member of Parliament from Shrewsbury. Through Pulteney's patronage, Telford became the Surveyor of Public Works for Shropshire in 1787. While serving in this position, he undertook a number of building projects. The first important one was the renovation of Shrewsbury Castle. Telford supervised the reconstruction of this abandoned ruin and turned it into a residence for his patron. The edifice even included a special addition known as Laura's Tower for Pulteney's wife.

Following the Shrewsbury Castle project, Telford acquired further work in the area. In 1788 he conducted the initial excavation of an old Roman City at Wroxeter. He also built the roof of St. Mary Magdalene's Church in Bridgnorth and served as a consultant on the repairs to the roof of St. Chad's Church in Shrewsbury, where he noted that the leaking roof needed substantial work. Ironically, three days after his report the old church collapsed entirely. In addition, Telford also helped to rebuild Shrewsbury Prison and repair St. Michael's Church in Madeley. In 1790 Telford designed a span to carry the London–Holyhead Road over the Severn River at Montford. This bridge was the first of forty that he helped to construct in Shrewsbury. His bridge at Buildwas became his first iron bridge, an influence from other iron bridges being constructed in the era.

By the early 1790s Telford's reputation had soared. He was a consultant on the renovation of London Bridge in 1800 and in the following year worked on the Caledonian Canal and thirty-two churches in Scotland. He also received an appointment to design and build the Ellesmere Canal, a project to connect the ironworks and mines of Wrexham with the town of Chester using the existing Chester Canal and the Mersey River. The construction of the canal required innovative engineering techniques that won Telford additional recognition. One such example was the Pontcysylite Aqueduct, an impressive structure that crossed over the Dee River at a height of 126 feet. Telford's engineering marvel employed a construction process whereby he made troughs from cast iron plates fixed in masonry mixed with bull's blood for additional skeletal strength. He also reinforced the joints with flannel soaked in syrup and boiled for hours. The aqueduct obtained the local title of the "waterway in the sky." Its symmetry and aesthetic appeal moved Sir Walter Scott to declare it to be a remarkable work of art. The Ellesmere Canal opened in 1805.

Shortly afterward, Telford obtained the commission to construct the Shrewsbury Canal, an important artery designed to haul huge amounts of coal and raw materials. The original engineer died and Telford stepped in. The seventeen-mile canal required extraordinary engineering skill to complete its eleven locks, eight lift bridges, and a nearly 1000-yard tunnel at Berwick. The canal remained in service until 1944.

Telford's canal and aqueduct phase continued for a number of years. Between 1796 and 1801, he built the Chirk aqueduct over the Ceiriog River. It was seventy feet high and consisted of ten spans, and is noteworthy because it is half in England and half in Wales. In 1810 he served as the engineer for the Gota Canal in Sweden. He also worked on aqueducts in Scotland and returned to Shropshire to construct his final but most impressive canal, the Birmingham and Liverpool Junction Canal (today a portion of the Shropshire Union Canal) from 1826 to 1835. Although he died before its completion, this project linked the Birmingham Canal network at Wolverhampton with the sea at Ellesmere Port and smaller canal tentacles along the route and continued its commercial traffic use until 1958.

Following his tireless efforts in canal and aqueduct construction, Telford turned to road building. The British government was so impressed with his previous work that it selected him for the important project to transform the London–Holyhead Road. Parliament appropriated the unheard of sum of 750,000 pounds for the endeavor. The road would become the ultimate achievement for a man whose crown already consisted of a number of priceless jewels. The port of Holyhead was the important embarkation point for the sea crossing form Wales to Dublin, Ireland. This connection had gained significance with the Act of Union in 1800. But the journey across Wales entailed traversing wild, rugged, and perilous terrain, hindering efforts to respond to the growing need for more rapid communication between England and Wales and Ireland. One of the main interests for the construction of the road was to speed mail service to Ireland. The highest speed obtained by staged coaches on the route until this time was approximately ten miles per hour. However, this pace dropped significantly when the coaches entered the mountains in Wales.

Telford surveyed the possible route and submitted his plans to Parliament in 1811. Parliament was slow to act and did not provide funds for an additional four years. Furthermore, seven turnpike trusts controlled the existing path route, and Telford had to employ extraordinary skills of negotiation to procure the entire route from the trusts. The portion of the road from London to Shrewsbury was not too difficult to construct. Indeed, an existing path dating back to the Roman era provided a clear route to follow. It was the part of the road from Shrewsbury to Holyhead (a distance of 106 miles) that presented the largest obstacle. Telford worked diligently to refashion the route. He used the existing path controlled previously by the turnpike trusts and reduced the gradients in key places, constructed bridges over the rivers, and attempted to ensure that travelers would have the smoothest ride possible. It should be noted that the A5 highway today follows Telford's route almost without modification. Interestingly, Telford employed a technique in road building as old as the Romans. He first placed a layer of stones on the road bed and then covered them with gravel to allow for proper drainage. This approach helped to ensure a long-lasting roadway. Today the route is basically unchanged, and Telford's roadway supports heavy vehicles and traffic that moves five times faster than the coaches of his day. The poet laureate, Robert Southey, used a pun to declare Telford as the "Colossus of Roads."

A second major challenge faced Telford. He had to construct a bridge across the Menai Straits from Bangor to the Isle of Anglessy. The purpose of the bridge was to replace the existing ferry that had to struggle against dangerous tidal and rapid currents that swirled in several directions. Indeed, in 1785 a vessel transporting fifty-five people capsized, stranding the passengers on a sandbar during a violent windstorm. By the time rescuers arrived the next day, they found only one survivor. Furthermore, the straits had to be open for shipping, which meant that a bridge had to be erected at least 100 feet above the water to permit the masts of vessels to pass safely underneath. The result of Telford's effort was the magnificent Menai Bridge, a suspension span that became a marvel of engineering skill and aesthetic beauty.

Construction on the Menai Bridge began in 1819 and was completed in early 1836 when a London mail coach crossed the bridge for the first time. Telford designed the bridge and secured contractors and labor to build it. He also created milestones along the way and designed the wrought-iron gates and toll houses that dotted the road. One of the old toll house boards depicted the type of traffic that crossed the bridge in its early days as well as the assessed tolls: a coach or carriage on springs (four shillings); a wagon or cart drawn by a horse or mule solely for the purpose of carrying or going to fetch lime for manure (one and one-half shillings); and a drove of cattle, pigs, sheep, or lambs (five shillings).

Thomas Telford's legacy in the field of engineering is nearly unfathomable. It is estimated that he was responsible for at least 1,100 bridges in Scotland alone and that 22,000 people could be seated in the churches he constructed or renovated. As a result, he obtained recognition for his achievements not only in his lifetime but even in more recent years. He is universally recognized as the father of civil engineering. In 1820 he was appointed as the first President of the Institution of Civil Engineers, a position he retained until he died in 1834. In a fitting tribute, he was buried in the nave at Westminster Abbey. Furthermore, In 1968 Dawley New Town renamed itself Telford in his honor, and in 1990 the city also designated one of its technology colleges as the Thomas Telford School. Thomas Telford's extraordinary engineering skills connected the disparate parts of Great Britain with a spider-like network of bridges, roads, canals, and docks and dotted many communities with new or improved houses of worship. The cumulative result of his work contributed in no small part to the nation's unprecedented economic growth in the first half of the 19th century.

Richard Trevithick (1771–1833)

As early as 1550 roads employing wooden rails called wagonways were commonly used in Germany. Horse-drawn wagons or carts traveled more easily on these pathways than on the dirt roads of the era. By the mid 1770s iron rails and wheels had replaced the wooden ones. In 1789 wagons with flanged or grooved wheels had appeared and provided greater traction on the rails. These developments, along with the invention and improvements of the steam engine throughout the latter half of the 18th century, provided a marriage of opportunity that Richard Trevithick would seize upon to create the first steam powered railroad locomotive.

Richard Trevithick was the son of a Cornwall mine manager. As a youngster, he proved to be more interested in leisure pursuits than schoolwork. He grew to be more than six feet tall, was alleged to be an outstanding wrestler, and possessed enough strength to hurl sledgehammers over the roofs of engine houses. After completing his basic education, he went to work for his father at the Wheal Treasury mine and demonstrated a keen insight regarding engineering principles. He became fascinated with steam power and made several improvements to mine engines. Trevithick believed that the application of high-pressure steam offered tremendous possibilities in the mining industry, particularly in the area of raising ore and refuse from mines. He soon developed such an engine that became greatly sought after in Cornwall and South Wales. In the space of two years he constructed thirty engines, each small enough to fit into an ordinary farm wagon for transport to the mines.

Trevithick realized that an impediment to his innovation was the strict hold that the Watt–Boulton team had on patent approvals on any apparatus that had a steam engine application. He sought ways to circumvent the Watt–Boulton patent by arguing that his high-pressure engine was a distinctive departure from his rivals' low-pressure engines. This success with a stationary engine led him to the idea of a steam locomotive. By 1796 he had produced a miniature operable one by putting the boiler and the engine in one piece. Hot water was placed in the boiler and a red-hot iron was inserted into a tube below. Thus, the heated water forced steam to rise and start the engine's operation. Steam from the cylinders was expelled to the atmosphere, eliminating the need for a condenser and producing more power than the much larger Newcomen or Watt–Boulton engines. As the latter's patents began to expire, Trevithick was in position to take advantage of the nation's insatiable demand for steam power.

Trevithick shifted his interest to create a larger version for transportation purposes. On Christmas Eve 1801 he unveiled his four-wheeled steam road carriage and drove seven friends on a short jaunt in Cornwall. His locomotive comprised a cylindrical horizontal boiler with a single horizontal cylinder let into it. The piston, propelled back and forth in the cylinder by the pressure of the steam, was linked by a piston rod and connecting rod to a crankshaft bearing a large flywheel. As the engine had no condensers and dispensed steam into the air with much noise, he called the device the *Puffing Devil*. This version was only capable of going short distances because it was plagued by inefficient steam production. Nonetheless, his initial success led him to take out patents for locomotive types of the engine in 1802.

Thus encouraged, Trevithick traveled to London to meet with several potential investors and scientists. He discovered that Watt had toyed with the idea of high-pressure steam for a locomotive but had abandoned the pursuit out of fear that it posed significant safety risks and would be prone to explosions. In 1803 a company agreed to finance his experiments, and Trevithick demonstrated his locomotive in London. Unfortunately, the engine failed to pull a carriage on several occasions, and he lost backing for the project. Trevithick then obtained financial support from Samuel Homfray, owner of the South Wales Penydarren IronWorks, in Merthyr Tydfil. Homfray bet 1,000 guineas with Richard Crawshay, owner of the Cyfarthfa Ironworks, that he would have a steam engine haul ten tons of iron from his works along the Methyr Tramway to Navigation House, Abercynon. The bet was accepted and local interest heated up as Trevithick readied his engine.

In early 1804 Trevithick's device with its single vertical cylinder, eight-foot flywheel, and long piston rod was ready. On February 14th people came from far and near to witness the challenge. Five trams of iron and seventy men constituted the load. Almost immediately after departure a near disaster occurred, as the locomotive's chimney struck a low bridge and each was destroyed. According to the conditions of the bet, Trevithick had to control his locomotive and make any needed repairs without assistance.

He hurriedly cleared the debris from the tracks, repaired his chimney, and then barreled down the tramway on the nine-mile journey at five miles per hour. He reached Abercynon without further incident. However, his locomotive, even without a load, could not make the return trip because of the steep gradients and sharp curves. Furthermore, his Penydarren locomotive only made three total trips. Each time the weight of the engine broke the cast iron rails. Homfray became discouraged, and consequently he pulled his support because he believed that the engine would not reduce his transportation costs. Nonetheless, Trevithick had proven that steam locomotives were a viable possibility.

After several problems with other investors, Trevithick returned to Cornwall and constructed a new locomotive called *Catch Me Who Can*. He built a circular tramway and in the summer of 1808 charged people one shilling apiece to take a ride at twelve miles per hour on his locomotive at Euston Square in London. Unfortunately, he faced the familiar problem of the breakage of the rails and he once again had to abandon his dream. With no source of income, Trevithick worked for a company who hired him to develop a steam-powered dredger to lift waste from the bottom of the Thames River. He was paid only sixpence for every ton of waste that he raised. Thus, in 1816 he left Britain and went to work as an engineer for a silver mine in Peru. For a decade, his steam engines proved successful, and the Peruvian government eventually awarded him mining rights. With his profits he acquired a copper and silver mine of his own.

Yet, fate intervened once again. In 1826 civil war erupted in Peru and he was called up to join Simon Bolivar's army. Instead he abandoned his investments and fled to Costa Rica and then Colombia, where he came across Robert Stephenson, son of George Stephenson. Robert Stephenson was supervising construction of a railroad in Colombia and remembered that Trevithick had met him as a small boy many years earlier. Stephenson paid the destitute Trevithick's fifty-pound passage back to England.

Once home in Cornwall, Trevithick's fortunes only soured further. In 1828 the House of Commons rejected a petition to grant Trevithick a pension, despite the fact that George Stephenson and other inventors stated that his work was key to the coming of the railroads. Nonetheless, Trevithick continued to have fresh ideas such as a new propulsion system for steamboats, an improved marine boiler, a recoil gun carriage, a device to provide heat for apartments, and a massive iron column to honor the passage of the Reform Bill of 1832. None of these plans gained financial backing, and Richard Trevithick died penniless in April 1833. No funds existed to bury him. Trevithick might have been buried as a pauper but a group of local factory workers in Cornwall stepped in and raised money to provide him with an honorable church funeral.

George Stephenson and others inherited the work done by Richard Trevithick concerning the development of the early railroad locomotive and acknowledged that he was the first to demonstrate successfully the application of high-pressure steam for the purpose of transportation on land. He also proved that his engine could have sufficient traction on iron rails, albeit initially on a normal gradient and even though weight of the engine presented problems with rail breakage. His other contributions in this area were the return flue boiler, the use of the steam jet in the chimney, and the coupling of the wheels of the engine. On the other hand, he also faced threats of competing patent claims, so often the curse of the early inventors in the Industrial Revolution. He once remarked that he had been disparaged by James Watt because he advocated the use of high-powered steam.

Richard Trevithick left few written details of his work other than patent applications and several letters. Yet he slowly gained a wider recognition of his accomplishments. The contemporary encyclopedist Abram Ries highlighted Trevithick with two pages of coverage in his *Cyclopedia* published in several volumes between 1810 and 1824. Robert Stuart penned a description and made a detailed engraving of

Trevithick's locomotive in 1824. In March 1868 *The Engineering Magazine* lauded Trevithick as the mastermind behind the locomotive. That accolade was followed by a biography of the inventor published by his son Francis in 1872. Additional honors and recognition followed beginning in the 20th century. In 1934 a monument was dedicated to Richard Trevithick on the site of the famous 1804 tram way run that set the stage for future locomotive developments. It is constructed of stones and rails taken from the site of the old tram road. A second plaque in his honor is located at the Navigation House Hotel in Abercynon. In 1935 The Trevithick Society For the Preservation and Study of Cornwall's Industrial Heritage was established. The Society sponsored a 2001 recreation of Trevithick's Christmas Eve 1801 "Puffing Devil" run. Finally, in 2004 the Royal Mint cast a special coin that commemorated the 200th anniversary of Trevithick's Penydarren locomotive nine-mile journey from Merthyr to Navigation House. Despite this adulation, Richard Trevithick remains the all-but-forgotten early significant contributor to the birth of the railroad era. Despite the fact that his life ended in poverty, Trevithick himself did not seem to have regrets regarding his pursuits, as he once remarked that his life had been honored by being a useful citizen, an accomplishment that could be equaled by no sum of money.

James Watt (1736–1819)

At the opening of the Manchester Mechanics' Institute in 1825, a banker named Benjamin Heywood remarked that the steam engine was a unique example of the wedding of science and art. He was in fact paying the highest tribute to James Watt, the Scotsman who had perfected the steam engine nearly a half-century earlier. Indeed, Watt's early life, study, and application seemed to prepare him for what was arguably the most significant development of the Industrial Revolution.

As a youth, Watt dabbled in a variety of technical fields such as wood- and metal- working and harmonics (the process of constructing stringed instruments such as guitars, fiddles, and organs) and scientific disciplines such as physics, chemistry, and mechanical engineering. He absorbed as much knowledge as possible about the scientific principles of these areas and then sought their practical application. In the mid-1750s he became an instrument maker for the University of Glasgow and subsequently joined the Lunar Society of Birmingham, so-called because its members—noted leaders of science and industry—convened on evenings of the full moon (perhaps the gentlemen relied on the better light of these nights to journey home after eating and imbibing together!). This association highlights his reputation for possessing a theoretical mind rather than his technical tinkering, a trait that set him apart from many contemporary mechanics and inventors. A close friend of Watt who met the inventor in his twenties later remarked that he was more than just a specialist with machines; having learned to speak French, Italian, and German, he was also considered to be a philosopher, one with a deep love of music and poetry—a truly universal man.

Watt's achievement at Glasgow had perhaps the most dramatic impact of any other single development of the Industrial Revolution. During the winter of 1764, Watt worked to repair a model of the Newcomen engine, perhaps inspired by a lecture on steam heat that he had recently attended at the university. He quickly spotted the flaws and inadequacy inherent in the inefficient engine, which he perhaps half-jokingly claimed required a coal mine to keep it running. He envisioned a means to make the engine more efficient by using the principle of latent heat developed by one of his associates, the chemist Joe Black. Watt deduced that it took more heat to re-warm the just-cooled cylinder than to inject steam, the process then in use to alternately heat and cool the cylinder and which wasted precious time and fuel.

He repaired the Newcomen model but pondered the problem he had observed for several months. During the spring of 1765, while taking a Sunday stroll, an idea popped into his head. The solution that he needed was two cylinders, one to stay consistently hot and another connected by a pipe and valve and being kept cold to serve as the condensing chamber. Thus, the great loss of steam that Watt had observed in the Newcomen engine would be alleviated, and his device required only one fourth of the fuel. In addition, the Newcomen cylinder had been open at the top, allowing atmosphere to do all the work. Watt opted to let the steam to do the same, sealing the top of the cylinder, a move that increased the steam pressure and introduced it alternately to the top and bottom of the piston. This modification greatly increased the power and efficiency of the engine.

Watt patented his separate condenser in 1769 but could not afford to further develop his engine. After one failed partnership he joined forces with a manufacturer, entrepreneur and fellow Lunar Society member Matthew Boulton. These two were complementary, yin and yang—Watt gloomy and negative, Boulton upbeat and full of energy. What Boulton provided to Watt was invaluable—monetary support, constant encouragement, and the use of his Soho Works, a factory near Birmingham where Watt could refine his prototype into a true steam engine. His innovations included the double powerstroke, a gearing mechanism that converted reciprocal motion to rotary motion to drive machinery, a governor to regulate the engine's speed, parallel motion to keep the piston rod vertical while being driven by an oscillating iron beam (previous engines had used awkward wooden working beams, usually a fir tree), and a gauge that provided information on the pressure and volume of steam—the real indicator of the power of the machine. The pair also brought in others to help perfect their creation. One such person was ironmaster John Wilkinson, whose experience with boring cannon led to the creation of close-fitting cylinders that further reduced potential steam loss.

During the early 1780s, the British government approved a series of patents for the adjustments Watt had made to the engine. During this period, Watt and Boulton established the profitable Boulton and Watt Company. They sold their revolutionary engines to anyone willing to purchase them—from potters to beer-makers. The pair installed their first engine in a coal mine and by 1800 fifty-two mines had adopted the devices. In addition, between 1787 and 1800, Watt engines were operating in at least eighty-four cotton mills. A Cartwright loom and a rolling mill and other factory operations were also being powered by steam. Indeed, the reaction to the Watt–Boulton collaboration was electrifying. Although there were approximately 120 Newcomen engines in operation in 1769, by 1781 the Watt–Boulton engines had appeared in growing numbers in saw mills, flour mills, and other industries not only in Great Britain but on the continent as well. Indeed, Richard Arkwright, the mastermind behind the factory system, purchased one of the Watt–Boulton engines for his mill in Nottingham. Watt and Boulton maintained their monopoly until 1800, when their patents expired even though they often had to go to court during the 1780s and 1790s to contest others who attempted to pirate their engine. By 1800 about 500 Watt–Boulton engines were in operation in Great Britain, although some 1,000 Newcomen and 30 Savery models were also still in use. However, the tremendous appeal of the Watt–Boulton engine soon rendered these other rivals virtually obsolete.

By the middle of the 19th century, steam power was the norm in the industrial process, and thus standards needed to be set regarding the capacity of engines. Watt had devised a means for measuring the output of steam power. Since horses had been used for several millennia to turn cranks, the term horsepower seemed to be a common and understandable measure. Watt coined the term and equated 33,000 foot pounds per minute as 1 horsepower—one foot pound being the amount of power needed to lift a single pound (one foot). The Watt–Boulton engine had a horsepower of 7,500. By the turn of the century Great Britain's total industrial horsepower derived from steam is estimated to have been between 20,000 and 30,000 horsepower, and by the mid-19th century the country's output was 500,000 horsepower. Boulton often bragged to his potential buyers (even to Czarina Catherine of Russia) that he had a product the entire world craved: power. For the first time, manufacturing was now possible on a large, industrial scale.

However, despite the tremendous contribution that the Watt–Boulton collaboration made to the age of industrialization, one drawback remained. Their engines were stationary and used low-pressure steam because Watt was fearful that high-pressure steam posed dangers and that the boilers might explode. Thus, until the Watt–Boulton patent expired, there was a delay in converting their idea to the next level, whereby lightweight engines mounted on wheels and using high-pressure steam might be used to pull or haul wagons or cars with cargo. Therefore, in the final analysis, the introduction of the railroad would have to wait. Indeed, when the Watt–Boulton patent lapsed, Richard Trevithick, a mining engineer from Cornwall, leaped to turn stationary into mobile application for steam power. Watt, ever the naysayer, once remarked that Trevithick's proper place was at the end of a rope.

In 1800, Watt retired and spent the last years at his home, Heathfield Hall, near Birmingham, where he died in 1819. His significant contribution of the refinement of the earlier steam engine prototypes, despite his reticence to use high-power steam, along with the financial and moral support of his colleague Matthew Boulton, cannot be overemphasized. Their collaboration truly ushered in the age of steam, an era that fueled remarkable industrial and economic expansion. Indeed, the watt designation as a unit of electrical power is named in his honor.

Eli Whitney (1765–1825)

Eli Whitney was an entrepreneur who used his extraordinary technical skills to make two significant contributions to the Industrial Revolution: the invention of the cotton gin and the introduction of the use of interchangeable parts. He grew up comfortably in an agricultural family in Massachusetts. Whitney abhorred farm labor but became fascinated with the operation of the simple machines that he observed operating on the farm. He had an instinctive understanding of mechanical principles and mechanisms. At the age of fifteen he became a nail maker and was so successful he could afford to hire an assistant. During the American Revolution he delved into hat pin making and had become a major manufacturer of pins by the end of the war. Ever energetic and resourceful, Whitney worked his way through preparatory school and gained admission to Yale. He subsidized his college expenses by repairing laboratory instruments and equipment. By 1792 he had obtained a law degree.

After completing his education, under the pretext of either teaching or beginning a law practice, he journeyed south to Savannah, Georgia where he met Catherine Greene, widow of Revolutionary War hero Nathaniel Greene. She offered free board on her plantation mansion that had been a gift to her late husband from the state of Georgia, in exchange for making and repairing items around the plantation.

Cotton was the main source of income. However, removing the seeds from the ripe cotton by hand was a tedious process, as one person could clean only a single pound of cotton a day and there was much waste. Whitney's imagination worked overtime. He envisioned how the tines of a comb passed through one's hair and wondered if the same procedure might be used to remove cotton seeds from the fiber. Using his mechanical gifts, he soon constructed a device based upon the comb principle and after some experimentation had his cotton gin in operation in 1793. His horse-drawn device contained spiked teeth mounted on a revolving cylinder turned by a crank which pulled the cotton fiber through small slotted openings to separate the seed from the fiber. In addition, a rotating brush pulled the remaining fibrous lint from the spikes eliminating much of the waste that had characterized the hand process. Whitney's invention cleaned an astounding fifty pounds a day.

Whitney soon formed a partnership with Phineas Miller and returned to New Haven, Connecticut to secure a patent for his machine. He and his partner produced a number of cotton gins and installed them for local planters for a fee of 40% of their profit. Unfortunately, the new U.S. patent law was weak at this time, and attentive competitors studied the operation of the gin and easily began to replicate it. Thus, many persons infringed on Whitney's invention and he soon exhausted himself fighting copiers in court, a struggle that cost him thousands of dollars. As a result, in 1798 he turned his back on the cotton gin enterprise and did not return to it until 1807 when his 1794 patent was eventually upheld by the courts.

The cotton gin made an immediate impact. The British had brought cotton to their markets as a result of their flourishing trade with India, the Middle East, and Egypt. Whitney's invention meant that the American South, which saw cotton introduced in 1786 in Georgia, would now begin to furnish the vast majority of the crop for Great Britain's growing textile industry. For example, in 1795 the British imported 7,000 tons of cotton from the United States. That figure rose dramatically to 96,000 tons in 1836 and 550,000 tons in 1860. The yield of cotton doubled each decade after 1850. By that date the United States exported 75% of the world's cotton supply. It was quickly realized that cotton was a commodity that had an elastic demand. In other words, as the price fell or purchaser's income rose, the demand for cotton grew proportionately. Cotton could produce a light, durable fabric for a large number of domestic and public uses, particularly clothing and garments. Clothing thus underwent significant improvement in both quality and quantity during the 19th century. Consequently, the cost of personal clothing declined and people could now afford both additional clothing and cleaning and washing of the garments. Another sidelight of the cotton boom was the adoption of cotton underclothing by the masses, a luxury enjoyed only by the upper classes until this time. The cotton gin, when married with the factory system and other textile inventions, meant that cotton production was the first growth industry of the modern world.

Despite his disappointment with the invention of the cotton gin, Whitney is a fine example of how timing is everything. The U.S. government was seeking a manufacturer to produce 10,000 flintlock muskets in a two-year period. Whitney took up the challenge even though he had no experience with firearms, no labor, no factory facility, and no raw materials to use in production. It was common knowledge that the best armories of the day had not yet produced 5,000 muskets in one year.

Whitney's persistence won the contract in 1798. The government was especially intrigued by his offer of the use of interchangeable parts to manufacture and repair muskets, an approach that made their construction more standard and simple. He convinced ten investors to finance a water-powered factory in New Haven. He did not use unique machinery but devised a division of labor that employed fifty workers to make particular, individual parts through simple, easy-to-complete tasks. His project took nearly ten years to complete but it resulted in the production of 15,000 flintlocks in two years. Ever wary of his cotton gin experience, Whitney kept his gun-making process and procedures secret. He never revealed the details of factory operations, and no descriptions or drawings of his facilities have ever been found.

Whitney was also an excellent public relations man. He made his first delivery of muskets in 1801 and provided a demonstration to Congress. Also in attendance were President John Adams and President-Elect Thomas Jefferson. His demonstration consisted of fastening separate flintlock mechanisms to the same musket using only a simple screwdriver. He impressed the audience, although in the 1960s researchers studying Whitney's records of the demonstration and those same muskets now housed in the Smithsonian concluded that the affair could not have been accomplished in the manner that Whitney had claimed and therefore was likely rigged. Nonetheless, his gun-making enterprises saved the government $25,000 a year.

Regardless of his delayed cotton gin profits and in spite of his possible duping of the government, Whitney was a technical pioneer and a leading light in the Industrial Revolution. His cotton gin ensured that the burgeoning demand for cotton could be met and the industry boomed, particularly in Great Britain. On a darker note, the cotton gin meant that Southern slavery would retain its profitability, even after the end of the importation of slaves in 1808. Slaves now concentrated on the planting, maintenance and harvesting of the cotton, activities much more conducive to human labor. The number of American slaves grew from 700,000 in 1790 to two million in 1820 and ultimately to four million on the eve of the Civil War. Furthermore, Whitney's use of interchangeable parts, initially spurred by the armament needs of the young nation, eventually was adopted in the broader industrial setting and became the standard for producing a multitude of machine parts.

Like his enterprising efforts, Whitney's personal life also had its highs and lows. There is speculation that he intended to marry his landlord Catherine Greene but his business partner, Phineas Miller, offered his proposal first. He did eventually marry Henrietta Edwards, a widow twenty years his junior with three children. Whitney died at the age of 59 of an incurable abdominal ailment. His new family controlled his factory operations known as Whitney Arms Company until Winchester Repeating Arms purchased it in 1888.

Notes

1. As quoted in http://shop.cieh.org/about_the_cieh/our_history/sir_edwin_chadwick.htm

2. As quoted in "Fitch's Steamboat," *The Scientific American*, Vol. 2, No. 4 (October 17, 1846), 25.

3. Samuel F. B. Morse Papers, Collection Highlights: The Impact of the Telegraph, Library of Congress, Washington, D.C. (http://memory.loc.gov/ammem/sfbmhtml/sfbmhighlights02.html).

4. Ibid.

PRIMARY DOCUMENTS

Document 1: French Road Building

This selection provides a praiseworthy assessment of the state and maintenance of roads in France during the late 19th century. The observation is that while conditions that acted on roads in France and the United States were not entirely identical, the United States might carefully observe the detail that French officials take regarding the cost, construction techniques, and preservation of the nation's road network.

> The French road system of to-day, says the New York *Sun*, was founded by the first Napoleon and finished by the third. During the last dozen years no important new roads have been opened, and few roads of any kind, the work now required being to keep up with the network already laid out. This splendid system of highways has raised the value of lands and contributed to the national wealth by putting peasant proprietors in easy communication with their markets.
>
> Typical French roads of the highest class are those in the Departments of the Loire and the Isere. In the Isere are perpetually snow-clad Alps, 11,000 feet high, and furious glacial torrents descend upon the roads now and then. Commercial Agent Loomis, of St. Etienne, says he has seen, after a summer rain of thirty-six hours, fifty yards of national road, including a small bridge, washed away by a torrent from a cloud-capped ice field, with an almost vertical fall of 2,000 feet, and yet has found the road repaired and made passable within three hours by the road men in that remote region.
>
> Thorough construction, vigilant watching, and prompt repair are the secrets of French success with roads. They are of three kinds, national, department, and township. The general rule in rural districts is to sacrifice the straight line in order to follow the valleys as much as possible, rising by gentle grades where this is required. Side-drainage is provided for, and the

road, of course, is highest in the middle, the sides sloping transversely about an inch to the yard.

Macadamizing is the rule of construction....

...For nearly half a century the French engineers have generally used, on roadways built for heavy traffic, basaltic rock, where it can be had nearby. It cost about $1,500 for the amount used on a mile of road, and Mr. Loomis says that it is not only far better, but about 30 per cent cheaper than the crushed granite formerly so much employed.

The cost of constructing a paved roadway Mr. Loomis puts at $2.35 per square meter, with 8 cents cost per year for repair, or, on a macadamized road, from 5 to 10 cents. Keeping in mind that a kilometer is six-tenths of a mile, we learn that the average cost of building a road per kilometer is $6,600, the valley roads costing about $4,000, and those in the mountains $9,000. The annual cost of repair is $4.40 per kilometer, while that of street paving per square meter is $2.43. These small estimates for the roads are largely due to the cheapness of labor in France, an ordinary workman getting 58 cents a day; a man and horse costing $1.55; a foreman, $30 per month; a supervisor, $600 per year; an engineer, $1,000, and a head engineer $2,000.

Durability, evenness and cleanliness are the attributes which General Knowles, of Bordeaux ascribes to the French roads of his district. "They are swept and watered every day, and kept in excellent order. No rugged eminences or depressions jar the nerves of the traveler riding over them. Neither dirt, decay, nor rubbish is visible to suggest neglect or bad care...."

...When money is appropriated for a road-building contract, one per cent is retained as a fund for the widows and orphans of those who are fatally injured while working on the roadways.

It is only fair to note that the superiority of the French, to our own roads, is largely due to the trifling damage caused by frost in France compared with that which almost destroys our roads every year....

Consul Trail, of Marseilles, says the annual cost of maintaining roads outside of the city in the Department of Bouches de Rhone, which is almost the size of Delaware, is $456,000 ...

...The paving of Paris is, of course, better known here than that of the French country roads, in its variation of stone, wood, asphalt, and gravel ...

The general conclusion is that the administration and engineering skill, characteristic of France in other matters is shown also in her system of road construction, which is not less remarkable for the excellence of its original construction that for its methods of prompt and thorough repair, which are especially worthy of imitation in America.

Source: "French Road Building," *Manufacturer and Builder* (Vol. 25, No. 11, November 1893), 244–245.

Document 2: Liverpool–Manchester Railway

The maiden journey on the Liverpool–Manchester railway in 1830 was a momentous event in the history of modern transportation. George Stephenson's well-staged event demonstrated the power and speed of the locomotive, captured the imagination of the British public, and was laced with drama, excitement, and even tragedy. The following account first appeared in Smiles, *Life of George Stephenson*, published in 1860.

> At length the line was completed and ready for the public ceremony of the opening, which took place on September 30, 1830. This important event attracted a vast number of spectators from all parts of the country. Strong palings were erected for miles along the deep cuttings near Liverpool, to keep off the pressure from the multitude and prevent them from falling over in the eagerness to witness the passing trains. Constables and soldiers were there in numbers to assist in keeping the line clear. The completion of the railway was justly regarded as an important national event, and the ceremony of the opening was celebrated accordingly. The duke of Wellington, the prime minister, Sir Robert Peel, secretary of state, Mr. Huskisson, one of the members for Liverpool and an earnest supporter of the project from the commencement, were amongst the number of distinguished public personages present.
>
> Eight locomotives constructed at the Stephenson works had been delivered and placed upon the line, the whole of which had been tried and tested for weeks before with perfect success. The various trains of carriages accommodated in all about six hundred persons. The "Northumbrian" engine, driven by George Stephenson himself, headed the procession; then followed the "Phoenix," driven by Robert Stephenson; the "North Star." By Robert Stephenson, senior (brother of George); the "Rocket" by Joseph Locke; the "Dart," by Thomas L. Gooch; the "Comet," by William Allcard; the "Arrow," by Frederick Swanwick; and the "Meteor," by Anthony Harding.
>
> The procession was cheered in its progress by thousands of spectators, - through the deep ravine of Olive Mount, up to the Sutton incline, over the Sankey viaduct, beneath which a multitude of persons had assembled, carriages filling the narrow lanes and barges crowding the river; the people below gazing with wonder and admiration upon the trains which sped along far above their heads at the rate of some twenty-five miles an hour.
>
> At Parkside, about seventeen miles from Liverpool, the engines stopped to take water. Here a deplorable accident occurred to one of the most distinguished of the illustrious visitors present, which threw a deep shadow over the subsequent proceedings of the day. The "Northumbrian" engine, with the carriage, containing the duke of Wellington, was drawn up on

one line, in order that the whole of the trains might pass in review before him and his party on the other. Mr. Huskisson had unhappily alighted from the carriage and was standing on the opposite road along which the "Rocket" engine was observed rapidly coming up. At this moment the duke of Wellington, between whom and Mr. Huskisson some coolness had exited, made a sign of recognition, and held out his hand. A hurried but friendly grasp was given, and before it was loosened there was a general cry from the bystanders, "Get in, get in." Flurried and confused, Mr. Huskisson endeavored to get around the open door of the carriage, which projected over the opposite rail; but in so doing was struck down by the "Rocket," and, falling with his leg doubled across the rail, the limb was instantly crushed. His first words on being raised were, "I have met my death," which unhappily proved too true, for he expired that same evening in the neighboring parsonage of Eccles. It was cited at the same time as a remarkable fact that the "Northumbrian" engine conveyed the wounded body a distance of about fifteen miles in twenty-five minutes, or at the rate of thirty-six miles an hour. This incredible speed burst upon the world with the effect of a new and unlooked-for phenomenon ...

It was anticipated that the speed at which the locomotive could run upon the line would be about nine or ten miles an hour; but the wisest of the lawyers and the most experienced engineers did not believe this to be practicable, and they laughed outright at the idea of an engine running twenty miles an hour. But very soon after the railway opening for traffic, passengers were regularly carried the entire thirty miles between Liverpool and Manchester in little more than an hour. Two Edinburgh engineers who went to report on the railway expressed their wonder at the traveling being smoother and easier than any that had hitherto experienced, even on the smoothest turnpikes of Mr. M'Adam. "At the highest speed of twenty-five miles an hour," they said, "we could observe the passengers, among whom a good many were ladies, talking to gentlemen with the utmost *sang-froid*."

Source: Smiles, *Life of George Stephenson* (1860), as quoted in James Harvey Robinson and C. A. Beard, *Readings in Modern European History*, Vol. II (New York: Ginn & Company, 1909), 407–409.

Document 3: Life in New England

This brief article appearing in the 1840s provides an interesting and upbeat first person observation of the vibrant, bustling pace of general economic activity and the state of the transportation network that had evolved during the early stages of the Industrial Revolution in America.

A gentleman traveling in New England reports "in raptures of the wonderful enterprise of the people." "Not only in manufactures," said he, "but in every branch of trade, and especially in agriculture.... Rough roads are made as smooth as bowling alleys. When you are on the railroad, all the population seems to be traveling. When you leave the cars, and get upon the cross roads, visit the farms, or look into the shops, the whole population seems at work, and hard work, too, with their coats off and 'fourteen hours a day' toiling for their bread."

Source: "Life in New England," *The Scientific American* (Vol. 2, No. 2, October 3, 1848), 9.

Document 4: The Factory System

The modern factory system pre-dated the wave of inventions that swept first Great Britain and later the Western world in the 18th and 19th centuries. Its origins can be found in the efforts of merchants and entrepreneurs who collected several more primitive machines such as looms in one facility and hired persons to work them. Following the introduction of the inventions of persons such as Hargreaves, Arkwright, and Compton, the concept of the factory with perhaps hundreds or thousands of machines became a reality. Richard Arkwright, certainly an imaginative and energetic businessman, is often given credit for first visualizing the potential of large factory enterprises, although his detractors, such as the writer of the account below, claim he pilfered the idea from other inventors. The following selection provides a brief summary of the emergence of the factory system and the intriguing personality, contributions, and biting criticisms of Richard Arkwright.

> Hitherto the cotton manufacture had been carried on almost entirely in the houses of the workmen; the hand or stock cards, the spinning wheel, and the loom required no larger apartment than that of a cottage. A spinning jenny of small size might also be used in a cottage, and in many instances was so used; when the number of spindles was considerably increased adjacent workshops were used. But the water frame, the carding engine, and the other machines which Arkwright brought out in a finished state required both more space than could be found in a cottage and more power than could be applied by the human arm. Their weight also rendered it necessary to place them in strongly built mills, and they could not be advantageously turned by any power then known but that of water.

The use of machinery was accompanied by a greater division of labor than existed in the primitive state of the manufacture; the material went through many more processes, and, of course, the loss of time and the risk of waste would have been much increased if its removal from house to house at every stage of the manufacture had been necessary. It became obvious that there were several important advantages in carrying on the numerous operations of an extensive manufacture in the same building. Where water power was required it was economy to build one mill, and put up one water wheel rather than several. This arrangement also enabled the master spinner himself to superintend every stage of the manufacture; it gave him a greater scrutiny against the wasteful or fraudulent consumption of the material; it saved time in the transference of the work from hand to hand; and it prevented the extreme inconvenience which would have resulted from the failure of one class of workmen to perform their part, when several other classes of workmen were dependent upon them. Another circumstance which made it advantageous to have a large number of machines in one manufactory was, that mechanics must be employed on the spot to construct and repair the machinery, and that their time could not be fully occupied with only a few machines.

All these considerations drove the cotton spinners to that important change in the economy of English manufacturers, the introduction of the *factory system*; and when that system had once been adopted, such were its pecuniary advantages that mercantile competition would have rendered it impossible, even had it been desirable, to abandon it. The inquiry into the moral and social effects of the factory system will be made hereafter. At present we observe that although Arkwright, by his series of machines, was the means of giving the most wonderful extension to the system, yet he did not absolutely originate it. Mills for the throwing of silk had existed in England, though not in any great number, from the time of Sir Thomas Lombe, who, in 1719, erected a mill on the river Derwent, at Derby, on the model of those he had seen in Italy.

...Wyatt's first machines, at Birmingham, were turned by asses, and his establishment, at Northampton, by water. So, Arkwright's first mill, at Nottingham, was moved by horses; his second, at Cromford, by water. "During a period of ten or fifteen years after Mr. Arkwright's first mill was built (in 1771), at Cromford, all the principal works were erected on the falls of considerable rivers; no other power than water having then been found practically useful. There were a few exceptions, where Newcomen's and Savery's steam engines were tried. But the principles of these machines were defective and their construction bad, the expense in fuel great, and the loss occasioned by frequent stoppages ruinous"...

Arkwright was now rapidly making a large fortune, not merely by the sale of his patent machines and of licenses to use them, but much more by the profits of his several manufactories, for, having no less enterprise than judgment and skill, and being supported by large capital and very able partners, he greatly extended his concerns, and managed them all with such ability as to make them eminently prosperous. He offered the use of his patents by public advertisements, and gave many permission to use them on receiving a certain sum for each spindle. In several cases he took shares in the mills erected; and from these various sources he received a large annual tribute ...

Arkwright continued, notwithstanding, his prosperous career. Wealth flowed in upon him with a full stream from his skillfully managed concerns. For several years he fixed the price of a cotton twist, all other spinners conforming to his prices. His partnership with Messrs. Strutt terminated about 1783, and he retained the works at Cromford, still carried on by his son; while Messrs. Strutt had the woks at Belper, which are yet conducted by the surviving members of their family. In 1786 Arkwright was appointed high-sheriff of Derbyshire; and having presented an address of congratulation from that county to the king on his escape from the attempt of Margaret Nicholson on his life, Arkwright received the honor of knighthood. Sir Richard was for many years troubled with a severe asthmatic affection; he sunk at length under a complication of disorders, and died at his house at Cromford, on the 3d of August, 1792, in the sixtieth year of his age.

I have found myself compelled to form a lower estimate of the inventive talents of Arkwright than most previous writers. In the investigation I have prosecuted, I have been guided solely by a desire to ascertain the exact truth. It has been shown that the splendid inventions, which even to the present day are ascribed to Arkwright by some of the ablest and best-informed persons in the kingdom, belong in greater part to other and much less fortunate men. In appropriating those inventions as his own, and claiming them as the fruits of his unaided genius, he acted dishonorably, and left a stain upon his character, which the acknowledged brilliance of his talents cannot efface. Had he been content to claim the merit which really belonged to him, his reputation would still have been high, and his wealth would not have been diminished.

That he possessed inventive talent of a very superior order has been satisfactorily established. And, in improving and perfecting mechanical inventions, in exactly adapting them to the purposes for which they were intended, in arranging a comprehensive system of manufacturing, and in conducting vast and complicated concerns, he displayed a bold and fertile mind andconsummate judgment, which, when his want of education and the influence of an employment so extremely unfavorable to mental expansion as that of his previous life are considered, must have excited the astonishment of mankind. But the marvelous and "unbound invention" which he claimed for himself, and which has been too readily accorded to him, - the *creative faculty*, which devised all that admirable mechanism, so entirely new in its principles, and characteristic of the first order of mechanical genius—which has given a new spring to the industry of the world, and which half a century has reared up the most extensive manufacture ever known—*this* did *not* belong to Arkwright. It is clear that some of the improvements which made the carding engine what it was when he took out his second patent were devised by others; and there are two prior claimants to the invention of spinning by rollers, one of whom had undoubtedly made it the subject of a patent thirty-one years before the patent of Arkwright ...

The most marked traits in the character of Arkwright were his wonderful ardor, energy, and perseverance. He commonly labored in his multifarious concerns from five o'clock in the morning till nine at night; and when considerably more than fifty years of age—feeling that the defects of his education placed him under great difficulty and inconvenience in conducting his correspondence, and in the general management of his business—he encroached upon his sleep in order to gain an hour each day to learn English grammar, and another hour to improve his writing and orthography! He was impatient of whatever interfered with his favorite pursuits; and the fact is too strikingly characteristic not to be mentioned, that he separated from his wife not many years after their marriage, because she, convinced that he would starve his family by scheming when he should have been shaving (it will be remembered that he was a barber), broke some of his experimental models of machinery. Arkwright was a severe economist of time; and that he might not waste a moment, he generally traveled with four horses and at a very rapid speed. His concerns in Derbyshire, Lancashire, and Scotland were so extensive and numerous as to show at once his astonishing power of transacting business and his all-grasping spirit. In many of these he had partners, but he generally managed in such a way that, whoever lost, he himself was a gainer. So unbounded was his confidence in the success of his machinery, and in the national wealth to be produced by it, that he would make light of discussions on taxation, and say that *he* would pay the national debt! His speculative schemes were vast and daring; he contemplated entering into the most extensive mercantile transactions and buying up all the cotton in the world, in order to make an enormous profit by the monopoly; and from the extravagance of some of these designs his judicious friends were of opinion that if he had lived to put them into practice, he might have overset the whole fabric of prosperity!...

Source: Baines, *History of Cotton Manufacture in Great Britain* (London, 1835), as quoted in J. H. Robinson & C. A. Beard, *Readings in Modern European History*, Vol. 1 (New York: Ginn & Company, 1909), 62–67.

Document 5: Female Inventors

This interesting brief observation in an important U.S. trade journal of the 19th century illustrates that American women wholeheartedly participated in the inventive spirit of the era, although it also suggests that serious concern existed regarding how much technical education they should be permitted to pursue.

> A Massachusetts woman has recently patented a self-fastening button which needs no buttonhole, holds fast, and yet unbuttons at a touch. An Iowan woman has devised a machine for making lace with 100 bobbins—lace handkerchiefs, collars, equal to the best imported articles. If this goes on, how long will it be before the sex will be demanding admission to our industrial schools, as already to our colleges?

Source: "Female Inventors," *The Manufacturer and Builder* (Vol. 6, No. 1, January 1874), 19.

Document 6: Reminiscence: *Among Lowell Mill Girls*

In the 1820s the Lowell Mill system opened in Massachusetts. By the early 1850s, Lowell's population had swelled to 33,000, of which 10,000 laborers made up the work force in its forty mill buildings. These factories housed 10,000 looms and 320,000 spindles. One of the unique aspects of the Lowell experience was the vision of its founder, Francis Cabot Lowell, and his associates to hire large numbers of young women in the mills. These single women, usually aged fifteen to twenty-five years but some as young as thirteen, came to the mills on a one- to three-year employment before returning home to marry. They lived according to strict regulations that dictated work, residence in boarding houses, and church attendance, rules intended to maintain both the productivity and the morals of the work force. Life for these women was essentially positive, although on several occasions in the 1830s they staged vocal public protests against the reduction in their wages. The selection below is a reflection of one woman's experience at Lowell. It should be emphasized that she did not mention the unrest but rather focused on the nature of the young women and the opportunities offered to them while employed in the factories. One point of interest was the mention of the visit to Lowell by Charles Dickens, whose observation of its life was a striking contrast to his opinion of contemporary British factory conditions.

> ...The place was named for Mr. Francis Cabot Lowell, whose improvements of the power-loom were such as to make him practically its inventor, and who was the originator of the cotton cloth manufacture, as now carried on in America. It is interesting to think of the cultured Boston gentleman in the seclusion of the room he had taken for his work, ... perfecting the details of his loom, and at the same time developing plans by which this new branch of industry should be made pleasant and remunerative to his countrymen, but more especially to his countrywomen, whose assistance he looked for in carrying out his project, In this connection arose questions which a man of large-hearted humanity, like Mr. Lowell could not but weigh with utmost care, as they concerned the well-being of those he meant to employ....
>
> Mr. Nathan Appleton, who was closely associated with Mr. Lowell, thus reports the result of their conferences on a point which justly gave them some anxiety.
>
> Here was in New England a fund of labor, well-educated and virtuous. The operatives of in the manufacturing cities of Europe were notoriously of the lowest character for intelligence and morals. The question, therefore, arose, and was deeply considered, whether this degradation was the result of the peculiar occupation, or of other and distinct causes. We could not perceive why this peculiar description of labor should vary, in its effects upon character, from all other occupations. The fund of labor, referred to by Mr. Appleton, meant the younger people of the rural districts, scattered abroad in villages and lonely farmhouses, who were, he says, induced to these mills for a temporary period. They were chiefly the young women of the land, who had been brought up to earn their own living in the fear and love of God, as their fathers and mothers had done before them.... A girl's opportunities for earning money were few, and the amount received was small for such employments as straw-braiding, binding shoes, and domestic labor. An occupation as easy as any of these, with a larger compensation, could now be offered her, and the project seemed to promise benefit to all concerned, while it would undoubtedly give the business of the country an unprecedented impetus.

...It was absurd to think that, as employments, their character could be intrinsically changed by the use of machinery, or by the bringing together of numerous worthy young women form country homesteads to pursue them socially in the mills.

The important thing would be, to keep the surroundings of any community thus formed free from all that could be harmful to personal character, and to leave it open in every direction to pure and healthful influences ... his first care was to place such guards around the every-day life of these young countrywomen of his as they would naturally find in their own homes. The corporation boarding system was to be established upon this idea. The houses were to be rented to matrons of assured respectability, many of whom would bring their own daughter with them....

... no immoral person was to be admitted to employment in the mills. In brief, these young girls were to be assured of an unobjectionable occupation, the privileges and wholesome restrictions of home, and a moral atmosphere as clear and bracing as that of the mountains from whose breezy slopes many of them were to come....

The cotton mill itself, as known in this country, was an original idea of Mr. Lowell. In Great Britain, the weaving, spinning, and so forth were done each as a separate business. His plan, adopted everywhere, was to have the raw cotton taken in from the picker on the lower floor of the mill, ascend in regular order through the processes of carding, spinning, and dressing, and come out of the weaving room in the upper story, finished cloth....

My mother's widowhood was the occasion of her removal to Lowell. Left without any means of maintenance for her large family, she bethought herself of the new manufacturing town ... she decided ... to go there and take charge of one of the boarding-houses....

A few young girls had followed my mother from our own neighborhood, but the most who lived with us were natives of Vermont or New Hampshire or Maine ... there was always a large preponderance in the community of intelligent and interesting young women....

The home life of the mill-girls as I knew it in my mother's family was nearly like this. Work began at five o'clock on summer mornings and at daylight in the winter. Breakfast was eaten by lamplight, during the cold in winter; in summer an interval of half an hour was allowed for it, between seven and eight o'clock. The time given for the noon meals was between half to three quarters of an hour. The only hours of leisure were from half past seven or eight to ten in the evening, the mills closing a little earlier on Saturdays. It was an imperative regulation that lights should be out at ten. During those two evening hours ... they gathered around the tables and sewed, and read, and wrote, and studied ... They made and mended all their own clothing—often doing a good deal of unnecessary fancy work besides. They took books from libraries; went to singing-schools, conference meetings, concerts and lectures; watched at night by a sick girl's bedside, and did double work for her in the mill, if necessary; and on Sundays they were at church, not difference in appearance from other well-dressed and decorous young women. Strangers who had been sitting beside them in a house of worship were often heard to ask, on coming out, But where were the factory-girls?

Lowell was eminently a church-going place.... The mill-girls not only cheerfully paid their pew-rents, but gave their earnings to be built into the walls of new churches, as the population increased. Their contributions to social and foreign charities also were noticeably liberal. What they did for their own families keeping a little sister at school, sending a brother to college, lifting the burden of a homestead debt from a parents old age was done so frequently and so quietly as to pass without comment....

While yet a child, I used to consider it special good fortune that my home was at Lowell. There was a frank friendliness and sincerity in the social atmosphere that wrought upon me unconsciously, and made the place pleasant to live in. People moved about their every-day duties with purpose and zest, and were genuinely interested in one another....

No child was continuously kept at work in the mills. The rule requiring all under thirteen years of age to go to school three months in the year was strictly enforced.... We were never unkindly treated. We had homes and careful guardianship; none of us knew what real poverty meant; and everything about us was educating us to become true children of the republic....

Whatever influence stirred the country deeply, moved us also. In the anti-slavery reform, especially, many were intensely interested. Petitions for the abolition of slavery in the District of Columbia grew yards in length, as they circulated through the mills. With some of the older ones, the question now and then pressed close, whether it was right to be at work upon the material so entirely the product of slave labor as cotton. But since the cloth woven from it was supposed to worn by the most zealous antislavery agitators, the question was allowed to pass as one too complicated for us to decide....

Lowell was one of the towns a foreign traveler in New England usually visited, as a matter of course. Charles Dickens came there in 1842, and made a report of his observations in the American Notes. The contrast between life in Lowell and in the great manufacturing towns of England he speaks of as the contrast between good and evil, the living light and the deepest shadow.... He mentions three things about the mill-girls at Lowell which he thought would strike his countrymen as remarkable: that some of them had pianos in their boarding-houses, that they subscribed to circulating libraries, and that they published a magazine among themselves, filled with original articles.... Mr. Dickens was pleased with his visit and writes, I solemnly declare that from all the crowd I saw in the different factories that day I cannot recall or separate one young face that gave me a painful impression.... He afterwards adds a paragraph which contains one significant fact in the life of the Lowell mill-girls; there is not manufacturing population in Lowell, so to speak: for these girls come from other States, remain a few years in the mills, and then go home for good.

And so it was. The girls always looked upon their life in the mills as a temporary one.... To the appellation mill-girl, or factory-girl, there is no objection, as indicating an occupation for the time being.... The young girls at work in the Lowell Mills were certainly not a class.... Certainly we mill-girls did not regard our own lot as an easy one, but we had accepted its fatigues and discomforts as unavoidable, and could forget them in struggling forward to what was before us. The charm of our life is that it had both outlook and outlet. We trod a path full of commonplace obstructions, but there were no difficulties in it we could not hope to overcome, and the effort to conquer them was in itself a pleasure.... To be identified with those who have won from a commonplace industry the means of making themselves and others happier, wiser, and better is reason for gratitude not unmixed with pride.

Source: "Among Lowell Mill Girls: A Reminiscence," *The Atlantic Monthly* (Vol. 48, No. 289, November 1881), 593–612.

Document 7: Thomas Hood, "Song of the Shirt"

Thomas Hood was a popular 19th-century English novelist and humorist. His works fall into both the Romantic and Victorian eras. After ill health forced him to turn to writing, he held positions as the subeditor or editor for several publications and in these roles gained an introduction to a number of important British literary figures of his time. In 1834 he published a popular novel, *Tylney Hall*. After 1840 he founded *Hood's Monthly Magazine*, a periodical that his son continued to publish following Hood's death. His most famous work is "The Song of the Shirt," a biting commentary on the dire conditions and exploitation in the British textile industries. In 1843 this work was initially published anonymously in *Punch*, the new British satirical magazine. It subsequently found an audience abroad in newspapers in the United States, German states, Italy, France, and Russia, all areas that were in the initial stages of industrialization. The selection below was part of a sermon preached in Syracuse, New York in 1845.

With fingers weary and worn,
With eyelids heavy and red,
A woman sat, in unwomanly rags,
Plying her needle and thread—
Stitch! Stitch! Stitch!
In poverty, hunger, and dirt,
And still with a voice of dolorous pitch
She sang the "Song of the Shirt."

"Work! Work! Work!
While the cock is crowing aloof!
And work—work—work,
Till the stars shine through the roof!
It's Oh! To be a slave
Along with the barbarous Turk,
Where woman has never a soul to save,"
If this is Christian work!

"Work—work—work,
Till the brain begins to swim,
Work—work—work,
Till the eyes are heavy and dim!
Seam, and gusset, and band,
Band, and gusset, and seam,
Till over the buttons I fall asleep,
And saw them in a dream!

"Oh, Men, with Sister dear!
Oh, men, with Mothers and Wives!
It is not linen you're wearing out.
But human creatures' lives!
Stitch—stitch—stitch,
In poverty, hunger and dirt,
Sewing at once, with a double thread,
A Shroud as well as a shirt.
But why do I talk of Death?
That phantom of grisly bone,
I hardly fear its terrible shape,
It seems so like my own –
It seems so like my own,

Because of the fasts I keep,
Oh, God! That bread should be so dear
And flesh and blood so cheap.

"Work—work—work!
My labour never flags;
And what are its wages? A bed of straw,
A crust of bread—and rags.
That shattered rood—this naked floor—
A table—a broken chair—
And a wall so blank, my shadow I thank
For sometimes falling there!
"Work—work—work!
From weary chime to chime,
As prisoners work for crime!
Band, and gusset, and seam,
Seam, and gusset, and band,
Till the heart is sick, and the brain benumbed,
As well as the weary hand.

"Work—work—work,
In the dull December light,
And work—work—work,
When the weather is warm and bright—
While underneath the eaves
The brooding swallows cling
As if to show me their sunny backs
And twit me with the spring.

"Oh! But to breathe the breath
Of the cowslip and primrose sweet—
With the sky above my head,
And the grass beneath my feet;
For only one short hour
To feel as I used to feel,
Before I knew the woes of want
And the walk that costs a meal!

"Oh! But for one short hour!
A respite forever brief!
No bless and leisure for Love or Hope,
But only time for Grief!
A little weeping would ease my heart,
But I their briny bed
My tears must stop, for every drop
Hinders needle and thread!"

With fingers weary and worn,
With eyelids heavy and red,
A woman sat in unwomanly rags,
Plying her needle and thread—

Stich! Stitch! Stitch!
In poverty, hunger, and dirt,
And still with a voice of dolorous pitch,—
Would that its tone could reach the Rich!—
She sang this "Song of the Shirt!"

Source: "The Rights and Conditions of Women," a sermon preached in Syracuse, NY, November, 1845, by S. J. May (cited in http://memory.loc.gov/cgi-bin).

Document 8: A Review of Japanese Industrial Advance

The following selection provided by a Japanese official is a brief summary of the phenomenal economic and industrial progress that Japan had achieved by the turn of the 20th century. The leap from a feudal to modern society in the space of less than a half century won the admiration and acclaim of the Western world.

> The first line of railway was constructed between Tokyo and Yokohama, eighteen miles, in 1872. Since that time the government railroads have been yearly extended at a varying rate of increase. The first private line was built in 1883, and covered sixty-three miles.... In 1890 we had 551 miles of government lines and 896 miles of private lines—total 1447 miles. Since the war with China marked development has been made, and in 1901 there were 1059 miles of government lines and 2966 miles of private lines—a total of 4025 miles....
>
> In 1890 or 1891 the weaving industry did not show any marked development, and the value of goods woven was about 30,000,000 or 40,000,000 yen. But recently, aided by the progress of applied chemistry, and also of technology, the industry has made considerable progress, and in 1899 its product was valued at 150,000,000 yen. During ten years the increase has been more than fourfold. Now, with the manufacture of cotton-yarn, it has become one of the principal industries of the empire.
>
> The cotton-spinning industry had its origin in 1880 or 1881, and developed gradually until, in 1890, the total number

of spindles reached 277,895, producing 5,132,588 kwan (about 42,000,000 pounds) of cotton yarn. But since, in 1894, the duty on exports of cotton yarn, and in April, 1896, that on the import of raw cotton, were removed, the industry made marked progress, and in 1901 the number of spindles in use daily reached 1,181,762, and the productive capacity had increased to 33,323,770 kwan (nearly 275,000,000 pounds). To-day cotton spinning has become the chief industry of the country.

Source: Stead (ed.), *Japan by the Japanese* (New York, 1904), as quoted in Robinson & Beard, *Readings in Modern European History*, Vol. II (New York: Ginn & Company, 1909), 430–431.

Document 9: Extracts from a Parliamentary Report on Child Labor

Before the end of the 18th century a number of reformers began to report on the plight of children, many as young as five or six years old, who worked in the growing number of factories and mills in Great Britain. These children labored long hours for little pay and often faced the wrath of the overseers of their work. By the early 19th century, Parliament appointed a number of commissions to interview the children who toiled in the mills and their family members to study the actual conditions under which they labored and determine appropriate reform measures to consider. The following excerpts come from an 1833 Parliamentary report on child labor.

> *The father of two children in a mill at Lenton deposed as follows:*
> My two sons (one ten, the other thirteen) work at Milne's factory at Lenton. They go to the mill at half past five in the morning; don't stop at breakfast or tea time. They stop at dinner at half an hour. Come home at a quarter before ten. They used to work till ten, sometimes eleven, sometimes twelve. They earn between them 6 s., 2d. per week. One of them, the eldest, worked at Wilson's for two years, at 2s., 3d. per week. He left because the overseer beat him and loosened a tooth for him. I complained, and they turned him away for it. They have been gone to work sixteen hours now; they will be very tired when they come home at half past nine. I have a deal of trouble to get them up in the morning. I have been obliged to beat 'em with a strap in their shirts, and to pinch 'em, in order to get them well awake. It made me cry to be obliged to do it.

Did you make them cry?

Yes, sometimes. They will be home soon, very tired; and you will see them.

I (i.e. the government inspector) preferred walking towards the factory to meet them. I saw the youngest only, and asked him a few questions, He said, "I'm sure I shan't stop to talk to you; I want to go home and get to bed; I must be up at half past five again to-morrow morning."

A family in the same town of Lento gave the following evidence:

The boy: I am going fourteen; my sister is eleven. I have worked in Milne's factory two years. She goes there also. We are both in the clearing room. I think we work too long hours; I've been badly with it. We go at half past five; give over at half past nine. I am now just come home. We sometimes stay till twelve. We are obliged to work over-hours. I have 4 s. a week; that is for staying from six to seven. The pay for overhours [sic] besides. I asked to come away one night lately, at eight o'clock, being ill; I was told, if I went I must not come again. I am not well now. I can seldom eat breakfast; my appetite is very bad, I have had a bad cold for a week.

Father: I believe him to be ill from being overworked. My little girl came home the other day cruelly beaten. I took her to Mr. Milnes; did not see him, but showed Mrs. Milnes the marks. I thought of taking it before a magistrate, but was advised to let it drop. They might have turned both my children away. That man's name is Blagg; he is always strapping the children. I shan't let the boy go there much longer; I shall try to apprentice him; it's killing him by inches; he falls asleep over his food at night. I saw an account of such things in the newspapers, and thought how true it was of my own children.

Mother: I have worked in the same mills myself. The same man was there then. I have seen him behave shocking to the children. He would take 'em by the hair of the head and drag 'em about the room. He has been there twelve years. There's [sic] many young ones in that hot room. There's six of 'em badly now, with bad eyes and sick headache. The boy of ours has always been delicate from a child. His appetite is very bad now; he does not eat his breakfast sometimes for two or three days together. The little girl bears it well; she is healthy. I would prefer their coming home at seven, without additional wages. The practice of working overhours [sic] has been constantly pursued at Milne's factory.

Source: Reports of Commissioners (1833): Factories, XX, as quoted in Robinson & Beard, *Readings in Modern European History*, Vol. II (New York: Ginn & Company, 1909), 283–285.

Document 10: The Opening of Japan

The torrid pace of continental expansion by the United States in the 1830s and 1840s had brought the nation to the California and Oregon shores and cast her gaze across the Pacific Ocean. In 1852 Commodore Matthew C. Perry, commander of the U.S. Navy East India Squadron, received orders to conduct operations in the Pacific for the purpose of surveying the China seas, Northern Pacific, and the Bering Straits and make direct contact with areas such as China and Japan, which had the potential of increased trading prospects with the United States. The contact had a great impact on both countries, but most specifically Japan. The latter experienced a political and cultural struggle that brought Japan into the modern era and resulted in that nation becoming a major industrial power in the space of just a few generations. The selections below are excerpted from the Secretary of the Navy Reports for the years 1852 to 1854 and provide a glimpse at the operational goals of Perry's fleet. Note that a slight hint of European and American smugness and superiority finds expression in portions of the reports.

Secretary of the Navy Report 1852

... During the past year the attention of this department, in conjunction with the Department of State, has been directed to the employment of the East India squadron in an enterprise of the great moment to the commercial interests of the country—the endeavor to establish relations of amity and commerce with the Empire of Japan.

... The extension of the domain of the United States to the shores of the Pacific, the rapid settlement of California and Oregon, the opening of the highway across the isthmus of Central America, the great addition of our navigation employed in trade with Asiatic nations, and the increased activity of our whaling ships in the vicinity of the northern coasts of Japan, are now pressing upon the consideration of this government the absolute necessity of reviewing our relations to those Eastern communities which lie contiguous to the path of our trade....

... That Oriental sentiment which, hardened by the usage and habit of centuries, has dictated the inveterate policy of national isolation in Japan, it is very apparent, will not long continue to claim the sanctity of a national right to the detriment of the cause of universal commerce and civilization, at this time so signally active in enlarging the boundaries of human knowledge and the diffusion of comfort over the earth. The day has come when Europe and America have found an urgent inducement to demand of Asia and Africa the rights of hospitality, of aid and comfort, shelter and succor, to the men who pursue the great highroads of trade and exploration over the globe....

The government of the United States has happily placed itself in the front of this movement; and it may be regarded as one of the most encouraging guarantees of its success, that the expedition which has just left our shores takes with it the earnest good wishes, not only of our own country, but of the most enlightened communities of Europe. The opening of Japan has become a necessity, which is recognized in the commercial adventure of all Christian nations, and is deeply felt by every owner of an American whale-ship, and every voyager between California and China.

The important duty has been consigned to the commanding officer of the East India squadron, a gentleman in every respect worthy of the trust reposed in him, and who contributes to its administration the highest energy and ability, improved by long and various service in his profession....

Secretary of the Navy Report 1853

... Commodore Perry was intrusted [sic] with the delicate task of endeavoring to open commercial intercourse with the Japanese government. After visiting several smaller islands and having favorable interviews with their inhabitants, he proceeded with the steams *Mississippi* and *Susquehanna*, and the sloops-of-war *Saratoga* and *Plymouth* to Yedo [sic] Bay, in Japan, where he arrived on the 8th of July last. After much effort, he succeeded in having an interview with one of the ministers of state, delivered in person a communication from the President of the United States proposing to form commercial relations with Japan, gave notice of his intention to return in the ensuing spring for a reply to his proposition....

Secretary of the Navy Report 1854

... Commodore Perry, with the steam-frigate *Powhatan*, as his flag-ship, ... arrived at Yedo [sic] Bay, Japan, on the 13th of February, for the purpose of fulfilling the plans of which he had notified them the year before, and endeavoring to establish commercial relations between Japan and the United States. By indomitable perseverance and remarkable management, he succeeded in finally overcoming the obstinacy and prejudices of the Japanese government, and induced it to enter into a treaty of amity and peace, by which two of its ports, Hakodade and Simoda, were opened to vessels, and shipwrecked mariners of American vessels are guaranteed to have ample protection and kind treatment on whatever part of the coasts they may be cast. The above-mentioned ports were fully surveyed by our vessels, and are represented to be very convenient and commodious. Presents were also exchanged between the Japanese government and the United States....

Source: *Report of the Secretary of the Navy, December 4, 1852* (Washington, D.C., 1852); *Report of the Secretary of the Navy, December 5, 1853* (Washington, D.C., 1853); *Report of the Secretary of the Navy, December 4, 1854* (Washington, D.C., 1854), Department of the Navy, Navy Historical Center, Washington, D.C. (http://history.navy.mil/bios/perry_mc_secnav.html)

Document 11: Gifts for the Emperor

Upon the conclusion of the negotiations with Japan in 1854, Commodore Matthew C. Perry's expedition, on behalf of the United States government, offered a number of interesting practical and elegant gifts to the Japanese Emperor, his wife, and leading members of the government. The following items represent a partial list of the gifts for some of the leading Japanese officials.

For the Emperor
Steam Engine and track
Telegraph
Audobon's birds
Colt's Revolver
Telescope
U.S. weights, measures & balances
Natural History of New York
Agricultural instruments
a stove
Box of Marichino
Box of Champagne
Barrel Whiskey
1 Box Tea

For the Empress
Flowered silk dress
Velvet Dress
Ladies Toilet box, guilded
One dozen bottles of essence

For the Commissioner Hayashi
Audonbon's Quadrupeds

Ivory Longnette
Rifle
Cotton Cloth
Clock
20 gallon Whiskey
Revolver
Tea Set for his Lady
Box of Champagne
1 box of cherry cordial
1 box Tea

For the First Councillor
Schoolcrafts Indians
Revolver & Rifle & Sword
Box of Cherry Cordial
5 Gal. Whiskey
1 Box Tea
1 Stove
1 Clock
Surf Boat

Source: List of Presents for the Emperor, Department of the Navy, Navy Historical Center, Washington, D.C. (http://www.history.navy.mil/biblio/biblio3/perry_gift.htm)

Document 12: "The Excursion"

William Wordsworth was one of the prominent Romantic poets who praised the power and beauty of nature. He published this poem in 1814 at a point in time when the Industrial Revolution was making its visible impact on Great Britain. Wordsworth's words paint a graphic picture of how the appearance of industrialization had begun to disfigure the British landscape, and he deeply mourns the disappearance of the rural and tranquil countryside he so admired.

Meanwhile, at social Industry's command
How quick, how vast an increase. From the germ
Of some poor hamlet, rapidly produced
Here a huge town, continuous and compact
Hiding the face of earth for leagues—and there,
Where not a habitation stood before,
Abodes of men irregularly massed
Like trees in forests, spread through spacious tracts.
O'er which the smoke of unremitting fires

Hangs permanent, and plentiful as wreaths
Of vapor glittering in the morning sun.
And, wheresoe'er the traveler turns his steps
He sees the barren wilderness erased,
Or disappearing, triumph that proclaims
How much the mild Directness of the plough
Owes to alliance with these new-born arts!
Hence is the wide seas peopled—hence the shores
Of Britain are resorted to by ships
Freighted from every climate of the world
With the world's choicest produce. Hence that sum
Of keels that rest within her crowded ports
Or ride at anchor in her sounds and bays;
That animating spectacle of sails
That, through her inland regions, to and fro
Pass with the respirations of the tide,
Perpetual, multitudinous!
I grieve when on the darker side
Of this great change I look; and there behold
Such outage done to nature as compels
The indignant power to justify herself;
Yea, to avenge her violated rights.
For England's bane.

Source: W. Wordsworth, "The Excursion," in W. Knight, L.L.D, ed., *Poetical Works* (Edinburgh: William Paterson, 1884), http://www.gutenberg.org/ebooks/10219

Document 13: Two Views of France in the 1780s

Arthur Young, the noted British agriculturalist, and Thomas Jefferson, the prominent member of the new American government, both journeyed to France in the late 18th century and recorded their observations of the conditions in France on the eve of the French Revolution. The first account below is Arthur Young's observation of conditions in Brittany in the fall of 1788 and along the Marne River in the summer of 1789, while the second is taken from a letter of Thomas Jefferson written while he was in Nice in the spring of 1788. Their views offer a stark contrast of opinion regarding the health and state of the French nation, which was on the verge of great political, economic, and social peril. The French Revolution and Napoleonic eras would consume the energy of the nation and delay the onset of the Industrial Revolution for more than a generation.

Arthur Young

To Combourg. The country has a savage aspect; husbandry not much further advanced, at least in skill, than among the Hurons, which appears incredible amidst inclosures [sic]. The people almost as wild as their country, and their town of Combourg one of the most brutal, filthy places that can be seen; mud houses, no windows, and a pavement so broken as to impede all passengers, but ease none. Yet here is a chateau, and inhabited....

To Montauban. The poor people seem so poor indeed; the children terribly ragged—if possible, worse clad than if with no clothes at all; as to shoes and stockings, they are luxuries. A beautiful girl of six or seven years playing with a stick, and smiling under such a bundle of rags as made my heart ache to see her. They did not beg, and when I gave them anything seemed more surprised than obliged. One third of what I have seen of this province seems uncultivated, and nearly all of it in misery. What have kings, and ministers, and parliaments, and States to answer; for their prejudices, seeing millions of hands that would be industrious idle and starving through the execrable maxims of despotism, or the equally detestable prejudice of a feudal nobility.

To Chateau Thiery ... I asked for a coffeehouse—not one in the town ... and not a newspaper to be seen by a traveler, even in a moment when all ought to be in anxiety. What stupidity, poverty, and want of circulation! ... To those who have been used to travel amidst the energetic and rapid circulation of wealth, animation, and intelligence of England, it is not possible to describe in words adequate to one's feelings the dullness and stupidity of France.

Thomas Jefferson

In the great cities I go to see what travelers think alone worthy of being seen; but I make a job of it and generally gulp it all down in a day. On the other hand, I am never satiated with rambling through the fields and farms, examining the culture and cultivators with a degree of curiosity which makes some take me for a fool, and others to be much wiser than I am. I have been pleased to find among the people a less degree of physical misery than I had expected. They are generally well clothed and have a plenty of food—not animal, indeed, but vegetable, which is just as wholesome. Perhaps they are overworked, the excess of the rent required by the landlord obliging them to too many hours of labor in order to produce that and wherewith to feed and clothe themselves. The soil of Burgundy and Champagne I have found more universally good than I had expected; and as I could not help making a comparison with England, I found that comparison more unfavorable to the latter than is generally admitted. The soil, the climate, and the productions are superior to those of England, and the husbandry as good except in one point, that of manure....

Source: A. Young, *Travels in France during the Years 1787, 1788, 1789* and *Works of Jefferson* (Ford, ed.), as quoted in Robinson & Beard, *Readings in Modern European History*, Vol. I (New York: Ginn & Company, 1909), 232–234.

Document 14: Robert Fulton's Voyage of *Clermont*

The rapid advance in transportation that occurred in the 19th century took a great leap forward with the famous trip of Robert Fulton's steamboat, the *Clermont*, from New York to Albany and back in 1807. His heralded journey proved the application of steam power to transportation and inspired a wave of steamship production that soon saw the rivers of America bustling with this new transportation technology. The following is a letter written by Robert Fulton to the editor of the *American Gazette* in September 1807 and recounts his momentous experimental trip and expresses his hope for the future success of steam power.

New York, September 15, 1807
Sir,
I arrived this afternoon, at four o'clock, I the steamboat from Albany. As the success of my experiment gives me great hopes that such boats may be rendered of great importance to my country, to prevent erroneous opinions and give some satisfaction to the friends of useful improvements, you will have the goodness to publish the following statement of facts:

I left New York on Monday at one o'clock, and arrived at Clermont, the seat of Chancellor Livingston, at one o'clock on Tuesday—time, twenty-four hours; distance one hundred and ten miles. On Wednesday I departed from the chancellor's at nine in the morning, and arrived in Albany at five in the afternoon—distance, forty miles; time, eight hours. This sum is one hundred and fifty miles in thirty-two hours, equal to near five miles an hour.

On Thursday, at nine o'clock in the morning, I left Albany, and arrived at the chancellor's at six in the evening; I started from thence at seven, and arrived at New York at four in the afternoon—time, thirty hours; space run through, one hundred and fifty miles, equal to five miles an hour. Throughout my whole way, both going and returning, the wind was ahead; no

advantage could be derived from my sails; the whole has therefore been performed by the power of the steam engine.
    I am, sir, your obedient servant,
Robert Fulton

Source: Reigert, *The Life of Robert Fulton* (1856), as quoted in Robinson & Beard, *Readings in Modern European History*, Vol. II (New York: Ginn & Company, 1909), 406–407.

Document 15: Opposition to the Ten-Hour Bill

In the first half of the 19th century the British Parliament enacted a large number of bills intended to improve the working conditions in the nation's factories, mills, and mines. In 1847 a measure was passed that prevented women and children from working more than ten hours a day. There was a fierce debate in Parliament prior to its passage, one that reflected the larger political struggle occurring in Great Britain between the more established landowners and the rising and influential manufacturing class. The former supported the bill, and the latter opposed it. The leading spokesman for the opposition was John Bright, who advanced the argument that Parliament should refrain from interference in such matters as the manufacturers themselves would certainly take the lead in reforming the conditions in the factories, mills, and mines. The following is a description of John Bright's approach in addressing his fellow members of Parliament on the issue.

> No one (the speaker said) would accuse him of a want of sympathy with the working classes; but this he would tell the House, that if they went on, at the bidding of the working classes, to legislate against the capitalists, they would find a very different feeling engendered among the latter towards the operatives, from which they now exhibited.... (In his own factory) they had a large infant school, together with a reading room and news room, and a school for adults, where the workmen attended after working hours. They had also a person employed, at a very considerable expense, who devoted his whole time to investigating the concerns of the workmen, and who was a kind of missionary among them. Not a few hundreds of pounds per annum were expended in promoting in this manner the interests of the workmen, and that, too, wholly independent of any act of the legislature. This was the case at many other wealthy factories; but he would warn the House that if they now armed the workmen against the capitalists by fixing by law ten hours, or

any other number of hours for the duration of labor, and thus interfered with the established custom of the kingdom, he believed it would be impossible that the feeling which hitherto existed on the part of the manufacturers towards the operatives would continue, should the workmen think that by coming to that House they could fix the time of work and the amount of wages. He thought, if such a result took place, that it would be the duty of the manufacturers—nay, that it would be absolutely necessary for them—to take such steps as would prevent the ruin from coming upon them which must result from the passing of this measure.

He would not detain the House further; but believing, as he did in his heart, that this proposition was most injurious and destructive to the best interests of the country; believing that it was contrary to all the principles of sound legislation, that it was a delusion practiced upon the working classes, that it was advocated by those who had no knowledge of the economy of manufactures; believing that it was one of the worst measures ever passed in the shape of an act of the legislature, and that, demands alike of the workmen and of the masters would compel them to retrace the steps they had taken; believing this, he felt compelled to give the motion for the second reading of this bill his most strenuous opposition.

Source: Hansard, *Parliamentary Debates* (3rd series), LXXXIX, as quoted in Robinson & Beard, *Readings in Modern European History*, Vol. II (New York: Ginn & Company, 1909), 285–286.

Document 16: The First Canal in America

The canal building age in America began in the late 18th century. The burst of construction continued for nearly four decades until the arrival of the steam-powered railroad system provided a more flexible, skeletal network for the transportation of goods and people over the vast stretches of the growing nation. However, it should be remembered that canals remained important to the economy, particularly in specific areas of the country, for more than a century following their first appearance on the scene. The following selection pays tribute to the significant role that canals continued to play in the nation's life in the late 19th century.

> The growing preservation and extension of our artificial waterways makes it of interest to note that July 19th was the one hundredth anniversary of the completion of the first canal in

America. It was in 1792 that Massachusetts had the honor of building the first artificial waterway, and although the canal was but five miles in length, it was a monument of the greatest importance. The object of the construction of this canal was to avoid the rapids at South Hadley. Another canal was shortly afterward built to avoid the Montagu Falls. These canals were the beginning of our national canal system and will always be famous. They are not now used.

It was fully a quarter of a century later that the Erie canal [sic] was built. Those opposed called it the "De Witt Clinton Ditch," owing to the fact that Governor Clinton was the sponsor of the movement. The canal was built in 1817, and was opened to navigation in 1825. The original cost was $8,000,000, but since then the State has spent nearly $90,000,000 on it. During the sixty-seven years of its existence, the income of the canal amounted to over $123,000,000. It is 300 miles in length, and was the first great enterprise of the kind carried out in the United States. Today we have 4,000 miles of canals in the country.

Source: "The First Canal in America," *Manufacturer and Builder* (Vol. 24, No. 11, November 1892), 242.

Document 17: Immigration

Immigration has been a significant issue in the American experience since the early days of the Republic. The wave of immigration that began in the 1840s gained renewed momentum following the Civil War and continued throughout the remainder of the 19th century. Europeans tended to dominate the immigrant pool entering the eastern shores of the United States. The selection below provides a brief snapshot and comparison of the source and numbers of European immigrants entering the country in a partial two-year span in the 1890s. Although the pace of immigration in this particular period had slowed for some nationalities, the numbers nonetheless speak to a continued steady stream of persons seeking a fresh start and new opportunity in the United States.

The stream of immigrants does not quite equal that of last year. In April, 1892, there came into the country 90,595 people; in April this year there came 75,261. So for the four months ending with April, the arrivals last year were 188,599, and this year 145,299. In certain nationalities there has been quite a falling off; for example, the following figures are for the four months of last year and this year:

	January–April 1892	January–April 1893
Germany	39,230	27,064
Poland	10,717	2,270
Russia	22,809	8,247
Austria-Hungary	28,012	15,174

The arrivals from Italy are somewhat greater, having risen from 24,969 to 26,422, and those from the United Kingdom have increased from 28,103 to 33,624.

Source: "Immigration in April," *Manufacturer and Builder* (Vol. 25, No. 7, July 1893), 143.

Document 18: Crime in America

In the late 19th century the rising rate of crime became a significant concern. Although a number of reasons were advanced for the increase, the most frequently cited ones were the density of population in America's urban areas, the continued influx of immigrants, and the dislocation and changes that modern industrial and commercial activities had wrought on the nation's society. The author, citing statistics from four U.S. census [sic] reports, below pines for the idyllic rural life of yesteryear and argues that city life and its new preoccupations had shattered the traditional family and moral underpinning of the country and contributed immeasurably to the increased crime rate in America.

Buckle in the first volume of the "History of Civilizations," assumes that crime among men is a fixed quantity, varying only with population. Whatever may be the truth as to the human race, doubts will arise when we consider any particular portion of that race. Our inquiry of census reports leads to the conclusion that in the United States, at least, crime is increasing, as is shown by these figures:

Year	Prisoners	Ratio to Population
1850	6,737	1 out of 3,442
1860	19,086	1 out of 1,647
1870	32,901	1 out of 1,172
1880	59,255	1 out of 860

... Statistics gathered by a Chicago newspaper from telegraphic reports of murders for the years 1881, 1882, and 1883 show an increase of more than 200 a year, from 1266 in 1881 to 1696 in 1883. Of this number, only 480 have suffered the death penalty—228 by legal execution, and 252 by lynch law....

The increase of population in the United States is much more rapid than would result from natural growth. Immigration introduces heterogeneous elements that do not readily assimilate. To the natural loss of interest that follows aggregation of even similar elements is superadded, I the case of the United States, the mingling of elements that lack the attractive force of a common origin, a common language, and similar habits and tastes. Many have come to us from the thronged cities where deprecation of the individual has already gone far beyond that which our people have attained, and their indifference adds new impetus to our own.... Many find little warrant for the hopes that inspired their emigration. Embittered by disappointment, they care less for their neighbors, add to the prevailing unrest, and easily enter on careers of crime. The presence of a disappointed element in our population probably has its effect upon the native element with which it mingles but does not affiliate.... For example, Iowa has 16.1 per cent, of foreign population, according to the census of 1880, with a little less than 16 per cent of foreign-born commitments to her penitentiaries; while Massachusetts, with 24,9 per cent of foreign population, has committed to her penitentiaries 34.9 per cent of foreign-born criminals.... For the United States, the commitments to penitentiaries are 19.2 per cent foreign-born, while 13.3 per cent marks the foreign-born share of the population....

But the statistics of each single state show increase of crime in excess of increase of population.... The growth of cities and towns at the expense of the rural population is marked. Thirty years have shown an advance of urban population from one-eighth of the entire population (12.5 per cent) in 1850 to nine-fortieths (22.5 per cent) in 1880. The quiet and simple life of rural districts feels the influence of the city, so that urban and suburban excitements reach the majority of an entire population.... City life lures the young from their homes long before their characters are solidified. Parental restraints are loosened. Parents dismiss their children from their thoughts under the glitter of a business career that opens before them. They have thought more of making them skillful accountants than men of stalwart honesty; their conversation has savored more of cash than of character; their counsels have led more frequently to shrewd bargains than to sterling integrity.... the home failing as a source of high moral purpose, parents look with leniency upon their sons' misdeeds, indirectly encourage vicious practices and condone offenses, until elders become involved in the crimes of their children.... The whirl and excitement of city life keep the flame constantly burning. The false side of social life allures the young man who has no abiding memory of a true home—a memory possible only to home who has known such a home not alone as a child in his tutelage, but as a young man participating in its hallowed scenes, himself a contributor to its blessedness....

Agricultural communities have ever been distinguished for good order and stability. Their communion is more with Nature than with men. Nature is unselfish, allays rather than irritates. Her friends are subject to few disturbances; the mind retains its equipoise; temptations are rare and seldom overpowering; small means satisfy few desires.... Mining, manufactures, commerce, and transportation will claim attention. Here association begins with work.... Separation into classes ensues; competition with the class stirs the blood; feverish excitement takes possession of all the faculties; rivalry provokes to jealousy....

Is this all theory? A study of manufacturing States in comparison with agricultural States will prove the theory founded in fact. For purposes of comparison I have taken the population above ten years of age of certain States, so as to exclude all who can be considered free from criminal acts. Taking first a group of mining States, we find that the criminals committed to prison were in these proportions: Nevada, 1 to 254; California, 1 to 268; Colorado, 1 to 416. A similar group of manufacturing States shows Massachusetts with 1 to 395; Rhode Island, 1 to 689; and Connecticut, 1 to 692. Another group, of partly agricultural and partly mining States, shows in Pennsylvania, 1 to 665; in Illinois, 1 to 687. A group of agricultural States shows Nebraska, 1 to 844; Minnesota, 1 to 1320; and Iowa, 1 to 1457....

...In the crowded factory villages, I the overcrowded boarding-houses with no home feeling to soothe the girl wearied by long hours of poorly paid toil, under the nervous excitements that constant indoor life increases, and with little brightness in the future prospect, will not temptation have an almost certain victory? ...The habit of carrying concealed weapons has doubtless grown out of the distrust of those whom we meet in crowded communities. King John, in addressing his chamberlain, utters a truth good for all time:

"How oft the sight of means to do ill deeds
Makes ill deeds done."

...Most if not all the causes of increase of crime are allied to the generic causes—increased density of population, with decreased individual responsibility and increased irritations growing out of, and inseparable from, the complexity of manufacturing and commercial activities....

Source: "Why Crime Is Increasing," *The North American Review* (Vol. 140, No. 342, May 1885), 456–463.

Document 19: Railroad Statistics

The rapid advance of the American railway system in the second half of the 19th century was a major impetus to the expansion of the American economy and the increased mobility of the population, as the cost of moving goods and persons over long distances decreased over time. The selection below illustrates this growth and provides a snapshot in 1893 of the size, health, and complexity of the railway network in the United States. The government went to great lengths to record the costs and expenses associated with the railway system. The piece also highlights that railway travel continued to have safety concerns by providing statistics regarding employee and passenger deaths and injuries for the year 1892.

> The following facts and figures are taken from the Seventh Annual Report of the Interstate Commerce Commission: The total railway mileage on June 30, 1892 was 171,363.52 miles; an increase of 3,100.78 miles; the total number of railway corporations was 1,822, being a net increase of 37 during the year; 899 maintained independent operating accounts, and 712 were independent operating companies.... There were 19 mergers, 17 reorganizations and 16 consolidations.... There were 560,958,211 passengers and 706,555,471 tons of freight reported as carried during the year ending June 30, 1892. The gross earnings reported were $1,171,407,343, and the operating expenses were $780,997,996, leaving net earnings of $300, 409,347, to which add $141,960,782 as income to railways from investments. After payment of ... fixed charges, ... dividends, ... and other payments, leaving a surplus of $14,636,656. The passenger revenue for the year was $286,805,708; and freight revenue amounted to $719,316,042. There were 821,415 persons employed in railway service at the end of that year, of whom 2,554 were killed in accidents and 28,267 were injured; 376 passengers were killed and 3,227 were injured. These accident statistics are carried out with considerable detail....

Source: "Railway Statistics," *Manufacturer and Builder* (Vol. 25, No. 12, December 1893), 275.

Document 20: The Tenements

Jacob Riis immigrated to the United States from Denmark in 1870. After struggling for several years, he took a position as a police reporter for the *New York Tribune* in 1877. His newspaper work brought him face to face with the dark underside of city life in New York City. He joined with a group of social reformers who launched a crusade for better living conditions for immigrants. He began writing down his observations and then used photography to provide the public with visual reality of the plight of the poor. He became a legend as a reporter, reformer, and photographer and received accolades from persons such as Theodore Roosevelt. The selections below are excerpts taken from three important late 19th century journals that published Riis' work exposing the harsh realities of the New York City tenements. The first two highlight the despair one normally associates with tenement life in the period. The third piece, however, although emphasizing the troubling aspects of immigrants living in the slums, also reveals some redeeming social values that emerged even in the midst of such wretched circumstances. Prior to his death in 1914, Riis compiled his writings and illustrations into the book *How the Other Half Lives*, an influential work that stimulated city leaders to pursue some reform measures.

How the Other Half Lives

New York alone, of the great cities of the world, has grown up with the century. The village of a hundred years ago is the metropolis of to-day. So fast a pace is not without its perils; in the haste to become great, our city has lost opportunities for healthy growth that have passed not to return....

It was in the old historic homes downtown that the tenement was born of ignorance and nursed in greed....

Turn but a dozen steps from the rush and roar of the elevated Railroad, where it dives under the Brooklyn Bridge at Franklin Square, and with its din echoing yet in your ears you have turned the corner from prosperity to poverty. You stand upon the domain of the tenement.... Like ghosts of a departed day, the old houses linger; but their glory is gone. This one, with its shabby front and poorly patched roof, who shall tell what glowing firesides, what happy children it once owned?.... Dirt and desolation reign in the wide hallway, and danger lurks on the rickety stairs.... A horde of dirty children play on the broken flags about the dripping hydrant, the only thing in the alley that thinks enough of its chance to make the most of it; it is the best it can do. These are the children of the tenement, the growing generation of the slums....

The cosmopolitan character of lower New York, as well as the constant need of the policeman and the use of iron bars, were well illustrated by the statement of the agent at one of my visits, that there were one hundred Irish, thirty-eight Italian, and two

German families in the court. It was an eminently Irish suggestion that the two German families were to blame for the necessity of police surveillance; but a Chinaman whom I questioned as he hurried past the iron gate of the alley was evidently of a different opinion, though he prudently hesitated to express it....

Perhaps this may be put down as an exceptional case; but one that came to my notice some months ago. In a Seventh Ward tenement was typical enough to escape that reproach. There were nine in the family: husband, wife, an aged grandmother, and six children; honest, hard-working Germans, scrupulously neat, but poor! All nine lived in two rooms, one about ten feet square that served as parlor, bedroom, and eating room, the other a small hall made into a kitchen. That rent was seven dollars and a half, more than a week's wages for the husband and father. That day the mother had thrown herself out the window, and was carried up from the street dead. She was "discouraged," said some of the other women from the tenement, who had come to look after the children while a messenger carried the news to the father of the shop....

That pure womanhood should blossom in such an atmosphere of moral decay is one of the unfathomable mysteries of life. And yet, it is not an uncommon thing to find sweet and innocent girls, singularly untouched by the evil around them, true wives and faithful mothers, literally like "jewels in a swine's snout" in these infamous barracks.

...The problem of the children becomes in these swarms, to the last degree perplexing. It is not unusual to find half a hundred in a single tenement. I have counted as many as one hundred and thirty-six in two adjoining houses in Crosby Street.

There was a big tenement in the Sixth Ward, now happily in the process of being appropriated by the beneficent spirit of business that blots out so many foul spots I New York—it figured not long ago in the official reports as "an out-and-out hogpen"—that had a record of one hundred and two arrests in four years among its four hundred and seventy-eight tenants, fifty-seven of them for drunken and disorderly conduct....

It is said that nowhere else in the world are so many people crowded together on a square mile as here. The average five-story tenement adds a story or two to its stature in Ludlow Street, and an extra building on the rear lot, and yet the sign "To Let" is the rarest of all there.... Through dark hallways and filthy cellars, crowded, as is every foot of the street, with half-naked children, the settlements in the rear are reached. Thieves know how to find them when pursued by the police, and the tramps that sneak in on chilly nights to fight for the warm spot in the yard over some baker's oven....

Life in the tenements in July and August spells death to an army of little ones whom the doctor's skill is powerless to save.... Fifty "summer doctors," especially trained to this work, are then sent into the tenements by the Board of Health, with free advice and free medicine for the poor ... but despite all efforts the grave-diggers in Calvary work overtime, and little coffins are stacked mountain-high on the deck of the Charity Commissioners' boat when it makes its semi-weekly trips to the city cemetery....

...But one tremendous factor for evil in the lives of the poor has been taken by the throat, and something has unquestionably been done, where that was possible, to lift those lives out of the rut where they were equally beyond the reach of hope and of ambition. It is no longer lawful to construct barracks to cover the whole of a lot. Air an sunlight have a legal claim, and the day of the rear tenement is past.... The dark, unventilated bedroom is going with them, and the open sewer. The day is not far distant when the greatest of all evils that now curses life in the tenements—the dearth of water in the hot summer days—will also have been remedied, and a long step taken toward the moral and physical redemption of their tenants.

These are the bright spots in the dreary picture; bright only by comparison.

Source: J. A. Riis, "How the Other Half Lives: Studies among the Tenements," *Scribner's Magazine* (Vol. VI, No. 6, December 1889), 643, 644, 647, 654, 657, 658, 660, 661.

Merry Christmas in the Tenements

Across the narrow yard, in the basement of the rear house, the lights of a Christmas tree show against the grimy window-pane. The hare would never have gone around it. It is so very small. The two children are busily engaged fixing the goldfish upon one of its branches. Three little candles that burn there shed light upon a scene of utmost desolation. The room is black with smoke and dirt. In the middle of the floor oozes an oil-stove that serves at once to take the raw edge off the cold and to cook the meals by. Half the window-panes are broken, and holes stuffed with rags. The sleeve of an old coat hangs out of one, and beats drearily upon the sash when the wind sweeps over the fence and rattles the rotten shutters. The family wash, clammy and gray, hangs on a clothes-line stretched across the room. Under it, at a table set with cracked and empty plates, a discouraged woman sits eying the children's show gloomily. It is evident that she has been drinking. The peaked faces of the little ones wear a famished look. There are three—the third an infant, put to bed in what was once a baby-carriage. The two from the street are pulling it around to get the tree in range. The baby sees it, and crows with delight. The boy shakes a branch, and the goldfish leaps and sparkles in the candle-light.... Outside the snow is falling. It sifts silently into each nook and corner, softens all the hard and ugly lines, and throws the spotless mantle of charity over the blemishes, the shortcomings. Christmas morning will dawn pure and white....

Source: Riis, "Merry Christmas in the Tenements," *The Century Magazine* (Vol. 55, No. 2, December 1897), 166, 182.

The Tenant

We have considered the problem of the tenement. Now about the tenant. How much of a problem is he? And how are we to go about solving his problems. The government "slum inquiry," of which I have spoken before, gave us some facts about him. In New York it is found 62.58 per cent of the population of the slums to be foreign-born, whereas of the whole city the percentage of foreigners was only 43.23. While the proportion of illiteracy in all was only 7.69 to 100, in the slum it was 46.65 per cent. That, with nearly twice as many saloons to a given number, there should be three times as many arrests in the slum as in the city at large need not be attributed to nationality, except indirectly in its possible responsibility for the saloons....

Jealousy, envy, and meanness wear no fine clothes and masquerade under no smooth speeches in the slums. Often enough it is the very nakedness of the virtues that makes us stumble in our judgment. I have in mind the "difficult case" that confronted some philanthropic friends of mine in a rear tenement on Twelfth Street, in the person of an aged widow, quite seventy I should think, who worked uncomplainingly for a sweater all day and far into the night, pinching and saving and stinting herself with black bread and chicory coffee as her only fare, in order that she might carry her pitiful earnings to her big, lazy lout of a son in Brooklyn. He never worked. My friends' difficulty was a very real one, for absolutely every attempt to relieve the widow was wrecked upon her mother heart. It all went over the river. Yet one would not have had her different.

Sometimes it is only the unfamiliar setting that shocks. When an East Side midnight burglar, discovered and pursued, killed a tenant who blocked his way of escape, a few weeks ago, his "girl" gave him up to the police. But it was not because he had taken a human life. "He was good to me," she explained to the captain whom she told where to find him, "but since he robbed the church I had no use for him." He had stolen, it seems, the communion service in a Staten Island church. The thoughtless laughed. But in her ignorant way she was only trying to apply the standards of morality as they had been taught her. Stunted, bemuddled, as they were, I think I should prefer to take my chances with her rather than with the woman of wealth and luxury who, some years ago, gave a Christmas party to her lapdog, as on the whole the sounder of the two, and by far the more hopeful.

All of which is merely saying that the country is all right, and the people are to be trusted with the old faith in spite of the slum. And it is true, if we remember to put it that way, - in spite of the slum. There is nothing in the slum to warrant that faith save human nature as yet uncorrupted....

Source: Riis, "The Tenant," *Atlantic Monthly* (Vol. 84, Issue 502, August 1899), 153, 161–162.

Document 21: Efficiency of Modern Industrial Methods

This selection by Charles A. Beard, the noted early 20th-century economic historian, praises the advent of modern machinery to harness power and increase the productivity of the work force. Citing statistics that emphasized the dramatic growth of the British economy, Beard argued that the inventions of the Industrial Revolution had reduced the amount of time humans devoted to sheer labor. This new paradigm thus allowed more opportunity for the pursuit of activities that would provide new meaning and satisfaction to life.

To show the expansion of trade following the new inventions is necessary to give a few statistics. When machinery was introduced into the textile industries the output of manufactured goods increased by leaps and bounds. In 1764 the cotton imported into England amounted to about 4,000,000 pounds; in 1841 it had increased to nearly 500,000,000 pounds. In 1792 the amount of cotton imported into Lancashire alone from the United States was 138,000 pounds; in 1800 it was 18,000,000 pounds. The wool imported into England in 1766 was only about 2,000,000 pounds; in 1830 the amount had risen to more than 32,000,000 pounds. In 1788 the iron output was 61,000 tons; in 1839 it was over 1,250,000 tons. One hundred years after Crompton invented his spinning mule there were in Lancashire 2655 cotton mills running a total of nearly 38,000,000 spindles and 463,000 power looms; in the twenty-two years from 1793-1815 English exports, according to official valuation, rose from 17,000,000 pounds annually to 58,000,000, in spite of the depression caused by the Napoleonic wars.

These figures give an inkling of the industrial transformation which followed the great inventions. Now let us turn to the real increase in the productive capacity of the individual. In other words, let us see whether productive capacity has grown more rapidly than the population. Unfortunately careful statistics are only of recent date, but we know that Hargreaves jenny worked, originally, only eight spindles. The number was gradually increased to one hundred and twenty, and by the beginning of the nineteenth century to two hundred. The jenny now has more than a thousand spindles, each revolving at the rate of ten thousand revolutions per minute. A man and two boys can tend to two thousand spindles.

The hand-loom weaver used to make from sixty to eighty throws of the shuttle per minute. Fifty years ago the best power loom made only one hundred throws; to-day the highest grade loom runs at the rate of about four hundred per minute, and along with the increase of the productive capacity of the machine there is a decrease in the amount of human labor required in the operations. Formerly one weaver tended but one loom; now one worker tends from two to ten looms, according to the grade of the goods. So great has been the increase in the efficiency of textile machinery that a single operative can supply two hundred and fifty persons with the necessary cotton garments, or three hundred persons with woolen clothing.

In every branch of industry attention has been devoted to increasing productive power, until almost marvelous results have been attained. In the continuation of the construction of the Cologne cathedral in 1870, two men with a steam crane lifted as much stone in a day as three hundred and sixty men could have done in the same time in the Middle Ages. The old craftsman produced at best a couple of pairs of shoes per day; the modern worker with machinery can turn out five hundred pairs a day. In one year six English workmen can produce enough bread to supply a thousand people for the same length of time. This includes all the labor from the breaking up of the soil to the delivery of bread to the consumer.

The extent to which mechanical power can be substituted for hand labor depends upon the ability of man to contrive machinery. Here is [sic] the material keys to the man's spiritual progress. The plowing of a furrow, the sowing of the seed, the reaping of the grain, its transportation from one market to another, the weaving of the fabric, and the making of a coat, all represent in the final analysis the application of so much power to matter. The past achievements of inventors have shown us that there are no limits to the ways in which the exhaustless forces of nature can be applied to do man's work. If we look back, we can see man struggling to maintain life by sheer strength of muscle; but if we look forward along the centuries of the future, we see the struggle for existence taking only a small portion of man's energy, leaving all the remainder of his powers of heart and brain free for the enlargement and enriching of life.

Source: Beard, *The Industrial Revolution* (London, 1901), as quoted in Robinson & Beard, *Readings in Modern European History*, Vol. II (New York: Ginn & Company, 1909), 71–72.

ANNOTATED BIBLIOGRAPHY

The sources listed below provide only a brief summary of the rich and large body of literature concerning the Industrial Revolution.

Books

General and Great Britain

Ashton, T. S. *The Industrial Revolution, 1760–1830.* Oxford: Oxford University Press, 1971. Stresses a definitive, sharp turn in economic activity in Great Britain after 1760.

Anderson, M. *Family Structure in Nineteenth Century Lancashire.* Cambridge: Cambridge University Press, 1971. Emphasizes the role that industrialization played in changing the nature of family life in this important early center of British manufacturing.

Beaudoin, S. M. *Problems in European Civilization: The Industrial Revolution.* New York: Houghton Mifflin Company, 2003. A recommended collection of brief but scholarly essays covering a variety of topics related to the Industrial Revolution.

Bentham, M., ed. *Arthur Young's Travels in France during the Years 1787, 1788, 1789.* London: George Bell and Sons, 1909. A fascinating compilation of Arthur Young's observations of French political, social, and economic life on the eve of the French Revolution.

Bland, C. *The Mechanical Age: The Industrial Revolution in England.* New York: Facts on File, 1995. Rich blend of themes, short biographical sketches, and key events in the first century of British industrialization.

Crouzet, F. *The First Industrialists: The Problems of Origins.* Cambridge: Cambridge University Press, 1985. A detailed account of the social and economic origins of the new men who founded the factories and mills that became the basis for the Industrial Revolution in Great Britain.

Clapham, J. H. *An Economic History of Modern Britain.* Cambridge: Cambridge University Press, 1930. Argues that no revolutionary development regarding economic and industrial growth took place in Great Britain in the 18th and 19th centuries.

Crafts, N. F. R. *British Economic Growth during the Industrial Revolution.* Oxford: Oxford University Press, 1985. Relies on national economic statistics not available to 18th and 19th century observers of British industrial growth.

Dale, H., & Dale, R. *The Industrial Revolution.* Oxford: Oxford University Press, 1992. A short but highly readable work that describes the most significant inventors and inventions during the Industrial Revolution.

Deane, P. *The First Industrial Revolution.* 2nd ed. Cambridge: Cambridge University Press, 1979. Revision of earlier 1969 work but still supports contention of a specific era that can be labeled as the Industrial Revolution.

Doty, C. S. *The Industrial Revolution.* New York: Holt, Rinehart, and Winston, 1969. General survey of the causes and course of the industrial revolution.

Dublessis, R. S. *Transformation to Capitalism in Early Modern Europe.* Cambridge: Cambridge University Press, 1997. Examines the role of consumer demand on the course of the Industrial Revolution.

Engels, F. Translated by W.O. Henderson and W.H. Chalons. *The Condition of the Working Class in England.* Stanford: Stanford University Press, 1968. An important contemporary work based on observations of the working class environment in Manchester during the middle of the 19th century, one that led to his famous collaboration with Karl Marx.

Flaherty, T. H., ed. *Time Frame AD 1800–1850: The Pulse of Enterprise.* Alexandria, Va: Time-Life Books, 1990. A brief, readable summary of the key industrial developments in the first half of the 19th century.

Flinn, M. W. *Origins of the Industrial Revolution.* London: Longman, 1966. An excellent treatment of the emerging Industrial Revolution in Great Britain with an emphasis on statistical analysis such as the standard of living, real wages, etc.

Hammond, J. L., & Hammond, B. *The Rise of Modern Industry.* London: Methuen, 1925. Addresses the enigma of the Industrial Revolution—the rise of great wealth and at the same time the appearance of unimagined poverty.

Hartwell, R. M. *The Industrial Revolution.* New York: Barnes and Noble, 1970. Stresses that while the growth of wealth and increase in poverty were obvious trends, in real terms the misery of the Industrial Revolution was no worse than the agrarian world preceding it.

Hays, W. P. *Samuel Morse and the Electronic Age*. New York: F. Watts, 1966. Examination of the impact of Morse's telegraph on the new age of communication.

Henderson, W. O. *The Industrial Revolution in Europe, 1815–1914*. Chicago: Quadrangle Books, 1961. General survey of the growth and spread of the Industrial Revolution in Europe in the 19th and early 20th centuries.

Hill, C. *Reformation to Industrial Revolution: The Making of Modern English Society*, 1530–1780, Vol. 1. New York, Pantheon Books, 1965. Excellent survey of British political, social, and economic picture in the two centuries leading to the Industrial Revolution.

Hobsbawm, E. *The Age of Capital*. London: Weidenfeld and Nicolson, 1962. Important work by a Marxist historian who traces the development of capitalism from the riotous days of 1848 until 1875.

King, S., & Timmins, G. *Making Sense of the Industrial Revolution: English Economy and Society, 1700–1850*. Manchester: Manchester University Press, 2001. Analyzes the Industrial Revolution from technological and theoretical conception and provides a number of primary documents for more detailed study.

Lampard, E. E. *The Industrial Revolution: Interpretations and Perspectives*. Washington, D.C.: Washington Service Center for Teachers, 1957. An older but still useful guide for new teachers of the Industrial Revolution.

Landes, D. *The Unbound Prometheus: Technological Change and Industrial Development in Western Europe from 1750 to the Present*. Cambridge: Cambridge University Press, 1965. A classic work that emphasizes the role of technological change to the transformation of economies in Great Britain and Western Europe.

Leone, B. *The Industrial Revolution: Opposing Views*. San Diego, Calif: Greenhaven Press, 1998. An engaging collection of pro and con opinions on economic change as stated by American observers such as Thomas Jefferson, Alexander Hamilton, Andrew Carnegie, and Eugene V. Debs.

Lipson, E. *The Economic History of England*. London: Longman, 1934. Emphasizes that the Industrial Revolution was another example of the natural flow of continuity and change in history.

Mantoux, P. *The Industrial Revolution in the Eighteenth Century: An Outline of the Beginnings of the Modern Factory System*. London: Cape, 1961. Early proponent of statistical analysis to argue for a series of long-term changes that prepared Great Britain for major economic growth in the last thirty years of the 18th century.

Marx, K. Translated by Samuel Moore and Edward Averling. *Capital*. Vol. 1. New York: International Publishing, 1967. Famous indictment of capitalism and the exploitation of labor in the 19th century.

Miller, J. H. *Charles Dickens: The World of his Novels*. Cambridge: Harvard University Press, 1958. Review of Dickens' contributions to make public the ills of British society that emerged during the Industrial Revolution.

Mokyr, J. *The British Industrial Revolution: An Economic Perspective.* 2nd ed. Boulder, Colo: Westview Press, 1999. Argues for a revolutionary interpretation of the Industrial Revolution because technological change and economic growth were clearly visible during the era.

Nardinelli, C. *Child Labor in the Industrial Revolution.* Bloomington: Indiana University Press, 1990. Separates fact from fiction regarding the issue of child labor and traces British legislative efforts to reform the use of children in factories.

Nef, J. U. *The Rise of the British Coal Industry.* 2 vols. Freeport, NY: Books for Libraries Press, 1922. Opines that the Industrial Revolution's origins date to the middle of the 16th century.

O'Brien, P. K., & Quinalt, R., eds. *The Industrial Revolution and British Society.* Cambridge: Cambridge University Press, 1993. Collection of essays regarding issues in the Industrial Revolution such as women's roles, parliamentary reform, crime and labor movements.

Rostow, W. W. *The Stages of Economic Growth.* Cambridge: Cambridge University Press, 1991 (reprint). Important work that stresses the five stages of economic change associated with industrialization.

Stalcup, B., ed. *The Industrial Revolution.* San Diego, CA: Greenhaven Press, 2002. An excellent work that compiles historical commentaries, selected biographies, and contested issues regarding the Industrial Revolution.

Stearns, P. *The Industrial Revolution in World History.* Boulder, CO: Westview Press, 1993. An important work that places the Industrial Revolution in a larger context as it spread its influence and had markedly different impacts across the globe.

Taylor, P. A. M. *The Industrial Revolution in Britain: Triumph or Disaster.* Boston: Boston Heath, 1958. Work debates the historical tension between those who embrace the positive aspects of the Industrial Revolution and those who emphasize its attendant economic and social ills.

Thomas, B. *The Industrial Revolution and the Atlantic Economy: Selected Essays.* New York: Routledge, 1993. Dismisses the revisionist views of the Industrial Revolution and emphasizes Great Britain's ability to sustain her economic growth in the latter half of the 19th century by dominating world trade and exchanging manufactured goods for needed foodstuffs.

Thompson, E. P. *The Making of the English Working Class.* London: Penguin, 1968. Work on the origins and growth of the British proletariat is representative of how in the 1960s the study of the Industrial Revolution split into smaller elements for examination.

Toynbee, A. *The Industrial Revolution.* London: Green & Company, 1894. The classic work on the Industrial Revolution, which places the starting point at 1760.

Weatherill, L. *Consumer Behavior and Material Culture in Britain, 1600–1760*. London: Routledge, 1988. Emphasizes the changing nature of Britain's consumer society during the transition to the Industrial Revolution.

Webb, S. & Webb, B. *The History of Trade Unionism*. London: Green and Company, 1884. Argues in a similar vein as the Hammonds text concerning the wide disparity between the wealthy and poor in the Industrial Revolution.

Wilson, C. *England's Apprenticeship, 1603–1763*. London: Longman, 1965. Traces roots of Britain's industrial development to the 1660s and argues that its dominance in international trade provided a foundation for rapid economic growth.

Wrigley, E. A. *Continuity, Chance, and Change: The Character of the Industrial Revolution in England*. Cambridge: Cambridge University Press, 1988. Essay that emphasizes the shift that occurred from a life based on the rhythm of nature to one in which humans regulated and dictated economic behavior.

United States

Ambrose, S. E. *Nothing Like It in the World: The Men Who Built the Transcontinental Railroad, 1863–1869*. New York: Simon and Schuster, 2000. An engaging work by one of America's leading historians who provides keen insight regarding the complex personalities and significant challenges involved in the gargantuan project to construct the transcontinental railroad in the 1860s.

Heilbronner, R. L., & Singer, A. *The Economic Transformation of America*. New York: Harcourt Brace Javonovich, 1977. Sees American industrial growth tied to a realignment of economic relationships surrounding work and institutional structures.

Hindle, B., & Lubar, S. *Engines of Change: The American Industrial Revolution, 1790–1860*. Washington, D.C.: Smithsonian Institution Press, 1986. Uses artifacts located in the Smithsonian to discuss technological development in America and from that point develops broader themes.

Knight, W. L. L. D., ed. *Poetical Works*. Edinburgh: William Paterson, 1884 (http://www.gutenberg.org/ebooks/10219). A collection of the poetry of William Wordsworth.

North, D. C. *The Economic Growth of the United States 1790–1860*. New York: W. W. Norton and Company, Inc., 1966. Emphasizes the role of social structures and sanctions in supporting industrial development.

Olson, J. S. *Encyclopedia of the Industrial Revolution in America*. Westport, CT: Greenwood Press, 2002. Useful compilation of selected topics related to industrialization in America from colonial times to the early 20th century.

Prude, J. *The Coming of the Industrial Revolution: Town and Family Life in Rural Massachusetts 1810–1860*. Cambridge, MA: Harvard University Press, 1983. Examination of the ways in which the arrival of industry changed the social and economic tempo of life in Massachusetts prior to the Civil War.

Biographies

Chernow, R. *Alexander Hamilton*. New York: Penguin, 2004. An insightful work that reveals the character of arguably our most brilliant founding father.

Dickinson, H. W. *James Watt*. Cambridge: Cambridge University Press, 1935. An older but interesting biography of the man considered the key to the depth and impact of the Industrial Revolution.

Fussell, G. E. *Jethro Tull: His Influence on Mechanized Agriculture*. Reading: Osprey Publications, 1973. An interesting work that attempts to separate fact from fiction regarding this often misinterpreted pioneer in modern agriculture techniques.

Latham, J. L. *Eli Whitney, Great Inventor*. Champagne, Ill: Garrard Publishing, 1963. Examination of the successes and disappointments of one of America's important inventors.

Unwin, G. *Samuel Oldknow and the Arkwrights: The Industrial Revolution at Stockport and Marple*. London: Longmans, Green and Company, 1924. Earlier work that discusses Arkwright's efforts to establish workable factory system in Great Britain.

Virginskii, V. S. *Robert Fulton, 1765–1815*. Springfield, VA: Amerind Publishing, 1976. A readable sketch of the many facets of Robert Fulton's life as an inventor and entrepreneur.

Western Europe, Latin America, India, Russia, and Japan

Bethell, L., ed. *The Cambridge History of Latin America*. Vol. 6. Cambridge: Cambridge University Press, 1986. Noteworthy source for the advance of industrialization in Latin America.

Blackwell, W. *The Beginning of Russian Industrialization 1800–1860*. Princeton, NJ: Princeton University Press, 1968. Interesting narrative of the important 19th century social and economic changes that prepared Russia for its entry into the industrial era.

Cipolla, C. M. *Before the Industrial Revolution: European Society and Economy, 1000–1700*. New York: W. W. Norton & Co. Inc., 1976. Excellent account of the pre-industrial world of Europe which provides a vivid contrast to the era of industrial change that followed.

Dore, R. P. *Aspects of Social Change in Modern Japan*. Princeton, NJ: Princeton University Press, 1965. Relates the impact of industrialization and modern economic developments to the rapid change in Japanese society.

Dunham, A. L. *The Industrial Revolution in France, 1815–1914*. New York: Exposition Press, 1955. Survey of the course of the Industrial Revolution in France from Napoleon to World War One.

Jansen, M. B., & Dozman, G. *Japan in Transition from Tokugawa to Meiji*. Princeton, NJ: Princeton University Press, 1986. Survey of the dramatic events that brought Japan into the modern, industrial era.

Lockwood, W. C. *The Economic Development of Japan: Growth and Structural Change* Princeton, NJ: Princeton University Press, 1968. Discusses the remarkable effort undertaken by Japan to alter its society and institutions as it entered the industrial era.

McKay, J. *Pioneers for Profit: Foreign Enterprise and Russian Industrialization*. Chicago: University of Chicago Press, 1970. Discusses the impact of foreign investment and technical skill in the early period of Russia's transition to industrialization.

Mosk, S. A. *The Industrial Revolution in Mexico*. Berkley: University of California Press, 1950. Excellent survey of Mexico's efforts, albeit largely unsuccessful, to make the transition to a modern industrial society.

Pomeranz, K. *The Great Divergence: China, Europe, and the Making of the Modern World Economy*. Princeton, NJ: Princeton University Press, 2000. A detailed work that argues that Great Britain and China had similar potential until the 18th century, but the former's resources, particularly coal, proved advantageous and allowed Britain to take the lead in industrialization.

Rostislav, A. *The Industrial Revolution and Social Progress in India*. New Delhi: People's Publishing House, 1970. An excellent survey of the relationship between economic and social change brought about by the arrival of industrialization in India.

Zelnick, R. E. *Labor and Society in Tsarist Russia: The Factory Workers of St. Petersburg, 1855–1870*. Stanford, CA: Stanford University Press, 1971. Highly specialized look at the beginning of the factory age in Russia.

Technology

Bruno, L. C. *The Tradition of Technology, Landmarks of Western Technology*. Collections of the Library of Congress, 1993. Combines an excellent narrative with intricate illustrations to emphasize the complex technical changes that stimulated and sustained the Industrial Revolution.

Buchanan, R. A. *The Power of the Machine: The Impact of Technology from 1700 to the Present*. London: Penguin, 1992. Highlights the important interaction between man and machine that powered industrial and economic change beginning in the 18th century.

Burns, W. E. *Science and Technology in Colonial America*. Westport, CT: Greenwood Press, 2005. Work dispels the notion that American colonists lagged behind in technical and scientific expertise by demonstrating important developments and discoveries in agriculture and early industry.

Cutliffe, S. H., & Reynolds, T. S. *Technology and American History*. Chicago: University of Chicago Press, 1997. Stresses the role that technology has played in the economic growth of the nation.

Eco, U. *The Picture History of Inventions*. New York: MacMillan Company, 1963. An interesting work which provides numerous and detailed illustrations of the significant inventions during the Industrial Revolution.

———. *Inventors and Discoverers Changing our World*. National Geographic Society, 1988. A work for the general public that nonetheless provides vivid imagery.

Karwatka, D. *Technology's Past*. Ann Arbor, MI: Prakken Publications, Inc., 1996. General survey of the role of technology through the ages with a special emphasis on technology in the Industrial Revolution.

Williams, T. *The History of Invention*. New York: Facts on File Publications, 1987. An engaging account of the relationship between invention and economic and societal change.

Documents

Clough, S., & Moodie, C. G. *European Economic History, Documents, and Readings: Major Developments from the End of the Middle Ages to the Present*. New York: D. Van Nostrand, 1965. Contains a number of valuable documents regarding the pre-industrial and industrial eras.

Pollard, S., & Holmes, C. *Documents of European Economic History, Vol. 1, The Process of Industrialization 1750–1850*. New York: St. Martin's Press, 1968. A significant collection of documents related to a number of European countries touched by the Industrial Revolution, particularly in the 19th century.

Robinson, J. H., & Beard, C. A. *Readings in European History*, 2 vols. New York: Ginn & Company, 1909. An important source for a variety of biographical, political and economic documents concerning the Industrial Revolution.

Stephenson, C., & Marcham, G., eds. *Sources of English Constitutional History: A Selection of Documents from 600 AD to the Present*. New York: Harper & Row Publishers, 1937. Important political documents related to the key economic changes brought about by the Industrial Revolution.

Commodore Matthew C. Perry's Expedition to Japan and Related Activities as Described in the Annual Reports of the Secretary of the Navy, 1852–1854, Navy Department Library, Department of the Navy, Navy Historical Center, Washington, D.C. (http://history.navy.mil/bios/perry_mc_secnav.html). Important accounts of Matthew C. Perry and his fleet as it pushed American economic and strategic power into the Pacific during the middle of the 19th century.

Samuel F. B. Morse Papers, Collection Highlights: The Impact of the Telegraph, Library of Congress, Washington, D.C. (http://memory.loc.gov/ammem/sfmhtml/sfbmhighlights01.html). Library of Congress site that provides detailed information regarding the interesting life of Samuel Morse and includes illustrations of his telegraph and early messages.

"The Rights and Conditions of Women," a sermon preached in Syracuse, New York, November 1845, by Samuel J. May (http://memory.loc.gov/cgi-bin). Library of Congress source that is part of a larger collection on the movement for women's suffrage and rights in the 19th and early 20th centuries.

Journals and Periodicals

The Atlantic Monthly, Vol. 48, Issue 289 (November 1881).
The Atlantic Monthly, Vol. 84, Issue 502 (August 1899).
The Century Magazine, Vol. 55, No. 2 (December 1897).
Harper's New Monthly Magazine, Vol. 67, No. 398 (July 1883).
Harper's New Monthly Magazine, Vol. 68, No. 408 (May 1884).
Manufacturer and Builder, Selected Issues (January 1863–April 1893).
The North American Review, Vol. 140, No. 342 (May 1885).
Scribner's Magazine, Vol. 6, No. 6 (December 1889).
Scientific American, Selected Issues (October 1846–June 1857).
Smithsonian, Vol. 36, Nos. 2, 10 &11 (May 2007, January 2008, and February 2008).

Documentaries

Burke, J. *Connections (BBC, 1978), Connections 2 (TLC, 1994),* and *Connections 3* (TLC, 1997). Innovative and highly acclaimed series on the relationship between science, technology and social change.

http://www.pbs.org/wgbh/amex. This PBS website contains a number of superb documentaries related to the age of industrialization in America. Examples include: *Chicago, City of the Century*; *New York*; and other pieces covering the transatlantic cable, transcontinental railroad, and biographies of persons such as Andrew Carnegie and John D. Rockefeller.

Websites

http://www.milestoneswebcom/features/telford.htm. An excellent overview of Telford's enormous contributions.

http://www.cis.yale.edu/amstud/inforev/riis/htm. Contains a wealth of information on Jacob Riis, one of America's premier social reformers.

http://www.cieh.org/htm. Site for the Chartered Institute of Environmental Health which contains excellent information regarding Edwin Chadwick's efforts to reform public health in Great Britain.

http://www.nps.gov/edis. Excellent site for study of the life and tireless inventive spirit of Thomas Edison.

http://www.history.rochester.edu/steam/thurston/1878. Lists a number of documents related to the history of the steam engine.

http://www.RobertFulton.org. Summary of the life and contributions of Robert Fulton.

http://cottontimes.co.uk/workers1/.html. Excellent source of information concerning the origin and growth cotton industry in Great Britain.

http://www.nps.gov/archive/lowe. Surveys the origins and life of the Lowell mills.

http://bbc.co.uk/history/historic_figures/tull_jethro.shtml. Informative summary of Jethro Tull's life.

http://bbc.co.uk/history/historic_figures/bakewell_robert.shtml. Highlights Bakewell's experiments with cattle and sheep.

http://www.bbc.co.uk/british/victorians. British Broadcasting Company site that looks at the impact of the Industrial Revolution in the Victorian Age.

http://www.yale.edu/ynhti/curriculum/units/1981. Provides suggestions for course topics and outlines related to the Industrial Revolution.

http://www.victorianweb.org/economics. Wide-ranging web site that addresses a number of topics related to the Industrial Revolution.

http://www.manchester2002-uk.com. Detailed account of the impact of industrialization on Manchester in the 19th century.

http://www.surreycc.gov.uk. Account of the impact of the Agricultural Revolution in Surrey County, England.

http://www.swetland.net/cumberland.htm. Discussion of construction of the first major turnpike in the United States.

http://www.pbs.org/wgbh/amex/tcrr. Excellent account of the building of the transcontinental railroad.

http://www.pbs.org/wgbh/amex/peopleevents/e_expo.html. A survey of the nation's 1876 Centennial Exposition in Philadelphia.

http://www.chicagohistory.org/hadc/chronology/html. Site provides details of the Haymarket Affair in Chicago.

http://www.eriecanal.org. Survey of the construction of the Erie Canal.

Annotated Bibliography

http://www.nrhs.com/archives/trainwreck.htm. Site provides interesting anecdotal information regarding railroad history.

http://www.pbs.org/empires/victoria/history. Surveys a number of topics related to the Industrial Revolution during the reign of Queen Victoria.

http://www.fordham.edu/halsall/mod/modsbook20.html. Internet modern history sourcebook—19th century Britain. Excellent resource for classroom use in teaching Industrial Revolution.

INDEX

accidents: railroads, 96–97; steamboats, 94
Adams, Henry: view on America at the turn of the 20th century, 115–116
Adams, John, 202
Agricultural Revolution, 25; agrarian worker productivity, 34–36; new farming techniques, 30–34. *See also* enclosure movement; seed drill; sheep breeding
Alison, William P., 171
Ambrose, Stephen, 97
American Federation of Labor (AFL), 106
American Philosophical Society, 108, 174
American Revolution, 81
American System, 110
American Telegraph Company, 183. *See also* telegraph companies
Ancien Regime, 121
Annals of Agriculture, 34. *See also* Young, Arthur
Appleton, Nathan, 103
Arkwright, Richard, 47, 157–160, 167–68, 176–77. *See also* factory system

Army Topographic Corps: survey of routes for transcontinental railroad, 98
Atlantic System, 18; exports, 19
atmospheric engine, 184–85. *See also* Newcomen, Thomas

Bakewell, Robert, 32–33. *See also* sheep breeding
Bank of England, 19–20; interest rates, 20; modern banking practices, 20
Bell, Alexander Graham, 108, 111
Bentham, Jeremy, 169. *See also* utilitarian thinkers
Bessemer, Henry, 105, 160–63. *See also* Bessemer process
Bessemer process, 161–63
Birkenshaw, John, 187
Blutcher, 186, 187. *See also* Stephenson, George
Boulton, Matthew, 198, 200. *See also* Watt–Boulton steam engine
Brace, Charles Loring, 114. *See also* Orphan Trains
Brady, Matthew, 182. *See also* daguerreotype
Bridgewater Canal, 55. *See also* Duke of Bridgewater
Brindley, James, 55

broad gauge, 164, 165
Brown, Moses: collaboration with Samuel Slater on Pawtucket Rhode Island mill, 82
Brunel, Isambard Kingdom, 163–66; Clifton Suspension Bridge, 163–64; early projects, 163–64; railway and steamship construction, 164–66
building construction, New York City, 114

Calhoun, John C., support for transcontinental railroad, 98
Canal du Midi, early French canal construction, 54
canals: Great Britain, 54–56; United States, 90–92, 191–92. See also Canal du Midi, Erie Canal
capitalism, birth of, 18–19
Carnegie, Andrew, 105–6
Cartwright, Edmund, 166–68
Catch Me Who Can (early locomotive), 195. See also Trevithick, Richard
Centennial Exposition (U.S.), 107–8, 153. See also Grant, Ulysses S.; Schwarzmann, Herman J.
Central Board of Health, 171
Central Pacific Railroad, 98–99. See also transcontinental railroad
Chadwick, Edwin, 63, 74, 168–72. See also Sanitation Commission
Charities, 114. See also Sisters of Charity
Chartist Movement, 73–74; six principles of, 74. See also People's Charter
Chicago Home Insurance Building, 162
child labor, 73; in France, 140; in Germany, 141; in Japan, 153–54
children, birthrates of, 15–16

Chinese labor, on the railroad, 97, 99
Civil War, impact on U.S. industrialization, 105–6
Clermont, 93–94, 172. See also Fulton, Robert; steamboats
Clinton, Dewitt, 91. See also Erie Canal
Clinton, George, 91
coal production: in Belgium, 131; in France, 127, 131; in Germany, 128, 130–31; in Great Britain, 41
Cobbett, William, 70. See also political reformers
Cockerill, William, 124
coke blasting, 53, 126
Collery, Charles, 33. See also shorthand sheep breed
colonial economy, 80–81; manufacturing, 82
Communist Manifesto, 140. See also Marx, Karl
Conditions of the Working Class in England, 72, 139. See also Engels, Friedrich
consumerism, pre-industrial, 21
Continental System, 122
Cooper, Peter, 95. See also *Tom Thumb*
Corliss steam engine, 108. See also Centennial Exposition (U.S.)
Cornell, Ezra, 182
Corn Law, 69–70, 74
cottage industry, 44
cotton (textile) industry: in Belgium, 130–31; in France, 128, 130–31; in Germany, 128–31; in Great Britain, 49–53, 130–31; in Japan, 151; in the United States, 105
cotton gin, 201; impact on exports, 201–202. See also Whitney, Eli
Coxe, Tenche, 84

Index

Credit Mobilier, 98
Crimean War, 146, 160
Cromford Mill, 158–69
Crompton, Samuel, 42 51; mule on continent, 122, 177
Crystal Palace, 2, 75, 119. *See also* International Exhibition of the Works of Industry of All Nations
Cumberland Road, 89. *See also* National Road

Daguerre, Louis, 182
daguerreotype, 182
Davis, Jefferson: support for transcontinental railroad, 98
Davy, Sir Humphrey, 186
Dickens, Charles, 63, 72–73, 171
Dishley Society, 33
Douglas, Stephen A.: support for transcontinental railroad, 98
Duke of Bridgewater, 54, 93. *See also* Bridgewater Canal
Duke of Wellington, 164, 189; praise of Richard Trevithick, 190
Duryea, Charles and Frank, 112
Dutch School of Learning, 150. *See also* Japan, opening of

economic theory, 42–44. *See also* "invisible hand"; *laissez-faire*; Malthus, Thomas; Ricardo, David; Smith, Adam; value, labor theory of
Edison, Thomas, 112, 116
education: in Japan, 152
Eiffel Tower, 136
electric trolley, 112
Elsworth, Annie: first telegraph message, 182
Embargo Act of 1807, 87
Empress Josephine, 179
enclosure movement, 27–30; parliamentary acts (1801, 1836, 1840, 1845), 29; Surrey County enclosures, 29–30. *See also* Agricultural Revolution
Engels, Friedrich, 71–72, 131, 139–40
entrepreneurship, 45
epidemic disease, 3, 170, 171
Erie Canal, 90–91
Essay on the Principles of Population, 69. *See also* Malthus, Thomas
Evans, Oliver, 175
Exposition of National Industry (Paris), 178

Factory Acts of 1833 and 1850, 73
factory system, 47, 59–61; early conditions, 60–61; first enterprise, 59; impact on church, 60; impact on workers, 60; wages, 61
families: before Industrial Revolution, 13
Fields, Cyrus, 183
"fire engine," 184. *See also* Savery, Thomas
Fitch, John, 93, 172–76. *See also* steamboats
Fitzherbert, Sir Anthony: *Boke of Husbandrie,* 28
Ford, Henry, 113
Franklin Institute, 108–9, 181
Fulton, Robert, 93–94, 168, 172, 175. *See also Clermont*; steamboats

Gale, Leonard, 181
gas-powered engine, 112
George III, 71, 159
George IV, 71. *See also* Great Reform Bill of 1832
Gladstone, William, 162, 172
Gould, Jay, 105

Grant, Ulysses S.: opening of Centennial Exposition, 97. *See also* Centennial Exposition (U.S.)
Great Britain (steamship), 165. *See also* Brunel, Isambard Kingdom
Great Eastern (steamship), 165. *See also* Brunel, Isambard Kingdom
Great Reform Bill of 1832, 71–72
Great Stink, 63
Great Western Railway, 164–65. *See also* Brunel, Isambard Kingdom
Great Western (steamship), 165. *See also* Brunel, Isambard Kingdom
Great White Fleet, 116
Greene, Catherine, 201, 203. *See also* Whitney, Eli
Grey, Earl, 169
Guericke, Otto, 18

Hamilton, Alexander, 84–87; *Report on the Subject of Manufacturing*, 86
Hargreaves, James, 51, 167, 159, 176–78. *See also* spinning jenny
Haymarket Affair of 1886, 106. *See also* strikes
Henry, Joseph, 180
Hering, Ralph, 135
Highs, Thomas, 157–59, 176
Homestead Strike of 1892, 106–7. *See also* strikes
Homfray, Samuel, 195
Howe, Elias. 110. *See also* sewing machine
Huskisson, William, 189. *See also* Stephenson, George

immigration: pre-Civil War, 104–5
Imperator, 166
industrial city: in 19th century, 62–64. *See also* Manchester

Industrial Revolution, historical interpretations of, 3–9. *See also* Toynbee, Arnold
interchangeable parts, 110, 202–203. *See also* Whitney, Eli
International Exhibition of the Works of Industry of All Nations, 2, 58, 74–75. *See also* Crystal Palace
International Telegraph Company, 183. *See also* Morse, Samuel Finley Breese
Irish labor, on transcontinental railroad, 97, 99
iron industry: in Belgium, 126; in France, 131; in Germany, 128, 130; in Great Britain, 52–53; in the United States during Civil War, 105
inventive spirit, 41–42
"invisible hand," 43. *See also* Smith, Adam
Iwakura Mission, 152. *See also* Japan, opening of

Jackson, Charles T., 180–81
Jacquard, Joseph-Marie, 131, 178–79
Jacquard Loom, 122
Japan, opening of, 150–51; business development, 151; child labor, 153; educational developments, 152; factory reform, 154; move to industrialization, 150–54; textile production, 151; worker conditions, 153. *See also* Dutch School of Learning; Meiji Restoration; Perry, Matthew; railroads; Tokugawa Shogunate
Jefferson, Thomas, 83–84, 86, 202
joint stock ventures, 125
Jupiter, 100. *See also* transcontinental railroad

Index

Kanagawa, Treaty of, 150. *See also* Japan, opening of
Kay, John, 42, 51, 157, 159, 176
Kelly, William, 162
Knights of Labor, 162
Krupp, Alfred, 124

labor unions, 106–7. *See also* American Federation of Labor (AFL); Knights of Labor; National Labor Union; trade unions
laissez-faire, 42, 68. *See also* economic theory; Smith, Adam
Lectures on the Industrial Revolution in England, 4. *See also* Industrial Revolution, historical interpretations of; Toynbee, Arnold
L'Enfant, Major Pierre-Charles, 85
Lincoln, Abraham: support for transcontinental railroad, 97
literacy: pre-industrial, 14
Liverpool to Manchester Railway, 57, 88. *See also* Stephenson, George
Livingston, Robert R., 168
London: in 19th century, 62–63
London Debating Society, 169
London–Holyhead Road, 190, 191. *See also* Telford, Thomas
Lord Palmerston, 171–72
Lowell, Francis, 102–3. *See also* Lowell Mill
Lowell Mill, 102–3; women workers at, 103–4
lower classes: pre-industrial, 15
Ludd, Ned, 70
Luddites, 70
Lunar Society of Birmingham, 197. *See also* Watt, James
Lyon weavers, 179. *See also* Jacquard, Joseph-Marie

Magnetic Telegraph Company, 183. *See also* Morse, Samuel Finley Breese

Malthus, Thomas, 68. *See also Essay on the Principles of Population*
Manchester (19th century), 64–66; efforts for reform, 66; immigrant labor, 65; lack of hygiene, 65; living conditions of workers, 65; textile mills, 64
Manifest Destiny, 97
Martin, Pierre-Emile, 162
Marx, Karl, 139. *See also Communist Manifesto*
McAdam, John L.: developments in road construction, 48, 56–57
McCormick, Cyrus: agricultural reaper, 111
Meiji Restoration, 151. *See also* Japan, opening of
Menai Bridge, 192–93. *See also* Telford, Thomas
middle class, pre-industrial, 13–14; education, 138; families, 135–36; leisure time, 138–39; rise of (19th century), 66–68, 137; standard of living, 137–38; women's roles, 136
Mill, John Stuart, 169. *See also* utilitarian thinkers
Mitsubishi Company, 151
Mormon workers: on transcontinental railroad, 99
Morse, Samuel Finley Breese, 110, 180–84. *See also* telegraph, Morse Code
Morse Code, 182
Muhammed Ali: impact on Industrial Revolution in Egypt, 144

Napoleon: abolition of Holy Roman Empire, 122; extension of French citizenship, 124
Napoleon III, 136
Napoleonic wars: impact on Industrial Revolution, 70, 87

National Labor Union, 106. *See also* labor unions
National Road, 89. *See also* Cumberland Road
navies, 55, 57
Neolithic Revolution, 1
Newcomen, Thomas, 123, 184–86, 194; engine repaired by James Watt, 198
New Leicester sheep, 33. *See also* Bakewell, Robert
newspapers, introduction of, 14
New York Manufacturing Society, 84
Norfolk System, 30–31

orphans, 114. *See also* Orphan Trains
Orphan Trains, 114
Owen, Robert, 69

Paine, Thomas, 169
Papin, Denis, 18
parliamentary acts. *See* Corn Law; enclosure movement; Factory Acts of 1833 and 1850; Great Reform Bill of 1832; Poor Law; Public Health Act of 1848; Reform Bills of 1867 and 1884; Ten Hours Act
patents, 109–10. *See also* Edison, Thomas
Paterson, New Jersey, 85
Paxton, Joseph, 74. *See also* International Exhibition of the Works of Industry of all Nations
Pawtucket, Rhode Island mill, 82. *See also* Brown, Moses; Slater, Samuel
Peele, Sir Robert, 168, 171. *See also* Great Reform Bill of 1832
Pennsylvania Packet, 174. *See also* Fitch, John
Perry, Matthew: opening of Japan, 150–51, 154

Perseverance, 175. *See also* Fitch, John
Peterloo Massacre, 70–71
pig iron production, 53
political reformers. *See* Cobbett, William; Engels, Friedrich; Marx, Karl
Poor Law, 49, 72
Poor Law Amendment Act, 169
Poor Law Commission, 169
population, pre-industrial, 11–14; Belgium, 125; Bradford, 47; colonial America, 80, 86; Europe in the 19th century, 135; France, 11–12, 127, 136; Glasgow, 47; Great Britain, 11–12, 59, 125; Italy, 11–12; Japan, 152, 154; Leeds, 47; Liverpool, 64–66; London, 12–14, 61–63; Moscow, 12; Paris, 13; population density of New York City, 114 Prussia, 12, 128; Russia, 12; Sheffield, 48; Spain, 11–12; United States in the 19th century, 113–14; Warsaw, 12;
power looms, 51, 167–68. *See also* Cartwright, Edmund
Priestly, Joseph, 169
Prince Albert, 62, 74–75
Public Health Act of 1848, 171
Pulteney, Sir William, 190
Punch magazine: comment on working conditions in Great Britain, 63, 77n25

Queen Victoria, 2, 58, 62, 74–75, 163, 183. *See also* Crystal Palace

railroads: accidents, 96–97; development in Belgium, 126, 130–31; in Brazil, 146; in France, 128, 130–31; in Germany 130–31; in Great Britain, 57–58, 130–31; in India,

Index

144; in Japan, 151; in Mexico, 146; in Russia, 146–47; in the United States, 94; early passenger travel, 101; impact on time, 58; Native American threat to, 99–100; railroad lines, 95, 96, 98, 101, 187–88; transcontinental railroad, 97–101
Railroad Act of 1862, 98
Reform Bill of 1832, 71–72. *See also* Great Reform Bill of 1832; Peele, Sir Robert
Reform Bills of 1867 and 1884, 140
Ricardo, David, 27
roads, pre-industrial, 14–15; early U.S. roads, 88; improved standards, 57; road construction techniques, 56. *See also* Cumberland Road; McAdam, John L.; National Road; Telford, Thomas
Rockefeller, John D., 105
Rocket, 189. *See also* Stephenson, George

Sanitary Commission: in Manchester, 66
sanitation, 64–65. *See also* Chadwick, Edwin; Great Stink; sewerage systems
Savery, Thomas, 42; improved draining of mines, 54, 184. *See also* "fire engine"
Schwarzmann, Herman J., 108. *See also* Centennial Exposition (U.S.)
science: impact on Industrial Revolution, 17–18
Scientific American, 109
seed drill, 31. *See also* Tull, Jethro
sewerage systems: in Europe 135. *See also* Chadwick, Edwin
sheep breeding, 33. *See also* Bakewell, Robert

Sherman, William Tecumseh, 97
Siemens, Charles and Ernest, 162. *See also* Bessemer, Henry; Bessemer process
silk exports: Japan, 153
Sisters of Charity, 114. *See also* orphans
skyscraper, 162
Slater, Samuel, 82. *See also* Brown, Moses; Pawtucket, Rhode Island mill
Smith, Adam, 27, 42–44, 155, 158. *See also* economic theory; *Wealth of Nations*
Smith, F. O. J., 181
socialist parties: in Russia, 149
Society for Useful Manufacturers, 85–86. *See also* Hamilton, Alexander
spinning frame, 158, 167. *See also* Arkwright, Richard
spinning Jenny, 176. *See also* Hargreaves, James
standard of living, 137–38
steamboats: accidents, 94; development of, 93–94, 172–75. *See also* Evans, Oliver; Fitch, John; Fulton, Robert
steam engine: early development of, 51, 54; 19th century growth of steam power, 131; Watt–Boulton, 197–200. *See also* Watt, James
Stephenson, George: development of modern railway system, 57, 94, 124, 165, 186–90. *See also* railroads
Stephenson, Robert: collaboration with George Stephenson, 165, 186. *See also* railroads
strikes: workers, 106. *See also* Haymarket Affair of 1886; Homestead Strike of 1892
Surrey County enclosures, 29–30. *See also* enclosure movement

Tariff of Abominations, 87
technological developments: transfer from Great Britain to the continent, 123–24; on the European continent (late 19th century), 134; in the United States (late 19th century), 111–12
telegraph: early device, 181; use in Crimean War, 183. See also Morse, Samuel Finley Breese; Morse Code
telegraph companies, 183. See also American Telegraph Company; International Telegraph Company; Magnetic Telegraph Company; Western Union
telephone subscribers: cities of Berlin, London, Paris, New York, and St. Petersburg, 111–12
Telford, Thomas, 56, 190–93; early church construction projects, 190; honors, 193; London–Holyhead Road, 190; Menai Bridge, 192–93; opposition to president of Institute of Civil Engineers, 193; participation in canal building, 190–92
Ten Hours Act, 73, 169
textile production: in Belgium, 130; in France, 127, 131; in Japan, 151; in Germany, 128–29, 131; in Russia, 146; in the United States, 131
Thomas, Sidney Gilchrist, 162
Thorton, 174. See also Fitch, John
Titanic, 166
Tokugawa Shogunate, 150–51. See also Japan, opening of
Tom Thumb, 95. See also Cooper, Peter
Tories, 71
Toynbee, Arnold, 3. See also *Lectures on the Industrial Revolution in England*

trade unions, 69, 106–7, 140
transcontinental railroad, 97–101. See also Ambrose, Stephen; Army Topographic Corps; Central Pacific Railroad; Chinese labor; Credit Mobilier; Irish labor; *Jupiter*; Manifest Destiny; Mormon workers; Railroad Act of 1862; Union Pacific Railroad; Whitman, Walt; Whitney, Asa
Transportation Revolution: Great Britain, 54–58. See also canals; railroads; steamboats
Treaty of Paris (1783), 81
Trevithick, Richard, 57, 187, 190, 193–97. See also *Catch Me Who Can*; railroads
Tull, Jethro, 31. See also seed drill
turnpike construction, 89. See also Cumberland Road; National Road

Union Pacific Railroad, 98. See also transcontinental railroad
urban growth, 19th-century United States, 113–14; problems in the cities: life expectancy, 114; overcrowding, 114
utilitarian thinkers, 169. See also Bentham, Jeremy; Mill, John Stuart

value, labor theory of, 43. See also economic theory; Smith, Adam
Van Buren, Martin, 181
Vanderbilt, Cornelius, 105
Vaucanson's loom, 179
Voight, Henry, 174

Walpole, Sir Robert, 29
War of 1812, 81, 86–87
Washington, George, 81
water frame, 58, See also Arkwright, Richard; factory system

Watt, James, 51, 197–200; concept of horsepower, 197; disagreements with Richard Trevithick; partnership with Matthew Boulton, 198–99; steam engine measures, 200; tribute by Benjamin Haywood, 197

Watt–Boulton steam engine, 194. *See also* Watt, James

Wealth of Nations, 43. See also Smith, Adam

Wedgewood, Josiah, 55. *See also* canals

Western Union, 183. *See also* Morse, Samuel Finley Breese; telegraph companies

Whigs, 71

Whitman, Walt, 100

Whitney, Asa: champion of transcontinental railroad, 97–98, 100

Whitney, Eli, 110, 111, 200–203. *See also* cotton gin; interchangeable parts

Wilkinson, John: close-fitting cylinders for steam engine, 199

Winchester Repeating Arms Company, 203. *See also* interchangeable parts; Whitney, Eli

Witte, Sergei, 148

workhouses, 17; Victoria, 169

working class, pre-industrial, 15; beggars and vagabonds, 17; family life, 16; illegitimacy, 16; marriage, 16

Wright, Wilbur, 116

Young, Arthur, 67, 121; discussion of new crops, 33–34. See also *Annals of Agriculture*

Zaibatsu, 151

Zollverein (German customs union), 121, 126, 128–29

About the Author

LEE T. WYATT III is a Visiting Professor at the University of Hawaii, Honolulu and also teaches history at Brevard Community College. A retired Army colonel, he is a former history faculty member at the United States Military Academy at West Point. He has written a multitude of journal and magazine articles, book reviews, and conference papers on military, world, and American history.